Best Groomed cross-country SKI TRAILS in

OREGON

Best Groomed cross-country SKI TRAILS in

OREGON

Includes Other Favorite Ski Routes

Mike Bogar

THE MOUNTAINEERS BOOKS

This book is dedicated to Mom,

who was too young when we lost her, and

to Dad, who is still going strong in his eighties.

Published by
The Mountaineers Books
1001 SW Klickitat Way, Suite 201
Seattle, WA 98134

© 2002 by Mike Bogar

First edition, 2002

Published simultaneously in Great Britain by Cordee, 3a DeMontfort Street, Leicester, England, LE1 7HD

Manufactured in the United States of America

Acquisitions Editor: Cassandra Conyers
Project Editors: Laura Slavik, Christine Ummel Hosler
Editor: Brenda Pittsley
Layout Artist: Kristy L. Welch
Mapmaker: Ben Pease
Photographer: All photos by the author unless otherwise noted.

Cover photograph: *Cross-country skiers on trail, Oregon.* © *Corbis/Vince Streano*
Frontispiece: *Skier at Mount Bachelor, Pole Pedal Paddle race*

Library of Congress Cataloging-in-Publication Data

Bogar, Mike, 1955–
    Best groomed cross-country ski trails in Oregon : includes other
favorite ski routes / Mike Bogar.— 1st ed.
        p.   cm.
Includes bibliographical references and index.
    ISBN 0-89886-801-7 (paperback)
    1. Cross-country ski trails—Oregon—Guidebooks. 2. Cross-country
skiing—Oregon—Guidebooks. 3. Oregon—Guidebooks. I. Title.
    GV854.5.O7 B64 2002
    796.93'2'09795—dc21

                                                    2002008326

CONTENTS

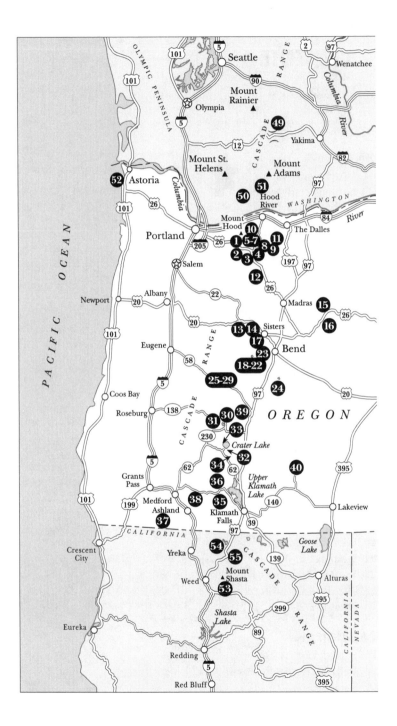

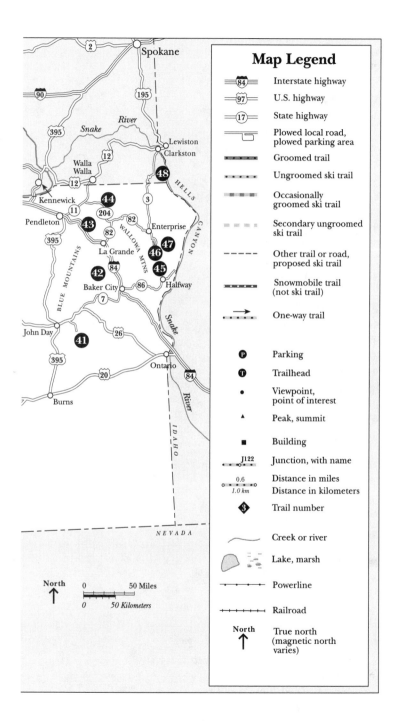

Map Legend

84	Interstate highway
97	U.S. highway
17	State highway
	Plowed local road, plowed parking area
	Groomed trail
	Ungroomed ski trail
	Occasionally groomed ski trail
	Secondary ungroomed ski trail
	Other trail or road, proposed ski trail
	Snowmobile trail (not ski trail)
→	One-way trail
P	Parking
T	Trailhead
•	Viewpoint, point of interest
▲	Peak, summit
■	Building
J122	Junction, with name
0.6 / 1.0 km	Distance in miles / Distance in kilometers
◆3	Trail number
	Creek or river
	Lake, marsh
	Powerline
	Railroad
North ↑	True north (magnetic north varies)

North
0   50 Miles
0   50 Kilometers

ACKNOWLEDGMENTS

I want to express my gratitude to fellow skiers who gave me advice on trails for this book. Chief among these were Einar Traa, who also was the first person I skied with in Oregon, and Bill Martin. Others include Bob Loper, Reider Peterson, Dick Knowles, Dick Kendall, Chuck Dunbar, Michael Babbit, Ellen Bartholomew, Dave Forkner, and Russ Barkman. Tom Gibbons, Jay Bowerman, and Gerry Smith contributed tidbits on the history of skiing in Oregon.

The many dedicated Forest Service personnel who enthusiastically shared their knowledge of ski trails were a valuable resource in completing this guide. I owe special thanks for such support to Mary Ellen Fitzgerald, Kevin Slagle, Ken Bronec, John Bambi, Jon Nakae, Steve Johnson, and Tom Lindy. Shaun Bristol at Fields Spring State Park was equally generous with his time.

Also, I am indebted to Stephanie Irving, who suggested I write this book and helped with its beginnings, and to Brenda Pittsley, who helped give sorely needed structure and coherence to the final manuscript. And I want to thank Christine Hosler, along with Laura Slavik and Cassandra Conyers, who patiently guided the book to completion. In addition, thanks to Ben Pease for producing the final maps in this guidebook.

Klindt Vielbig and John Lund also deserve recognition. I often referred to their earlier trail guides while researching this guidebook. My deep appreciation of their contributions to skiing in Oregon continued to grow as I came to understand the challenges faced in such a project.

I want to extend thanks to my siblings and friends who offered encouragement during the writing process or who have shared a mutual love of skiing with me over the past 25 years. Finally, thanks to those volunteers who have spent hundreds of hours helping to develop and maintain many of the ski trails in this book. Foremost of these are my fellow members of the Teacup Lake chapter of the Oregon Nordic Club, a group that has given me rewarding opportunities to make a contribution to Nordic skiing.

INTRODUCTION

People of all ages are attracted to cross-country skiing as a means of enjoying the outdoors in winter. Many others are attracted to the sport because it is an excellent aerobic exercise. A less tangible but equally important attraction is the exhilaration that comes from gliding over snow. It is possible to shuffle along on skis, but it is a lot more fun to glide. Novice skiers quickly learn that gliding in tracks set by other skiers makes for a better day than breaking new tracks in soft snow. When they do this, they are taking advantage of the simplest form of ski trail grooming. Ski trail grooming is the packing and preparation of snow to enhance the gliding experience.

Many ski courses have been groomed simply by skiers skiing through fresh snow to set a track. As late as the 1960s, the Norwegian army groomed cross-country racecourses by skiing in formation to pack ski tracks and poling lanes. In the past forty years, trail grooming has become more elaborate. Many trails are groomed with snow-mobiles pulling grooming sleds and commercial areas often use large machinery costing hundreds of thousands of dollars, all for the sake of making it easier to glide on skis.

In the 1960s, the Oregon Nordic Club used the Norwegian army's method to groom their 4-kilometer training course near Government Camp on Mount Hood. The state's first machine-groomed trails were probably set in 1965. Oregon rancher John Day bought two Ski-Doos, built a track-setting sled, and set tracks at Crater Lake. In the late 1960s, Day promoted the sport of cross-country skiing by hauling a snowmobile around Oregon and grooming for special events. Jay Bowerman, a member of the U.S. biathlon team, bought one of Day's Ski-Doos and groomed a training course at the base of Mount Bachelor in 1968. Parts of his trails were incorporated into the trail system at Mount Bachelor Ski Area when it started grooming cross-country trails in 1976.

Oregon now has nearly a dozen commercial ski areas and resorts with groomed cross-country ski trails. Volunteers or municipal groups groom trails at another half dozen locations. Oregon's commercial and noncommercial groomed trail venues run the gamut from Mount Bachelor Ski Area's 50-kilometer trail system with a full-service Nordic center to very small areas that are groomed only sporadically. Nearly all

Downhill tuck

these venues are described in this guide. A few areas with groomed trails in southern Washington and northern California are also included.

Oregon has fewer groomed ski trails than Washington because, unlike Washington, Oregon does not have a state-supported grooming program. Oregon skiers compensate by taking advantage of hundreds of miles of groomed snowmobile trails. Many of these are included in this guide. Finally, this guide also covers a selection of ungroomed trails. Most are popular trails where the tracks set by skiers are generally very good. These trails give skiers benefits similar to groomed trails and expand the range of available ski opportunities.

This mix of groomed ski trails, ungroomed ski trails, and groomed snowmobile trails is designed to encourage skiers to explore. There should be no division between skiers of groomed trails and skiers of ungroomed terrain. Fun skiing can be had on all types of trails. Skiers who will only ski meticulously groomed trails miss a host of opportunities. And those who refuse to try groomed trails seldom experience the thrill of great glide.

TWO WAYS TO SKI

There are two distinct forms of cross-country skiing. The traditional technique is *diagonal stride*, which involves striding forward on cross-country skis using alternating poling movements and generally keeping the skis parallel. *Skating*, first popularized as a racing technique in the 1980s, uses a side-to-side motion to keep the skis gliding continuously. The skills learned for diagonal stride and skating complement each other, and the best skiers use and enjoy both techniques.

Diagonal stride refers to the alternating action of arms and legs during striding. Each stride includes a kick followed by a glide phase on the opposite ski. The center portion of the ski, called the grip zone, is flattened against the snow during the kick. The ski base in this section is patterned or waxed to grip the snow and prevent the ski from slipping backward. The grip zone is lifted from the snow during the glide phase, and the ski glides on its smooth tip and tail. The longer the glide phase lasts, the less energy a skier needs to move forward. Learning to balance and glide on one ski during the glide phase is the single most important skill for efficient diagonal stride. Mastering this skill is easiest on groomed tracks, but it pays off on all trails.

Diagonal stride is also called *classic skiing*, though classic skiing is actually a broad term that refers to all the techniques commonly used before skating was popularized. These techniques include diagonal stride, double-poling, and herringbone.

The side-to-side leg movements of the skating technique resemble those of an ice skater. Skating is faster than diagonal stride because the skis never stop gliding to grip the snow—skating skis do not even have a grip zone. Skating caught on as a racing technique after American Bill Koch used it to help win the cross-country skiing World Cup in 1982. Koch was also a champion classic technique skier, winning a silver medal in the 1976 Olympics before experimenting with skating. Skating is now popular with many recreational skiers who don't race. They are attracted to the speed and often find it easier than diagonal stride. The side-to-side gliding used in skating requires wide, firmly packed trails, and its rising popularity has motivated many ski areas to groom wide trails with snow machines similar to those used on alpine slopes.

TRAILS

Cross-country skiers take advantage of all kinds of trails, groomed and ungroomed. Many fine tours follow forest roads. Generally, such trails have gentle turns and are best for long, easy skiing. The most enjoyable trails are those that were designed for skiing. Well-designed trails roll and twist and constantly change direction. This is more interesting and challenging than plodding in a straight line. When a trail in this guide is described as "designed for skiing," expect it to have a lot of turns and short ups and downs. These will be gentle hills and wide turns if it is a novice trail and short, steep hills and sharp curves if it is an advanced trail.

Most chapters in this guidebook describe areas with several ski trails and multiple loop options. Most of Oregon's groomed cross-country trails are included, as are a variety of interesting trails that are not groomed. Trails are suited to a range of skill levels. The ungroomed trails in this book are generally well marked and have little avalanche danger or other hazards.

In most areas, cross-country ski trails are marked with blue diamonds. Many trails are also rated for difficulty and marked with standard symbols for Easiest, More Difficult, and Most Difficult.

A dozen chapters in this book describe ski routes that at least partially follow snowmobile trails. Snowmobile-club volunteers groom these trails—if you ski on them, appreciate their efforts. Stay to one side when snowmobiles are passing and be friendly to other users.

Snowmobile trails are usually marked with orange diamonds and often include junction numbers, which help with routefinding. Snowmobile club maps showing groomed routes and junction numbers are usually available at major trailheads.

WEATHER

The dominant weather factor in the Cascade Range is warm, moisture-laden air moving eastward from the Pacific Ocean. This air rises over the western slopes, cools, and loses its moisture. The result is huge snowfall and relatively warm winter weather west of Cascade passes. The trade-offs are plenty of cloudy days and occasional rain while skiing. The heavy precipitation on the western slopes fosters dense forests of Douglas fir, hemlock, and red cedar with thick undergrowth. For skiers, dense forests limit views and make it difficult to ski off-trail.

Across the Cascade passes, the eastern slopes are a stark contrast. Air moving over the crest has lost most of its moisture and cools as it descends the eastern side. The result is colder, drier conditions and a fraction of the precipitation. In places, eastern slopes receive only an eighth of the moisture that falls west of the crest. The result is fewer clouds and more sunshine. Eastern slopes are characterized by widely spaced, drought-tolerant lodgepole pines and sparse vegetation on the forest floor. The mountains of northeast Oregon, influenced less by the Pacific Ocean and more subject to northern weather systems, are even colder and drier than the eastern Cascades.

Mount Hood above Cooper Spur

Easy skiing on groomed ski trails

Weather reports are now available 24 hours a day. Use them to track major storms and avoid dangerous conditions. However, it is hard to predict local conditions in the mountains, especially in western Oregon. Skiers may leave town under rainy skies and find clear weather at the trailhead. Be flexible. Consider driving farther east for potentially better weather. If weather is marginal, ski closer to the trailhead than planned. Light rain or falling snow does not have to ruin a ski trip—skiing is still enjoyable if you are properly dressed.

LESSONS

Skiers are more likely to enjoy the gliding aspect of the sport if they practice good skating or classic skiing technique. Unfortunately, many people ski for years with inefficient technique. Lessons with a competent ski instructor can help. Experienced instructors go beyond the basics of a snowplow turn and a herringbone step to focus on balance and to help a skier appreciate gliding on skis. Great racers do not necessarily make great instructors, but many of the best instructors have some race experience. While trying to ski fast, they learned to appreciate efficient technique and practiced the skills needed to develop it.

Most commercial areas offer ski lessons, and some have excellent instructors. Cross-country ski clubs often provide lessons or can recommend a good local instructor.

EQUIPMENT

Basic cross-country equipment includes skis (with permanently attached bindings), boots, and poles. The boot clips into the binding near the toe, leaving the heel free to move up and down. There are a few common binding designs, and boots must match the binding type. Boots are the most overlooked equipment consideration. Poorly fitting boots will result in a miserable ski tour. For track skiing and most touring, avoid stiff, heavy boots. Most skiers are better off with light- or medium-weight boots. Fewer pounds on the feet make a big difference in fatigue after a few hours of skiing.

For classic skiing technique, ski bases have a grip zone under the foot. This zone grips the snow during the kick phase of the diagonal stride. For best performance, grip is provided with a sticky kick wax that is rubbed on the grip zone. The kick wax must be selected to match snow conditions.

No-wax skis have a molded grip pattern that eliminates the need for a kick wax. This makes sense for touring and casual track skiing in the Cascades, where wet and variable snow can make wax selection frustrating. No-wax skis nearly guarantee good grip without the frustration of waxing, but at the expense of dramatically reduced glide.

The skating technique requires skis that glide well. Skating skis do not have a grip zone. Instead, the bases are coated tip-to-tail with a hard wax that improves glide. Skating skis are normally shorter and stiffer than classic skis.

CLOTHING

Proper clothing is key to comfort and avoiding hypothermia while skiing. Wool is the traditional winter weather fabric, as it provides insulation when wet. But wool is being replaced by synthetic fabrics as the best choice because they insulate and have the advantage of wicking moisture away from the body. After all, it is better to be dry and warm than wet and warm. Avoid cotton clothing, including blue jeans. Cotton holds water and provides no insulation when wet.

Use layers to adapt to your activity level and weather conditions. Start with lightweight long underwear that wicks moisture away from the skin. Polypropylene, silk, Capilene®, and CoolMax® fabrics are good choices. Cover this with an insulating layer made of wool, fleece, or a synthetic material. Your activity level affects how much insulation is required from this layer. Be prepared to add an outer layer for wind and rain protection, often a serious consideration in Oregon. An outer layer includes both pants and a jacket. A breathable material, such as

Gore-Tex®, is best. If you plan to stay active, avoid starting out overdressed. Overheating can create a chilling layer of sweat next to the skin. Skiing warms you up quickly.

Racers and other skiers who ski hard are often seen in skintight Lycra®. Lycra offers little insulation but is not just for the callipygian skier. Worn over long underwear, Lycra can be comfortable, can facilitate sweat evaporation, and can minimize overheating during strenuous activity. It is inadequate for casual skiing in cold weather. Since Lycra provides little wind protection, men should wear briefs with a front wind panel under Lycra tights.

Finally, bring dry clothes to change into after a ski tour. Slightly damp clothes can be chilling during après ski activities and the drive home.

Racer wearing a Lycra racesuit

SNO-PARKS

Most parking areas in Oregon's snow zones are state sno-parks. Failure to display a sno-park permit in these areas from November 15 to April 30 can result in a fine. Sno-park permits can be purchased at state Department of Motor Vehicles offices, commercial ski areas, and sporting goods stores. In 2002, daily permits cost $3 and annual permits cost $15. Most sales agents add a service fee. The permits are valid at more than ninety sno-parks throughout Oregon and at sno-parks in Washington, Idaho, and California. Permits from those states are valid in Oregon as well.

Oregon's sno-park program is self-supporting. Funds from permit sales are used only for plowing and maintaining sno-parks. Unlike other states, Oregon does not use sno-park funds to support trail grooming.

Vehicle break-ins at winter sno-park areas are a persistent problem. Many break-ins are accomplished simply by smashing a side window. Thieves are looking for money and items that are easy to sell. Do not leave cash or valuables in a vehicle. To help prevent future problems, report all incidents to law enforcement authorities.

PAYING FOR SKI TRAILS

A Swedish friend quips, "Snow is free, but groomed trails do not fall from the sky." Trail grooming costs money. Skiers who enjoy the trails should do their part to cover expenses. Commercial cross-country ski areas charge trail-use fees, just as alpine areas charge lift fees. Do not use the trails without purchasing a trail pass. Volunteer groups that groom trails rely on membership dues and user donations. Look for donation boxes at Teacup Lake, Virginia Meissner, Meacham Divide, and Trillium Lake. As of

Ski tracks

2002, the recommended minimum daily donation was $3 per person. This may be less than the cost of a latte on the way to the mountain. Set an example and contribute your share every time you use the trails or check with the volunteers about an annual membership.

The state of Oregon does not fund any ski trail grooming, but the state transportation department administers a snowmobile trail grooming program funded through snowmobile gas taxes and license fees. Skiers often use these groomed trails and several are described in this book.

Washington State Parks supports cross-country trail grooming throughout Washington, including at three areas described in this book (Wind River, Pineside, and Fields Spring). Grooming is funded mostly through Washington sno-park permit sales. Oregon permits are valid at these locations, but do not support the grooming.

SKI CLUBS

Cross-country ski clubs provide opportunities for meeting other skiers, learning about trails, and enjoying a variety of ski experiences. Club-sponsored tours are a great way to discover new trails and enjoy the camaraderie of other skiers. Perhaps more importantly, most clubs try to promote cross-country skiing through trail development, education, and special events. Clubs are a great vehicle for getting more enjoyment from the sport and giving something back in return.

The Oregon Nordic Club (ONC) is a unique ski club with eleven chapters throughout the state. Three chapters maintain groomed ski trails that are open to the public. Other chapters help maintain Forest Service ski trails and shelters, give lessons, and organize ski events. Most chapters have day tours every week and occasional overnight ski tours. Contact information for the ONC chapters and other Oregon ski clubs are listed at the back of this book (see Appendix D).

SKIING WITH CHILDREN

Teaching Children to Ski (1980), by Norwegians Asbjorn Flemmen and Olav Grosvold, is an excellent guide for those who ski with young children. Unfortunately, the English translation is out of print. One key guideline from the book is "Learning is more important than teaching." This is a reminder not to obsess over whether young children are "doing it right." Put them in fun situations on snow, and their natural desire to learn will help them develop the skills they need.

Children ages 8 and older may enjoy an organized ski program. Spending time on snow with other kids makes skiing more interesting. Programs for children are harder to find in Oregon than they are

Skier in the children's program at Teacup Lake

in New England or the Midwest, where large populations live near ski destinations. Check with your local parks department or ski club. The Bend Parks and Recreation Department runs a fine program for kids and some ONC chapters have youth groups. These programs usually depend on volunteers, so if you want an active group in your area, be prepared to donate some time.

DOGS

Dogs do not belong on most ski trails. They especially do not belong on groomed trails. They damage prepared tracks, which encroaches upon other skiers' enjoyment of the trails. Dogs are a safety hazard where skiers are moving quickly. Other skiers do not enjoy encountering a barking dog or feces in the trail. Complaints about dogs and irresponsible owners have grown over the years. National forests in central and southern Oregon have addressed the problem by closing large areas to dogs during winter months. Violations can result in fines. Continued problems are likely to lead to closures in other areas. If you must ski with a dog, choose seldom-used trails to avoid causing problems.

WINTER DRIVING

Many skiers consider the potential hazards of skiing, but forget that the most dangerous part of most trips is the drive to and from the trails. Safe winter driving requires traction tires with good tread. Keep a snow shovel, tire chains, emergency flares, and blankets or a sleeping bag in the car. Practice installing tire chains in dry conditions—a cold, slushy roadside is a miserable place to learn. Above all, reduce speed on snow and ice. Four-wheel drive will not keep you out of a snowbank or a serious accident if you drive too fast.

TRAIL SAFETY

Most of the trails in this book have little avalanche danger or risky stream crossings. Exceptions are mentioned in the text. Still, any adventure in winter has hazards. Understanding these hazards is the first step toward avoiding potentially life-threatening situations. Planning ahead helps ensure a safe trip. Remember that days are short in winter. Plan your ski day to finish well before dusk. Check weather forecasts before a trip. If bad weather is possible, choose a route that makes it easy to return to the trailhead quickly.

In Oregon, the greatest danger for skiers is hypothermia, the lowering of the body's core temperature. Wet clothes and wind dramatically increase heat loss and the potential for hypothermia. Symptoms of mild hypothermia include shivering, slurred speech, clumsiness, and unclear thinking. Mild hypothermia is hard to diagnose, but must be treated before becoming life threatening. If possible, a victim should change to dry clothes and seek warm shelter quickly.

Dehydration is often overlooked as a winter hazard. During vigorous skiing in cold weather, the body can lose more than a liter of water per hour. If not replenished, the fluid loss will hamper muscle activity. Severe cases can damage the kidneys and other vital organs. Dehydration also reduces the body's thermal control functions and increases the risk of hypothermia and frostbite. Thirst lags behind water requirements. Do not wait until you are thirsty. Drink some water every twenty to thirty minutes while skiing.

Deer wintering near Wallowa Lake

MAPS

Routefinding is generally easy at both commercial and club-operated ski areas. Most have trail signs at junctions and provide trail maps that are sufficient if you stay on groomed trails. But carry a compass anyway in case you get confused and wander from the trail. The maps in this book show trails and key land features. Remember that trails may have changed after the book was printed.

Snowmobile trails and ungroomed Forest Service trails may be less easy to follow than trails in developed ski areas. Most routes in this book are well marked, but you are responsible for knowing where you are. The maps in this book will help you to identify intersections. Carry a contour map for more detailed routefinding. Some ski trails are not shown on contour maps, and you may need both a trail map and a topographical map.

THE TEN ESSENTIALS

Each cross-country skier should carry these ten essential safety items for outdoor activities:

1. **Extra clothing.** More than is needed for the anticipated conditions.
2. **Extra food.** Extra means more than needed for a pleasant trip. Water is essential, too.
3. **Sunglasses.** Very important for alpine snow travel.
4. **Pocketknife.** Innumerable uses.
5. **Firestarter.** A candle or chemical fuel works well.
6. **First-aid kit.** Learn basic first-aid skills.
7. **Matches in a waterproof container.** Use the windproof, waterproof variety.
8. **Flashlight.** Include spare batteries.
9. **Map.** Know how to read it.
10. **Compass**. Know how to use it.

And I like to add:

11. **Chocolate.** Never leave home without it.

Do not count on maintaining a fire in a winter storm, especially in the Cascades. It is safer to count on extra warm clothes and food to preserve and generate body heat. Carrying a lightweight emergency shelter or vapor barrier bag is another smart idea. In the Cascades, pack a scraper and a commercial wipe-on liquid or wax designed to prevent ice buildup on ski bases.

It is easy to get confused in an emergency situation. A map and compass can help save your life, but only if you know how to use them. Develop confidence in your skills by taking time to practice on easy tours. In unfamiliar territory, verify your location periodically. If you do get lost, it is easier to determine your position if you know where you were thirty minutes ago.

USING THIS BOOK

Each chapter in this guide begins with at-a-glance information to help you compare ski areas and pick one that fits your needs and interests. The following is an explanation of how the information was determined.

DISTANCE

Distances are specified for round-trip tours from the trailhead, which is usually next to a sno-park or Nordic center. Most chapters describe areas with several routes. For these, the range of available tour distances from the trailhead is listed. Loops often can be combined to create longer tours. Trail distances are usually given in miles. Ten commercial or club-operated areas use kilometers to mark trail distances. Metric measurement is standard practice at Nordic centers, a result of the influence that European immigrants had on skiing in this country. For these areas, key trail distances are given in both kilometers and miles.

Commercial and club-operated ski areas advertise the total length of groomed trails in kilometers. This is useful for comparing areas with many connecting trails and numerous loop possibilities. For these areas, the total distance of groomed trails is also listed in the chapter header. The total distance might be less than what is advertised by the ski area, as ski areas recount some sections as part of multiple loops, which can lead to an exaggeration.

TRAILS

Groomed ski trails. Trails are machine-groomed specifically for cross-country skiing. These trails usually have a grooved lane for easy classic skiing. Tracks may be groomed with a large snow machine or by a snowmobile pulling a small grooming sled. Some groomed trails are only groomed occasionally.

Ungroomed ski trails. Trails are not groomed mechanically. Most ungroomed trails included here have little avalanche risk or other hazards and usually have a good track set by weekend skiers. These trails are often excellent for classic skiing, but are too narrow for skating.

Groomed snowmobile trails. Trails are groomed wide with large snow machines operated by snowmobile clubs. Skiers and snowmobilers share these trails, which are good for skating. No classic tracks are set, but classic ski touring works well here too. Trails are groomed once or twice each week, but may get rough after heavy snowmobile use on weekends.

Other. Two alpine ski areas groom maintenance roads that are also cross-country ski trails. A third ski area grooms a long trail from alpine runs to a sno-park. This "runout" is also a cross-country trail. These wide trails are good for skating or classic touring.

TRACK QUALITY

Trail design and width, snowfall, temperature, the type of grooming equipment, and grooming frequency all affect track quality. Quality is a subjective evaluation, especially for ungroomed ski trails. The track quality listed at the beginning of the chapters is to help skiers compare trails and ski areas. Actual track quality may vary from day to day. Evaluations range from poor to excellent for both classic skiing and skating. Since skating requires a wider, firmer trail than classic skiing, ratings are given for both types of skiing. The descriptions here provide a rough guide to how the trails were evaluated.

Classic Skiing

Excellent. The track has a classic lane with machine-set grooves and firm poling lanes. The tracks are seldom icy because the grooming machine tills the snow surface to break up ice.

Very Good. The classic lane is machine-set or consistently well set by other skiers. The poling lanes may be soft or the tracks may be icy in certain weather conditions.

Good. Ski tracks are consistently well set by other skiers, though the poling lane is likely to be soft. Or the trail is machine-groomed without a classic lane, but it is easy to keep the skis pointed forward.

Fair. The trail has tracks set by other skiers that are often rough and hard to use.

Poor. The trail has no classic lane and the surface is often rutted or bumpy. It is difficult to keep skis pointed forward.

Skating

Excellent. The trail has a firm and smooth skating platform at least 12 feet wide. It is seldom icy because the grooming machine grinds ice on the track surface. Turns are designed for high-speed skating.

Good. The trail has a firm and smooth skating platform at least 10 feet wide. It may be prone to icy conditions.

Fair. The skating platform is less than 10 feet wide or soft or bumpy conditions are common.

Poor. A soft skating platform or icy ruts are common.

No skating. Trails are too narrow for skating. Grab your classic skis.

SKILL LEVEL

Routes in this book are rated according to the skill level required to ski a trail with confidence. The ratings are novice, intermediate, and advanced. These ratings assume a skier is in reasonably good shape and that there are no severe trail conditions, such as an icy track. Remember that trail conditions are extremely variable and affect trail difficulty. Icy tracks can turn an intermediate hill into a harrowing toboggan run. Snowmobile trails are sometimes flat and smooth, and sometimes filled with ruts. Be aware of trail conditions and adapt your trail choice accordingly. Skill ratings are also affected by distance. Long tours on novice terrain are rated at a higher skill level.

Novice: Novice skiers range from first-time skiers to those who are mastering basic uphill and downhill skills. Some novice trails are flat, but most include short uphill and downhill sections. These short hills require the novice to use the herringbone, an uphill step with the ski tips spread apart, and the snowplow, a downhill technique with the skis forming a wedge to control speed. Novice tours are generally less than 5 miles long.

Intermediate: Skiers should be able to ski up moderate hills and use a snowplow to turn effectively on downhill turns. Expect a few sharp downhill turns. Tours of more than 5 miles on otherwise novice terrain are rated intermediate.

Snow pockets near Fish Lake

Advanced: Skiers should be able to stop quickly on downhills, execute sharp turns, and always be in control. Expect steep or long uphill and downhill sections and sharp downhill turns.

ELEVATION

The elevation for a ski area is noted for the Nordic center or the sno-park.

MAXIMUM ELEVATION GAIN

Elevation gain is the difference between the highest point and the lowest point within a trail system. Cumulative climb can be much more in hilly terrain. Most areas with multiple loops have at least one loop with much less elevation gain than the maximum for the area. A novice trail rating is a good indication that a trail does not have significant elevation gain.

SEASON

For groomed trails, the season noted is the period when trails are likely to be groomed. The start of the season is typically as soon as there is sufficient snow to set good tracks. The end of the season is generally determined by skier attendance. Grooming often stops long before the snow has melted.

For ungroomed trails, ski seasons listed here are based on average annual snow conditions, but snow levels vary widely from year to year. The season beginning and ending dates may be off by a month in either direction but are useful for comparing ski areas. If in doubt, check with the local ranger station. Early and late in the season, be prepared to change plans if you misjudge the snow level.

SERVICES AND FACILITIES

Cross-country ski facilities range from winter resorts and commercial Nordic centers to simple warming huts or just an outhouse. Commercial Nordic centers rent skis and sell snack food. Full-service centers offer lessons, sell warm food, and provide a gathering place for skiers. These are great places to enjoy the camaraderie of other skiers.

Resorts have overnight accommodations, usually in simple cabins. Most have a restaurant. Some rent skis and have groomed ski trails. Others cater primarily to snowmobilers, while also welcoming skiers.

Warming huts usually have a heater or wood stove but no ski rentals

Gray Jay (a.k.a. Camp Robber, Whiskey Jack)

or food sales. Some chapters in this book note Forest Service lookout towers or rustic cabins that are available for overnight rental. These do not have electricity or running water.

HOURS

Days and hours of operation are noted for commercial ski areas and some lodges. An NA (Not Applicable) designation usually means the trails are in a noncommercial area and skiing is restricted only by the amount of daylight.

FEES

Most commercial areas charge a fee for trail use. If you are unwilling to pay this fee, ski elsewhere. With your fee you will receive a trail pass that should be worn in a visible location while skiing. Full-day trail fees for the 2001–2 ski season are noted here. Rates may increase. Most commercial areas offer discounts for half-day, senior citizen, and student passes. Multiday and season passes are usually available as well.

Volunteer-operated ski areas request a donation for trail use. Look for a donation box near the trailhead. The recommended donation is usually three dollars per person. Donations are on the honor system. Set an example by letting others see you put money in the donation box. If you regularly ski at one of these areas, support grooming by becoming a member.

INFORMATION

Phone numbers or websites are listed for ski areas, lodges, or land agencies.

LAST WORDS

Two last bits of advice: Go out and ski. It is the best way to become a better skier. And don't forget to play. Cross-country skiing is more than getting there and back. Take every opportunity to have fun on the way.

A NOTE ABOUT SAFETY

Safety is an important concern in all outdoor activities. No guidebook can alert you to every hazard or anticipate the limitations of every reader. Therefore, the descriptions of roads, trails, routes, and natural features in this book are not representations that a particular place or excursion will be safe for your party. When you follow any of the routes described in this book, you assume responsibility for your own safety. Under normal conditions, such excursions require the usual attention to traffic, road and trail conditions, weather, terrain, the capabilities of your party, and other factors. Because many of the lands in this book are subject to development and/or change of ownership, conditions may have changed since this book was written that make your use of some of these routes unwise. Always check for current conditions, obey posted private property signs, and avoid confrontations with property owners or managers. Keeping informed on current conditions and exercising common sense are the keys to a safe, enjoyable outing.

—*The Mountaineers Books*

KEY

Trail type
G Groomed ski trail
S Groomed snowmobile trail
U Ungroomed ski trail

Ability
N Novice
I Intermediate
A Advanced

Fees
D Donation for trail use
NFP Northwest Forest Pass required for parking
(Most other areas require sno-park permit)

Chapter	Area	Trail Type	Tour length (miles)	Ability	Elevation (feet)	Fees (2002)	Notes
MOUNT HOOD							
1	Government Camp	U	1.2–3.5	N–I	3630		Short loops and one long trail.
2	Summit Ski Trail	G,U	2	N–I	3660		Good skating on ski area road. Wetland meadows.
3	Trillium Lake Basin	G,U	3–12	N–I	3810	D	Views of lake, Mount Hood. Groomed weekly. Busy on weekends.
4	Pioneer Woman's Grave	U	1–5.7	N–I	4157		Easy-to-reach Mount Hood views, pioneer history.
5	White River	U	1–3	N	4240		Continuous views, busy on weekends.
6	Mount Hood Meadows	G	1.9–3.1	N–A	4580	$10	Nordic center, ski rentals, lessons, excellent grooming. Sahalie Falls.
7	Heather Canyon	G	4.4	I	4580		Steady climb, views, good skating, some alpine skier traffic.
8	Teacup Lake	G	0.6–5.6	N–A	4350	D	Volunteer-operated, warming hut, varied terrain. Groomed one or two times per week.
9	Pocket Creek	U	2–10	N–I	3800		Roads to views, intermediate-level trail through trees.

10	Cooper Spur	U	6–14	N–A	3810		Long uphill on road, Mount Hood views. Ski to rental cabins.
11	Billy Bob	S,U	3–8	N–A	3960	NFP	Fire lookout tower. New ski trails added 2001.
12	Skyline	S	8–13	I	3640		Long tour to Little Crater Lake. Fire lookout tower.
SANTIAM PASS							
13	Hoodoo	G	1–5	N–A	4700	$7	Ski rentals. Good grooming on lower trails. Ride lift to upper trails for views.
14	Ray Benson	U,S	4–9.7	N–A	4800		Loops in forest and old burn area, views of Mount Washington and Three Fingered Jack.
CENTRAL OREGON							
15	Bandit Springs	U	1.5–5	N–A	4520		Varied terrain. Snow coverage variable.
16	Walton Lake	U	3.6–6.7	N–I	5540		Open terrain, reliable snow.
17	Three Creek Lake	S,U	3.1–12.2	I–A	5150		Snowmobile trail to base of Tam McArthur Rim. Ski trails with views of Mount Jefferson.
18	Mount Bachelor	G	0.6–7.5	N–A	6350	$11	Nordic center, ski rentals, lessons, reliable snow, excellent grooming, open daily.
19	Dutchman Flat	U	2.5–6.5	N–I	6300		Reliable snow, views of the Three Sisters and Broken Top.
20	Elk Lake Resort	S	22	I–A	6300		Road tour with long hill 11 miles to resort, restaurant.
21	Wanoga	S	1–8.5	I–A	5480		Mount Bachelor views, good skating close to Bend. Snowmobiles. Dogs allowed.

#	Name					D	Description
22	Virginia Meissner	G	3–10	N–A	5350	D	Volunteer maintained. Rolling loops on mostly forest roads. Day-use shelters.
23	Tumalo Falls	U	1–5.8	N–I	4740		Road to waterfalls. Two easy forest loops. Snow level marginal.
24	Paulina Lakes	S	6–10.6	N–A	5600		Lakes in giant volcanic crater. Ski 3 miles to resort, restaurant. Day tour to rim.
WILLAMETTE PASS							
25	Pengra Pass	U	2.4–8.4	N–I	5000		Narrow forest trails and snow-covered roads. Lean-to shelters.
26	Willamette Pass	G	1.7–5	N–A	5100	$6	Ski rentals, hilly trails, good skating.
27	Shelter Cove	G	1–4	N	4750		Very easy trails along lake, great views, ski rentals, cabins.
28	Odell Lake	G	1–6	N–I	4800	$5	Resort, restaurant at trailhead. Ski rentals. Many short loops.
29	Crescent Lake	S	14.8	I	4820		Loop around lake, views, good skating.
SOUTHERN OREGON							
30	Diamond Lake	G,U	5–9.5	N–I	5200		Resort, restaurant, easy trails. Most grooming is for special events.
31	Three Lakes	U,S	4.6–7.6	N–I	5390		Varied trails, creek headwaters. Ski to overnight cabin.
32	Crater Lake, South	U	2–15	N–A	7100		Stunning views.
33	Crater Lake, North	S	5.4–18.4	N–I	5794		Snowmobile trail to crater rim.
34	Annie Creek	S	2.9–6.5	N–I	4358		Skating. Alternative to Crater Lake Rim in bad weather.

#	Name						Description
35	Lollipop Loops	U	5.7–7.2	N–I	4645		Rolling loops mostly on forest roads.
36	High Lakes	U	3.6–6.6	N–A	5050		Varied loops, Mount McLoughlin views, day-use shelter.
37	Grouse Gap	G,U	4.4–6.7	N–I	6680		Groomed ski area road and ungroomed loop, open terrain. Shelter.
38	Buck Prairie	U	4.5–6	N–I	5180		Loops on forest roads.
39	Walt Haring	G	2.1–8.8	N–A	4820		Roads in pine plantation. Volunteers groom occasionally.
40	Woods Line Linear Park	U	6–17.6	N–I	5220		Former railroad line. Flat. Long ski to trestle.
NORTHEASTERN OREGON							
41	Summit Prairie	S	5.6	I	5720		Easy skiing, open terrain, cold snow.
42	Anthony Lakes	G	1.3–7	N–A	7146	$8	Nordic center, lessons, ski rentals. Excellent grooming. Easy-to-reach views.
43	Meacham Divide	G	1.6–12	N–A	4131	D	Volunteer-maintained, mostly forest roads, scenic overlooks.
44	Spout Springs	G,U	2.8–4.5	N–I	5050	$5	Ski rentals, lunchroom.
45	Clear Creek	U	0.6–7.4	N–A	3740		Easy riparian trails and challenging forest trails.
46	Wallowa Lake Tramway	G	2.5	N–I	8150	$16	Ride tramway to incredible views encompassing four states. Rough ski trails.
47	Salt Creek Summit	U	1.3–5.6	N–A	6100		Views from old burn areas.
48	Fields Spring	G	1–4	N–I	3990		State park, scenic overlooks of Blue Mountains, wild turkeys.

SOUTHWEST WASHINGTON AND OREGON COAST							
49	White Pass	G	2–10	N–A	4500	$8	Nordic center, ski rentals, lessons, café, varied trails, excellent grooming.
50	Wind River	G	1.2–11	N–I	3000		Groomed weekly. Views on long loop.
51	Pineside	G	1.5–7	N–I	2760		Groomed weekly. Look for Big Tree.
52	Oregon Coast	U		I	sea level		Unique skiing.
NORTHERN CALIFORNIA							
53	Mt. Shasta	G	0.6–3.8	N–A	5254	$14	Nordic center; ski rentals, lessons, varied trails, excellent grooming.
54	Juanita Lake	G	6–10	I	4268		Lovely lake, marginal snow, infrequently groomed.
55	Four Corners	S	10.8	I	5314		Good skating. Snowmobiles.

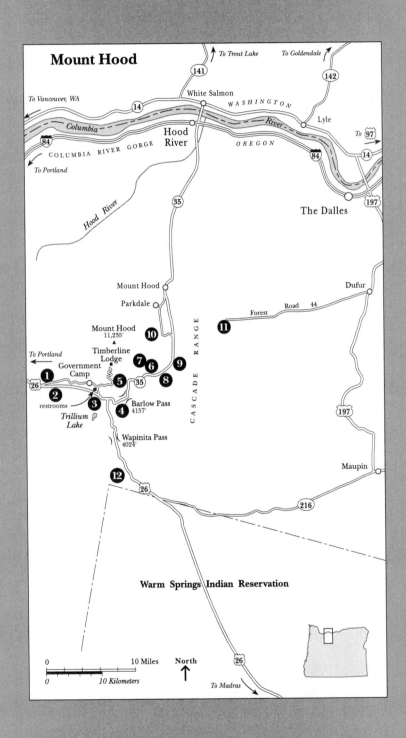

Mount Hood

Majestic Mount Hood is arguably the prettiest peak in the Cascades. It is also the primary cross-country destination for skiers from Portland and the Columbia Gorge area. The mountain has three areas with groomed cross-country trails and many miles of fine ungroomed trails in Mount Hood National Forest. Most ski routes are near 4000 feet in elevation.

Wet Cascades snow is the norm here. Clouds tend to hang over westside slopes. Westside trails near Government Camp have great skiing but more than their share of clouds and light rain. Heading around the mountain on Highway 35 improves the likelihood of sunny weather. White River, between Highway 26 and Mount Hood Meadows, commonly marks the transition zone between overcast skies and only partial clouds.

The common route to Mount Hood from Portland is on Highway 26, through Sandy, Zigzag, and Government Camp. Cross-country equipment can be rented in Sandy and Government Camp. Weekend traffic can be heavy on the road. The 12 miles between Welches and Government Camp see many winter accidents, a consequence of drivers who are unprepared for winter or unwilling to slow down. Most of the traffic is heading to alpine ski areas and lets up from late morning until about 4 P.M. If skiing on the east side of the mountain, consider approaching via Interstate 84 to Hood River, and then heading south on Highway 35. This adds about 30 miles to the overall distance for Portland skiers, but avoids the worst traffic problems. The ultimate way to avoid heavy traffic is to ski on weekdays.

Overnight accommodations are available in Government Camp and along Cooper Spur Road, off Highway 35. For a real treat, spend a night at the historic Timberline Lodge, uphill from Government Camp. The beautiful timbered lodge, excellent restaurant, and spectacular mountain views combine for an unforgettable visit. Clubs that ski on Mount Hood include the Mazamas, the Bergfreundes, and the Ptarmigans, as well as Oregon Nordic Clubs from Portland, Teacup Lake, and The Dalles.

1 GOVERNMENT CAMP

Distance: 1.2–3.5 miles
Trails: Ungroomed ski trails
Track Quality: Fair classic skiing, no skating
Skill Level: Novice to intermediate
Elevation: 3630 feet
Maximum Elevation Gain: 950 feet
Season: Late November to late March
Services and Facilities: Near restaurants, ski rentals, lodging
Hours: NA
Fees: Sno-park permit
Information: Mount Hood Information Center, (503) 622-7674

Fifty miles southeast of Portland, Government Camp packs restaurants, lodging, shops, mountain views, and a network of ungroomed ski trails into a small area. Some trails are within walking distance of the town center. Loops near the west end of town include novice trails as well as tougher, narrow trails through the forest. As the name implies, the Crosstown Trail traverses from one end of town to the other. The Huckleberry Inn, on the loop road through Government Camp, is open 24 hours and is a good stop for huckleberry pie and milkshakes. Clear days here are cherished for spectacular views of Mount Hood's south side, amply making up for the frequent cloudy days.

There are trailheads at three sno-parks. Trails also can be reached from residential streets, but parking is not allowed on these streets. The Glacier View Sno-Park offers easy access to novice and intermediate trails. It is on the north side of Highway 26, 0.3 mile west of Government Camp. From Portland, turn left from the highway across from the entrance to Ski Bowl West. Drive to the end of the plowed area, usually 0.2 mile from the highway.

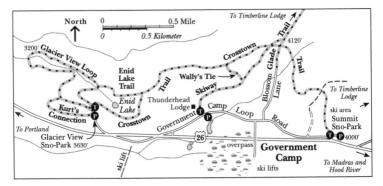

To reach the second trailhead, continue east on Highway 26 for 0.3 mile beyond the Glacier View turn to a blinking yellow light. Turn left onto Government Camp Loop Road. Drive 0.2 mile to the sno-park, which is just a wide section of the loop road near the Thunderhead Lodge. Skiway, an intermediate-level trail, climbs from this sno-park to provide access to the middle of the Crosstown Trail. The third trailhead is at Summit Sno-Park. Continue another 1.2 miles on Highway 26 to a second blinking light and turn left into the large sno-park next to a small downhill ski area. This sno-park has public restrooms. Ski up the left side of the ski slope, climbing 200 feet to the east end of the Crosstown Trail.

Glacier View Loop. Three loops begin at the Glacier View Sno-Park. The longest is Glacier View Loop. Climb the snow bank at the end of plowing to reach the trailhead. Ski the 2-mile Glacier View Loop clockwise by starting on an old road that was part of the original highway. The road gently loses 200 feet in elevation. This section is good for novices. Just before some powerlines, the trail turns right into the woods, follows some tricky terrain, and then climbs an equestrian trail back to the trailhead. This "off-road" leg requires intermediate ski skills.

Kurt's Connection. Kurt's Connection, a 0.5-mile trail, branches off Glacier View Loop to form an excellent 1-mile beginners' loop. Ski on the old highway 0.5 mile to Kurt's Connection on the left. This short trail was designed for skiing with twisty turns and hills that challenge, but it should not intimidate beginners as it winds east back to the sno-park.

Enid Lake Loop. Enid Lake Loop is a 1.2-mile intermediate route. The trail starts on the right a few feet past the end of Glacier View Sno-Park and follows the Crosstown Trail through mature pine forest. It quickly passes a trail on the left, which is the loop's return leg and part of Glacier View Loop. Continue straight 0.1 mile to the edge of Enid Lake and a view of Mount Hood. Beyond the lake, the trail climbs through forest and marsh to a junction with the Enid Lake Trail. Turn left and ski west, descending to merge with the Glacier View Loop and winding uphill to the sno-park.

Crosstown Trail. Constructed in 1994, the Crosstown Trail is Government Camp's backdoor trail. Crossing uphill of town, its west end is at Glacier View Sno-Park. From here, its first 0.5 mile is also the south leg of the Enid Lake Loop. It twists through the forest, climbing steadily as it leads east. At 1.2 miles and 1.5 miles the Crosstown Trail reaches junctions with Wally's Tie and Skiway, two intermediate trails to the right that climb from near Thunderhead Lodge. Skiway follows the lower course of the Timberline Tramway, built in 1950. The tramway used a city bus suspended from cables. Plagued by mechanical and financial problems, it closed quickly and was torn down.

Creek crossing along Crosstown Trail

Just beyond the junction with Skiway, the Crosstown Trail meets the Glade Trail, a steep downhill run from Timberline Lodge to Blossom Lane in Government Camp. At this point, the Crosstown Trail stops climbing and traverses the hill to Summit Ski Area, with views uphill of Mount Hood and across the highway to Multorpor Mountain. Ski down the easy slope at the ski area to Summit Sno-Park. Traveling in the opposite direction, the Crosstown Trail is a fun, intermediate downhill run to Glacier View. If the trail is icy, the downhill sections require advanced skiing skills.

2 SUMMIT TRAIL

Distance: 2 miles
Trails: Groomed ski area road and ungroomed trail
Track Quality: Fair classic skiing, good skating
Skill Level: Novice to intermediate
Elevation: 3660 feet
Maximum Elevation Gain: 150 feet
Season: Late November to mid-March
Services and Facilities: Alpine ski lodge
Hours: NA
Fees: Sno-park permit
Information: Mount Hood Information Center, (503) 622-7674

This hilly, 1-mile maintenance road between Ski Bowl West and East (formerly Multorpor) is also a marked Forest Service ski trail. Large alpine grooming equipment runs over the road daily. This creates a fine skating trail, and cross-country racers like to use it for midweek skating workouts. The road is also the west half of a popular 2-mile beginner ski tour. The east half is not groomed.

Most grooming occurs at night, but exercise caution by getting well off the road if you encounter one of the big snow machines in operation. Ski area personnel occasionally run snowmobiles between the ski areas. Move to one side when you hear one coming. Horse-drawn sleighs also may pass, especially on weekends.

The groomed road can be reached from sno-parks at Ski Bowl

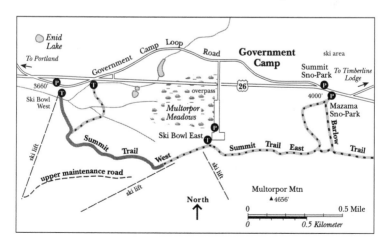

Forest Service cabin near Summit Trail East

West and Ski Bowl East. From Portland, drive east on Highway 26 to Government Camp, 50 miles from Portland. The well-marked west entrance to Ski Bowl is on the right just before Government Camp. To reach the east sno-park, continue on the highway 0.3 mile and turn left on the Government Camp Loop Road. Drive 0.7 mile to a right turn to Ski Bowl East and cross the highway on an overpass. The short road ends at the sno-park and Ski Bowl East lodge.

The official trailhead from Ski Bowl West is at the east end of the long sno-park, near the highway. Summit Trail starts on an ungroomed road that leads 0.3 mile to the groomed road. This access is fine with touring equipment, but soft snow will hamper skaters on the ungroomed section. Skaters can reach the ski trail from the edge of the alpine ski area. Walk between the ski lodge buildings. Ski to the left, staying away from the bottom of the ski lift, to a groomed maintenance road on the left. The road climbs steeply for 0.1 mile to a viewpoint of the alpine run. The road turns left and climbs less steeply. In another 0.1 mile, the ungroomed road from the official trailhead is on the left. Some racers use this 0.1-mile section for uphill interval training, but normal people have better ways to spend their time.

The groomed road winds east for 1 mile, with two short steep hills. Its east end is just above a lower lift terminal and lodge at Ski Bowl East. Most skaters turn back here and enjoy laps along the road. Multorpor Meadows, wetlands preserved by The Nature Conservancy, is between the east end of the groomed road and the highway. It is buffered from the ski area by a strip of trees and brush. It is rewarding, though awkward on skating skis, to leave the groomed trail and check out the meadows. Look for otter tracks, with a characteristic pattern of alternately running and sliding across the snow.

The ski area does not open until afternoon Monday through Thursday. If skiing before downhill skiers are on the slopes, strong skiers can venture uphill from the east end of the groomed road. Follow the lift line 300 feet to another maintenance road on the right, which climbs 0.5 mile to an alpine run high above the west lodge. Do not ski on or across the ski run. Return downhill on the road, which is used by a few alpine skiers.

Skiers with touring equipment can continue 1 mile east on the ungroomed portion of Summit Trail. From the end of the groomed road, the trail descends around the bottom of the lift and past the Ski Bowl East lodge. The obvious trail sign is up a hill beyond the lodge. The trail follows an easy road east and north through tall trees. In 1 mile, it reaches Forest Service cabins and a short climb to Mazama Sno-Park.

Forty years ago, the Cascade Ski Club had a ski jump on Multorpor Mountain. Look up the slope from the Ski Bowl East lodge. The wood structure on the partially wooded hill to the left of the ski run was the judges' tower. Trees now obscure the jumping hill, which was to the left of the tower.

3 TRILLIUM LAKE BASIN

Distance: 3–12 miles
Trails: Groomed and ungroomed ski trails
Track Quality: Good classic tracks, no skating
Skill Level: Novice to intermediate
Elevation: 3810 feet
Maximum Elevation Gain: 400 feet
Season: Early December to mid-April
Services and Facilities: Rental cabins along ski trails
Hours: NA
Fees: $3 per person suggested donation, sno-park permit
Information: Mount Hood Information Center, (503) 622-7674

Trillium Lake Basin, easily reached from Portland, is Mount Hood's most well-known cross-country ski destination. A stunning view of Mount Hood from Trillium Lake Dam highlights any tour in the basin. Most trails are on Forest Service roads and are suitable for novice skiers. However, all tours start with a challenging descent from the sno-park. The most popular trails are groomed weekly for classic skiing. Donations are requested to help cover costs. Visit on weekdays if you want to enjoy the basin's beauty in relative solitude.

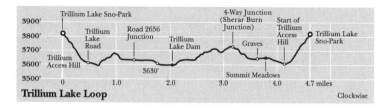

Trillium Lake Loop

Clockwise

Trail grooming, begun in 1992, has dramatically improved the quality of ski tracks here. A local cabin owner does the grooming. The Forest Service administers the program, but it is not government funded. Expenses are paid by donations from Government Camp businesses and skiers. Unfortunately, few skiers put money in the donation boxes near the trailheads. Help ensure the program can continue by donating a few dollars every time you use the trails.

The basin is accessible from two sno-parks on Highway 26. The larger and more popular is Trillium Lake Sno-Park. It provides the most direct route to the Trillium Lake Loop and the viewpoint at the dam. Follow Highway 26 for 50 miles from Portland to Government Camp. Drive 1.5 miles beyond Government Camp and turn right into the sno-park. Mazama Sno-Park, the smaller sno-park, is in Government Camp, 1.5 miles northwest of Trillium Lake Sno-Park.

Trillium Access Hill and Red Top Meadows. Two routes, Trillium Access Hill and Red Top Meadows, descend into the basin from the Trillium Lake Sno-Park. Both descents will challenge beginners. Because it is wide and well packed, most skiers prefer the Trillium Access Hill. It starts at the west end of the sno-park near the entrance. Look for the donation box at this trailhead. The trail drops immediately with short steep sections and long moderately steep sections. The hill may be congested with skiers and, unfortunately, loose dogs. The Forest Service is considering restrictions to reduce the dog problem. Use snowplow braking to descend safely. If necessary, remove your skis and walk along the edge of the road where you will be safely out of the way and will not damage the trail. The road levels in 0.3 mile. Continue 0.2 mile to a junction with the Old Airstrip Road. The rest of the tour is generally easy. Beginners will find the rewards of skiing in the basin are worth the challenge of the initial descent.

Red Top Meadows begins at the far end of the sno-park from the highway entrance. It is less steep than Trillium Access Hill, but is ungroomed and has sharp, narrow turns that require good downhill skills. The bottom half is part of a snowmobile route. In 0.7 mile, the trail connects to the bottom of Trillium Access Hill. Turn left and ski to

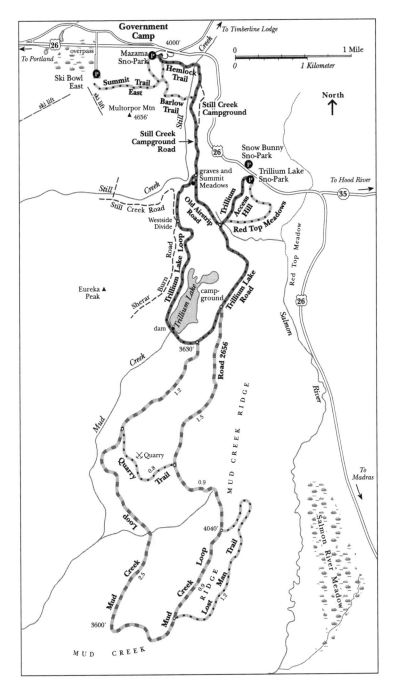

the Old Airstrip Road junction. This junction is the start and finish of the Trillium Lake Loop.

Trillium Lake Loop. Groomed weekly, this is the most popular tour in the basin. The 3.7-mile loop (4.7 miles round trip from the sno-park) can be skied in either direction. To quickly reach rental cabins near Summit Meadows, turn right. For the shortest trip to the dam, follow Trillium Lake Road as it curves left. The road drops gently and then climbs 100 feet. A long downhill is followed by rolling terrain to the dam, 1 mile from the start of the loop.

Even first-time visitors may recognize the view from the dam of Mount Hood looming above Trillium Lake. It has been captured in numerous classic photographs. Stay off the lake; the ice may be thin, especially near the outflow. This is a good spot for lunch. It is also a good turnaround point for beginner skiers and those preferring an easy day. Continuing around the loop is 2.7 miles, with more hills.

The loop continues across the dam and climbs a moderately steep hill. The forest is closer here, a contrast to more open trail before the dam. The road reaches a four-way junction 1.2 miles from the dam. On the left, Sherar Burn Road climbs to Kinzel Lake, which is 20 miles round trip. The road continuing straight ahead is Still Creek Road. It descends to the creek in 1 mile. Most skiers decide the side trip to the creek is not worth the climb back to the junction.

Continue on the Trillium Lake Loop by turning right and descending from the junction. If the track is icy, winding downhill is tricky, but regular trail grooming makes this descent smoother and safer than it would be otherwise. In 0.2 mile the road levels and winds past rental cabins. It ends at a T intersection at the edge of Summit Meadows, once a bustling stop on the old Barlow Trail. The volunteer groomer occasionally wanders off the main trail and sets ski tracks in the meadows.

To the right of the intersection are three pioneer graves. One infant was buried in 1847. A second was buried in 1882 at the base of a tiny pine tree, now more than 100 feet tall. The picket fence around the graves may be under snow, but a faded sign on the pine tree marks the site. The third grave is that of Perry Vickers, Mount Hood's first alpine guide. This colorful figure built Summit House and was host to thousands of immigrants before the final leg of their trek to Oregon City. Vickers was one of Mount Hood's early murder victims. His story and the fascinating history of the Barlow Trail are described in Jack Grauer's *Mount Hood, A Complete History* (self-published, 1975).

A left at the T leads to Still Creek Campground and the Mazama Sno-Park. Skiers returning to Trillium Lake Sno-Park turn right and head south on the flat Old Airstrip Road along the edge of the meadows. In 0.5 mile, this road returns to the bottom of Trillium Access Hill, completing the loop. Trillium Lake Sno-Park is to the left, up the hill. Stay to the right side to avoid collisions.

Mud Creek Loop. Mud Creek flows from Trillium Dam and through a large basin bordered on the east and south by Mud Creek Ridge. Three ski trails along the ridge have some of the area's most enjoyable terrain, as well as a solitude that is uncommon on the lake loop. One, the Mud Creek Loop, is occasionally groomed.

To reach the Mud Creek Loop, ski clockwise on the Trillium Lake Loop. A half-mile before the dam, Road 2656, the Mud Creek Ridge Road, angles left. It heads south, climbing the ridge with views of Mount Hood to the north. After 2.4 miles of climbing, the roast crests 400 feet above Trillium Lake Road. The road descends and loops north through rolling terrain with more Mount Hood views. At 7 miles, it reconnects with Trillium Lake Road, 0.2 mile before the dam. Mud Creek Loop is not technically difficult, but the length and climb make it difficult for beginners.

Quarry Trail. Two options off the Mud Creek Loop are the Quarry and Lost Man Trails; neither is groomed. The Quarry Trail is a short cutoff from Mud Creek that starts at 1.5 miles on the loop's east leg. It starts with an exciting downhill into a gravel quarry. Open slopes in the quarry are good places to play and practice skills. The trail joins a narrow road and climbs to the west leg of Mud Creek Loop. This 0.8-mile cutoff can be used to bypass 4.2 miles of the Mud Creek Loop.

Summit Meadows in the Trillium Lake Basin

Lost Man Trail. Lost Man Trail is a 1.2-mile branch off the east leg of Mud Creek Loop. From the Quarry Trail junction, continue southeast for 0.9 mile. Near the high point of the road, the north-end junction with the Lost Man Trail is on the left. The trail drops through a few curves, turns sharply south, and continues gently downhill. It passes meadows, clear-cuts, and a view of Mount Jefferson on the way to its lower junction with Mud Creek Ridge Road.

Mazama Sno-Park. An alternate starting point for Trillium Basin Trails is Mazama Sno-Park, a small lot along the shoulder of Highway 26 in Government Camp, across from the Summit Sno-Park public restrooms. Two trails, one groomed and one ungroomed, lead to the basin. Both are narrower and more challenging than the access hill from the Trillium Lake Sno-Park. Trillium Lake and Mud Creek tours are 2 miles longer from Mazama than they are from Trillium Lake Sno-Park.

Hemlock Trail and Barlow Trail. Hemlock and Barlow Trails start at the west end of Mazama Sno-Park. The ancient little snow cat used for trail grooming is often parked here. Weathered writing bears testament to its Coast Guard service in the Arctic decades ago. Its oversize cabin heater, designed for arctic weather, keeps the volunteer driver from sending the old machine to the scrap pile.

From the trailhead, descend past Forest Service cabins to a junction in 0.1 mile. There is a box for trail grooming donations here. To the right is Summit Trail, leading to Ski Bowl (Chapter 2). Bear left on Barlow Trail and immediately curve right. The trail drops quickly, flattens, and reaches a junction in 0.3 mile. Hemlock, the groomed trail, veers left. It is the easier descent route. It has steep sections but is less serpentine than the Barlow Trail. In 0.4 mile, it connects to Still Creek Campground Road. Turn right, pass through the campground, and follow the road 0.9 mile to Summit Meadows and the pioneer graves.

From the junction with the Hemlock Trail, the ungroomed Barlow Trail continues past a steep connector to Summit Trail and down a winding hill that sometimes resembles a toboggan run. It ends at Still Creek Campground, 0.6 mile from Summit Meadows.

Snowmobiles. Snowmobiles are allowed in the basin, but few will be encountered. There are not enough miles of trails to attract many riders. Occasionally, the snowmobile club grooms the road from the Trillium Lake Sno-Park and along Mud Creek Ridge. Red Top Meadows Trail is the designated snowmobile route into the basin. Summit Meadows and Still Creek Campground are closed to snowmobiles. The status quo is reasonable for skiers and snowmobilers. Periodic efforts to ban snowmobiles have not generated enthusiasm because conflicts are rare. There also have been suggestions to develop a route into the basin from Frog Lake, a popular snowmobile area. Such a route would transpose Trillium Basin into a snowmobile highway between Frog Lake and Government Camp. The Forest Service has not endorsed this plan and skiers should help them resist such proposals.

Night Skiing. Skiing to Trillium Dam on a night with a full moon is an exciting experience. On a clear night, moon shadows bounce across the snow. On a cloudy night, lights at Timberline Lodge give the mountain an eerie appearance reminiscent of a Tolkien story. Time a tour so the moon is well above the horizon. Bring flashlights and other essentials. Stay on the road to the dam. Other trails are too dark and winding.

4 PIONEER WOMAN'S GRAVE

Distance: 1–5.7 miles
Trails: Ungroomed ski trails
Track Quality: Good classic skiing, no skating
Skill Level: Novice to intermediate
Elevation: 4157 feet
Maximum Elevation Gain: 467 feet
Season: Early December to early April
Services and Facilities: None
Hours: NA
Fees: Sno-park permit
Information: Mount Hood Information Center, (503) 622-7674

Pioneer history, an easy-to-reach view of Mount Hood, and a delightful winding loop through clearings and over streams combine for a charming ski tour. Beginners can ski 0.5 mile to the mountain viewpoint. Most novices will be able to reach a pioneer gravesite and lovely creek crossing by descending a road for 2.1 miles. Add the Beaver Marsh Loop for a round trip of nearly 6 miles. Though the road is usually no problem for novice skiers, its long descent can be challenging when icy.

Drive 2 miles east from Government Camp on Highway 26 to Highway 35 and head north toward Hood River. Ignore a sign for Pioneer Woman's Grave in 0.2 mile. It marks the end of an access road that is closed in winter. Continue to the Barlow Pass Sno-Park 2 miles from Highway 26. Turn right and drive 0.2 mile to a small parking area. Barlow Pass Sno-Park is the high point on the old Barlow Road, the first wagon route across the Cascades and part of the Oregon Trail. Built in 1846, the wagon route offered an alternative to the dangerous and expensive boat trip through the Columbia Gorge.

Several trails start here. Trails east of the parking area are narrow or steep and tracks are often rough. The gentler Buzzard Point Trail on the road to the Pioneer Woman's Grave usually has decent tracks. The first skiers through new snow should try to set good, evenly spaced tracks.

Buzzard Point Trail. Buzzard Point Trail begins at the south end of the sno-park, opposite where the access road enters. It follows an old section of Highway 35 built in the 1920s. It descends gradually across a wooded slope 0.5 mile to a wide bend to the right. A clear-cut slope opens the forest for a view of Mount Hood. Few trails offer such a view for so little effort. On the up-slope side of the trail, a spring and cistern made this a popular stop on the old highway. The spring is under several feet of snow during much of winter. There are other viewpoints on the tour, but none have such an unobstructed view of the mountain.

The road rounds Buzzard Point, hardly noticeable, and drops more steeply. A hairpin turn at 1.4 miles is followed by a gradual downhill. The road flattens and at a wide bend to the left passes the first junction with the Beaver Marsh Trail. Continue on the road. A sign marking the Pioneer Woman's Grave is on the left, 75 feet past the junction. Since the sign is only 5 feet high, it may be buried by snow. In 1924 engineers surveying the original route of Highway 35 found a grave marker commemorating "a good woman" who died along the old Barlow Road.

In another 100 yards beyond the grave, Buzzard Point Road crosses the East Fork of the Salmon River. This is a particularly pretty winter scene, if the snow is not deep enough to hide the river from view. The second junction with the Beaver Marsh Trail is just beyond. The road

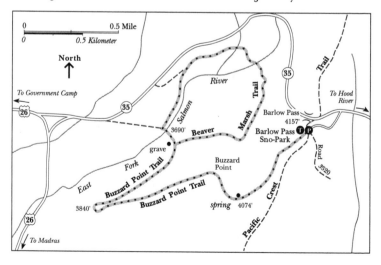

View from a clear-cut along the Buzzard Point Trail

continues to Highway 35, but there is no good reason to ski that section. If time or energy is short, return the way you came, 2.1 miles to the sno-park. Unless the road is icy, the 467-foot descent from the sno-park to the grave is not especially noticeable. Returning uphill, the same slope seems much steeper.

Beaver Marsh Trail. For a longer tour, turn onto the Beaver Marsh Trail and ski the loop clockwise. Just 100 yards from Buzzard Point Road, pass a fairly obscure section of the old Barlow Road. The trail may be difficult to follow here. Continue straight and look for blue diamond markers. In 0.4 mile, bear right on a narrow road. After crossing a stream, the loop returns to off-road trail marked by blue diamonds. The Beaver Marsh Trail crosses two branches of the East Fork of the Salmon River as it winds through thin second-growth forest and along the edge of two clear-cuts. Near the end of the 1.5-mile loop, the trail narrows, drops downhill, and crosses a clearing to regain the Buzzard Point Road. Turn left to return to the sno-park.

From the west side of the parking lot, the original descent route of the Barlow Road is an unmarked but obvious trail that drops quickly. It is historically interesting, but not a good ski route. The trail lacks adequate drainage, and water troughs create holes and soft spots in the snow.

The Barlow Road section that climbs from the east is across the access road near the entrance to the sno-park. Two other ski trails start near here. Forest Road 3520, starting 50 yards closer to the highway, drops down a steep hill and leads to meadows at Devil's Half-Acre and a 2.5-mile loop. A signboard marks the Pacific Crest Trail, a challenging narrow trail through the woods that is part of a loop to Twin Lakes.

5 WHITE RIVER

Distance: 1–3 miles
Trails: Ungroomed ski trails
Track Quality: Fair classic skiing, no skating
Skill Level: Novice
Elevation: 4240 feet
Maximum Elevation Gain: Up to 600 feet
Season: Early December to early April
Services and Facilities: Outhouse
Hours: NA
Fees: Sno-park permit
Information: Mount Hood Information Center, (503) 622-7674

Few views of Mount Hood surpass those from the broad, snow-covered White River Canyon. The mountain greets visitors from the sno-park and stays visible throughout the ski tour. The incredible scenery and gentle terrain make this sno-park very popular. Visit on a weekday if solitude is important. Blanketed by snow, the White River looks deceptively serene and docile, belying its power to wash tons of mud across the highway after heavy rains. White River often marks the transition zone where westside clouds give way to the blue sky that is more common on the east side.

From Portland, follow Highway 26 to Government Camp and continue east 2 miles. Exit on Highway 35 toward Hood River. In just over 4 miles, the entrance to White River West Sno-Park is on the left, 200 yards before the highway crosses the White River. The sno-park is

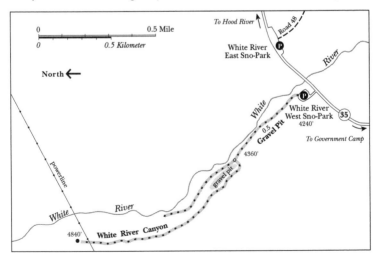

often congested with skiers, walkers, and dogs. Many are there just to enjoy the view near the sno-park. A second sno-park, White River East, is just across the bridge on the right side of the highway.

Gravel Pit. An easy 1-mile round trip up the broad river valley to the gravel pit is one of Mount Hood's most popular beginner ski tours. It climbs gently from White River West Sno-Park, gaining a mere 120 feet. Just ski uphill from the sno-park, with the river on the right. Mount Hood looms ahead the entire way. The normally well-packed route follows an old quarry road 0.5 mile to the pit. Do not expect solitude except on some weekdays. Likewise, do not expect nice ski tracks. Early tracks in new snow quickly take a beating. The pit is actually an open bank facing the river. Its 30-foot wall is good for practicing downhill skills and for just playing on skis.

White River Canyon. Beyond the gravel pit, the crowd thins out. There are two options for a longer tour up the canyon. The easier route to the right stays on the river flats, continuing another mile toward glacial moraines left by White River Glacier. Enjoy views of Mount Hood and the increasingly steeper canyon. As you go higher, the steep walls across the river have avalanche potential after heavy snowfall. Stay off these slopes and away from their base. The second option to the left is 3 miles round trip and requires intermediate skills, especially on the downhill return. Climb the bank at the southeast end of the pit and continue uphill on the bench above the river. The trail is not marked, but the trees are well spaced and routefinding is easy. In 1 mile, pass under the powerlines to Mount Hood Meadows Ski Area and continue a short distance for an excellent view of the canyon. The return along the same route is a quick downhill.

Some skiers cross the river and return downhill along the flats on the opposite side. This adds variety to the tour, but exercise caution and make sure a snow bridge is solid before crossing.

Stories of groomed tracks at White River are not worth getting excited about. A snowmobile club occasionally grooms Forest Road 48 from White River East Sno-Park, which connects to many miles of snowmobile trails. They sometimes also set a ski and snowshoe track along a short loop, but this is only done three or four times during the winter. White River East is less crowded than the west sno-park. Forest Road 48 is an easy but not terribly interesting tour. A better option is to play in the open areas and gullies near the river. The White River area has several other forest trails, most notably the Yellowjacket Trail, a challenging route from Government Camp to White River best done with a car shuttle. Klindt Vielbig describes these trails in *Cross-Country Ski Routes: Oregon* (The Mountaineers Books, Seattle).

Mount Hood above White River Canyon

6 MOUNT HOOD MEADOWS

Distance: 3–5 kilometers (1.9–3.1 miles); 13 kilometers total
Trails: Groomed ski trails
Track Quality: Good classic skiing, excellent skating
Skill Level: Novice to advanced
Elevation: 4580 feet
Maximum Elevation Gain: 280 feet
Season: Early December to late March
Services and Facilities: Ski rentals, lessons, lunchroom, snacks
Hours: 9:00 A.M.–4:00 P.M., Wednesday through Sunday
Fees: $10, sno-park permit
Information: Mount Hood Meadows Ski Resort (503) 337-2222,
ext. 262, *www.skihood.com/nordic.htm*

The commercial Nordic Center at Mount Hood Meadows Ski Resort is at Hood River Meadows, the resort's lower base of operations. It is named after nearby meadows bordering a tributary of the East Fork Hood River. The base includes one major ski lift and a small alpine service center at the west end of a huge parking lot. The Nordic Center is at the east end, away from most of the activity. Since the early 1990s, the Nordic operation has expanded from a few kilometers of haphazardly groomed trails to 13 kilometers (8 miles) with

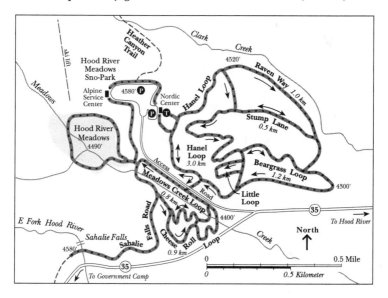

exceptional grooming. Trails are 18 feet wide and are excellent for skating. Most trails run through wooded terrain and are not particularly scenic, though there are a few outstanding viewpoints.

From Portland, drive east on Highway 26 through Government Camp. One mile beyond the Trillium Lake Sno-Park, exit right onto Highway 35 toward Hood River. In 8 miles, pass under the Mount Hood Meadows overpass. Continue 1 mile to the Hood River Meadows access road. Turn left and drive 0.5 mile uphill. At the start of the huge parking area, turn right into a small annex lot by the Nordic Center. On busy weekends, the road between Highway 26 and the overpass is prone to serious traffic congestion. An alternative is to follow Interstate 84 to exit 64 in Hood River, and then drive south on Highway 35 for 32 miles. The Hood River Meadows access road is on the right, just past the Teacup Lake Sno-Park. From Portland, the drive through Hood River adds nearly 30 miles each way, but avoids the traffic problems encountered along Highway 26.

Since 2000, the Nordic Center has been located at the annex lot, away from the hubbub of the alpine area. It is not elaborate but provides a comfortable place to rest or have lunch. It has running water and heated restrooms, welcome amenities on cold days. Each year the Nordic Center hosts a series of four ski races in which most entrants use the skating technique.

The Nordic trail system is split by the ski area access road. The Nordic Center and the most popular loops are on the east side of the road. The most scenic spots, as well as a short trail featuring exciting downhill turns, are on the west side. A spur with snow ramps to the access road connects west- and eastside trails. Remove skis and walk across. It is also possible to ski around the parking lot on an uninteresting groomed trail that passes through congestion near the alpine service center.

Skier crossing Hood River Meadows

Eastside Trails. The eastside trails were developed in the early 1990s and include three main loops. From the Nordic Center, follow signs to the Hanel Loop and ski 0.2 kilometer to a T intersection that starts the loop. Most of this rolling loop is one way headed clockwise. Only the first 0.3 kilometer to the right from the T is two way. This section is the route to the west side trails. From the T, the 3-kilometer (1.9-mile) Hanel Loop drops through two hills and turns sharply right at the first junction. Stay right for more rolling downhill skiing and then a long climb back to the T. This is a challenging loop for beginners, but the wide trails are forgiving.

The east leg of Hanel Loop has junctions with four trails on the left. These trails connect to form loops that descend between 100 and 200 feet and then climb back to the Hanel Loop. The first junction off Hanel Loop is Raven Way, a 1-kilometer intermediate trail with fast downhill sections. It connects to Stump Lane, which climbs 0.5 kilometer back to Hanel Loop. Farther south, the north leg of the 1.2-kilometer Beargrass Loop drops from the Hanel Loop. The loop crosses a creek near its bottom, and then its south leg, which is a one-way trail, climbs back to the Hanel Loop. Stump Lane and the north leg of Beargrass Loop can be skied in either direction. A short connector between these two trails makes other loops possible. Beginners should descend on Stump Lane, as it is the gentlest of the three possible downhill routes.

Westside Trails. The lovely meadows for which Hood River Meadows is named are west of the access road below the main parking lot. Almost 2 kilometers of flat trails are groomed here. Meadows Creek flows through these meadows but is mostly hidden under deep snow. On a clear day, you'll be treated to unforgettable views of Mount Hood. These trails are not groomed until 5 feet of snow cover them.

A trail from the busy alpine service center drops steeply to the meadows from the parking lot, but it is better to use the access road crossing from the Nordic Center. After crossing the road, turn right and ski parallel to the access road on Meadows Creek Loop. The section along the road may have gravel that has been tossed by road plows. This intermediate 0.8-kilometer loop shares a leg with Cheese Roll Loop, an advanced trail. Cheese Roll has tight hairpin downhill turns and must be skied counterclockwise. Skiers with strong downhill skills will love it. Ski within your ability to stop quickly, as there may be a skier sprawled across the trail on a turn.

Sahalie Falls. Sahalie Falls Road is technically not part of the fee system trails, but it is usually groomed. It is an out-and-back trail on the west side of the access road. It is the obvious road heading uphill from near the entrance to the meadows. It climbs easily for 1.6 kilometers to a bridge across the East Fork Hood River, just below stunning Sahalie Falls. The 80-foot-high waterfall is especially impressive in winter. Sahalie is a Chinook Indian word meaning "high." In spring, look for dippers, dark sandpiper-like birds that walk underwater. A pair often nests under the bridge. On the return, enjoy a view of Mount Hood from the lower road. Skiers who choose not to pay the trail fee can ski in deep snow along the side, off the groomed tracks.

7 HEATHER CANYON

Distance: 4.4 miles
Trails: Groomed ski area runout
Track Quality: Good classic skiing, good skating
Skill Level: Intermediate
Elevation: 4580 feet
Maximum Elevation Gain: 850 feet
Season: Mid-December to late April
Services and Facilities: None
Hours: NA
Fees: Sno-park permit
Information: Hood River Ranger District, Mount Hood National
    Forest, (541) 352-6002

The Heather Canyon Runout is a 2-mile ski trail that channels alpine skiers from the bottom of Heather Canyon's expert ski runs to the Hood River Meadows parking lot (Chapter 6). The trail is also a fine out-and-back cross-country ski route that climbs steadily along the banks of Clark Creek. The climb has steep sections, but the effort is rewarded with views of the rushing creek, steep canyon walls, and Mount Hood rising above the canyon. Mount Hood Meadows Ski Resort grooms the runout, maintaining a wide trail with a firm and smooth base. The result is a trail well suited for ski touring and skating, though the downhill return is fast and requires intermediate skills.

Skiers must be alert for alpine skiers coming downhill. There is plenty of room on the wide trail to avoid collisions. Though the trail feels steep for cross-country skiers, it is a gentle slope for alpine skiers and they cannot pick up a lot of speed. Often, a cross-country skier skating back to the parking lot can catch up to and pass the lift skiers. There is very little downhill traffic for the first 1.6 miles. At that point, the Heather Canyon Runout is only 200 yards from the lower terminus

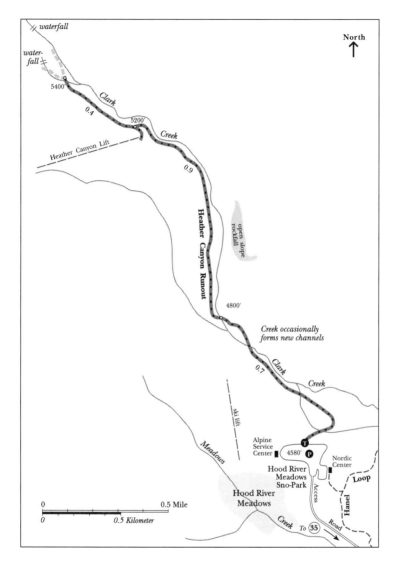

of the Heather Canyon Lift, installed in the mid-1990s. Most alpine skiers exit the runout and head for that lift, leaving the long section to the parking lot in relative solitude. More skiers will be encountered beyond the lift, but it is still far from being crowded.

Follow driving directions in chapter 6 to the Hood River Meadows Sno-Park. The Heather Canyon trailhead is on the north side of the large parking lot, 200 yards from the east end of the lot. Climb the snowbank next to the lot to reach the trailhead. On many weekends, the

Mount Hood above Heather Canyon

lot fills with lift skier traffic. To be considerate, cross-country skiers should bear right as they enter the lot and park near the east end. This leaves parking space closer to the alpine facilities for the area's paying customers, and it is little effort to ski 200 yards along the north side of the lot to reach the Heather Canyon Runout. The ski area posts avalanche conditions at the trailhead. The most dangerous chutes are in the upper canyon, but the whole canyon should be avoided when risk is high or when avalanche control work is in progress.

From the trailhead, ski northeast for a short distance. Early in the season, the trail quickly encounters a small channel that was carved by rain-swelled Clark Creek on Thanksgiving Day 2000. It is impossible to cross this channel without getting wet feet until there are several feet of snow. The creek goes where it will and in any year could abandon this channel or create new ones. In another 100 yards, the trail curves northwest and skiers are treated to the first of several open views of Mount Hood. At 0.2 mile, it reaches the main channel and continues uphill along its bank, providing numerous opportunities to enjoy the creek's beauty. At about 1 mile from the trailhead, the trail passes steep open slopes to the east, just across the stream.

The trail continues to climb, with Clark Creek on the right and several views of Mount Hood. At 1.6 miles, a sign marks a trail to the Heather Canyon lift on the left. The side trail angles back and up a small hill. The lift is tucked in the trees, hidden from view. Without the sign or a few skiers heading up the side trail, it could be overlooked. Heather Canyon Runout continues for another 0.4 mile with more excellent Mount Hood views. This section will have more skiers coming downhill, and it is best to stay to one side of the trail.

Skiers have three choices at the end of the trail. The first is to turn around and enjoy a 2-mile downhill run to the parking lot. The second is to veer left and climb a ridge for a better view of the canyon. Watch for alpine skiers coming down in this area. In the spring, listen for the sound of cascading water and follow it to a small waterfall on the ridge. The third choice is to continue along Clark Creek. It may be necessary to break trail in deep snow. The canyon gets narrower and the walls get steeper. Continuing far in this direction requires knowledge of avalanche conditions and proper backcountry equipment. Another waterfall can be heard far up the canyon, but it is on a steep slope and cannot be reached.

8 TEACUP LAKE

Distance: 1–9 kilometers (0.6–5.6 miles), 20 kilometers total
Trails: Groomed ski trails
Track Quality: Very good classic skiing, fair skating
Skill Level: Novice to advanced
Elevation: 4350 feet
Maximum Elevation Gain: 445 feet
Season: Early December to early April
Services and Facilities: Warming hut, outhouse
Hours: NA
Fees: $3 per person suggested donation, sno-park permit
Information: Teacup Lake chapter, Oregon Nordic Club,
  www.teacupnordic.org

The trails at Teacup Lake are an excellent example of what volunteers can do. The Teacup Lake chapter of the Oregon Nordic Club developed and maintains 20 kilometers of groomed trails at what has become a favorite destination for many skiers. Some trails follow roads, but most were designed to be ski trails. There are scenic spots and views of Mount Hood, but trails with a mix of flats, rolling hills, and

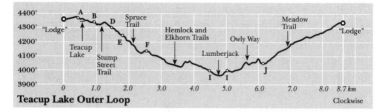

Teacup Lake Outer Loop   Clockwise

some challenging sections are the main attraction. A trailer serves as a warming hut and a gathering place for the ski community. There is a Teacup Lake along the trails, but it was named for its size and is easy to overlook. Dogs and snowshoes are not allowed on the trails.

Volunteers often groom with a snowmobile, but it is impossible for them to handle 20 kilometers of trail regularly. Most grooming is done with a large snow machine, hired on an hourly basis. The club also pays for trail maps, heater fuel, trailer repairs, toilet paper, and a host of other expenses associated with the ski area. Membership dues and donations pay for these expenses. Teacup volunteers ask that everyone contribute by either joining the club or making a donation every time they use the trails. The current suggested minimum is $3 per person.

Teacup's terrain and grooming are excellent for classic skiing and fair for skating. The trails are narrower and less meticulously groomed than trails at commercial ski areas. Most are 9 feet wide, though a few are groomed wider with a second pass. The trails are groomed for Saturday skiing. When finances permit, they are groomed again during the week or on Sunday. Summer work parties clear trails so they can be groomed with minimal snow accumulation, well before other Mount Hood trails are skiable.

The Teacup Lake Sno-Park is on the south side of Highway 35, 10 miles east of Government Camp and 1 mile past the Mount Hood Meadows overpass. It is on the right, 0.1 mile past the turn to Hood River Meadows. If the lot is full, use the Clark Creek Sno-Park across the highway. From Hood River, drive 32 miles south on Highway 35 to the sno-park on the left. The trailhead is near the east end of the sno-park. If touring on nearby ungroomed trails, turn left at the signboard and look for blue diamonds.

For the groomed trails, turn right at the signboard and follow a wide trail 0.4 kilometer to the "lodge," which is actually a trailer. The donation box and an outhouse are here. The trailer is open as a warming hut on most weekends. It is a good place to stow gear, have lunch, and meet other skiers. The club hopes to replace the trailer with a cabin closer to the sno-park, but that will take time, money, and permission from the Forest Service.

The club has been grooming trails at this location since 1977. Skiers used to park along the highway until the sno-park was built in 1987. The club started with a few trails and then partnered with the Forest Service to develop quite a system. Unlike other ski clubs, Teacup sponsors few tours and holds few meetings. Their efforts are focused on the trail system and special events. These include a ski clinic in early December and a race in late January that attracts competitors ranging from beginners to skiers of national stature. A Saturday ski program for 8- to 12-year-olds will continue as long as volunteers are available. The club performs a great public service at Teacup, so be nice to the volunteers. Better yet, pitch in and lend a hand with the work.

Numerous connecting trails create a variety of loop possibilities. Some basic routes are described here, but use a trail map to create your own. Trail junctions are marked with letters and trail names to help with routefinding. Most trails are one-way; heed the signs. Trails that are not shown on the map are groomed occasionally. Both the club and the groomer like to play with new possibilities. If you encounter an unmarked junction, just ski on to a marked junction to get reoriented.

All loops start at the lodge/trailer and most are skied counterclockwise. From the trailer, ski south on Teacup Road. This road crosses Meadows Creek and then climbs gently uphill to connect to other trails.

Wahoo. Kids love this 0.7-kilometer loop with the descriptive name. Ski 0.3 kilometer from the trailer on Teacup Road. Turn left for a fast and challenging drop into Wahoo Gulch and then a short, steep climb after crossing Meadows Creek. Stay to the left to loop back to the trailer.

Lakeside and Tea Time. This is a good, 2.4-kilometer (1.5-mile) beginner loop that does not wander far from the trailer and has Mount Hood views. Ski 0.3 kilometer from the trailer on Teacup Road and turn right onto Lakeside. Ski past tiny Teacup Lake on the right. In winter, it looks like a small meadow. Lakeside descends to Nordic Way in an open area with a view of Mount Hood. Turn right onto Nordic Way and in 25 yards turn left onto Tea Time. After a short, steep dip and then a short, steep climb, Tea Time meanders on gentle terrain for nearly a kilometer before looping back to Nordic Way. Turn right and ski up a steep 0.2-kilometer hill to the high point on the Teacup trail system. It is a steady climb on a wide road. Take your time and you will reach the top. Skiers affectionately call the hill Tom's Terror after Tom Gibbons, an early driving force in developing the Teacup trails. The "terror" refers to him more than the hill. Turn left and ski 0.5 kilometer down Teacup Road to the trailer.

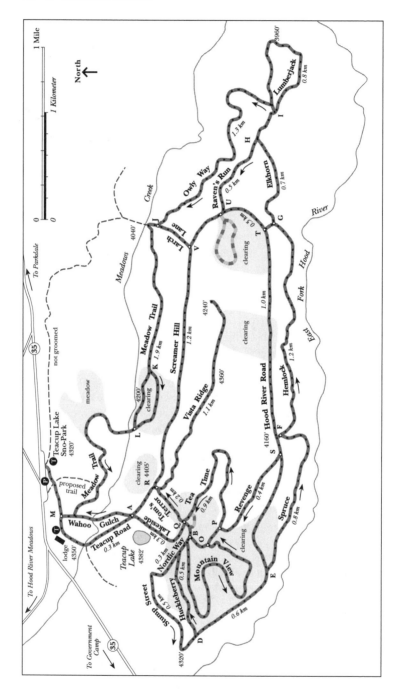

Outer Loop. A loop around the perimeter of the Teacup ski area is 8.7 kilometers (5.4 miles). It is an intermediate tour, but sections of the loop will test intermediate skiers in icy conditions. The loop uses twelve different trails. The simple directions are to start up Teacup Road from the trailer and stay right on the groomed trails at all marked intersections. More specifically, ski up the Teacup Road and down Lakeside to Nordic Way. Turn right and enjoy a view of Mount Hood. Ski 0.3 kilometer on Nordic Way, which curves sharply left on a downhill into Stump Street. Stump Street descends into Hood River Road at the westernmost point on the Teacup trails. Follow the road southeast for an easy 0.6-kilometer to Spruce, which drops sharply to the right on a challenging intermediate hill. Spruce and the next trail, Hemlock, parallel the East Fork Hood River, which can be heard but not seen on the right. Spruce and Hemlock combine for 2 kilometers of twisting trail with several steep up and down sections. Hemlock climbs steeply to Elkhorn, which leads east to Lumberjack, a trail that drops to the easternmost and lowest point on the Teacup trails, nearly 400 feet below the trailer. Turn right onto Owly Way, a 1.3-kilometer trail with steep ups and downs that leads west to Larch. Turn right onto Larch, which leads a few yards to the Meadow Trail, a 1.9-kilometer trail with a long, gradual climb back to the trailer.

Long Beginner Loop. This 6.3-kilometer (4-mile) loop is easy skiing and has views of Mount Hood but requires some endurance. Ski up Teacup Road from the trailer and turn right onto Lakeside. After passing tiny Teacup Lake, Lakeside curves left and descends to Nordic Way. Turn right, enjoy a view of Mount Hood, and follow Nordic Way until it curves left into Stump Street. The downhill turn at the beginning of Stump Street will challenge beginners. Stump Street drops to Hood River Road. Ski east on Hood River Road, passing below small clear-cuts on the left. Hood River Road curves northwest for a fine view of Mount Hood and reaches trail junction V (2.7 kilometers from Stump Street). This is at the bottom of Screamer Hill. Do not go up Screamer Hill. Turn right onto Larch Lane, which quickly curves left onto the Meadow Trail. The Meadow Trail heads west 1.9 kilometers through forest and along the edge of a large meadow, climbing gradually to the trailer.

Screamer. Screamer Hill is not a ski loop, but it is a trail that skiers should know about. It is a 1.2-kilometer hill along the Teacup–Hood River Road. Reach the top of Screamer, which is also the high point on the Teacup trails, by skiing uphill 0.5 kilometer on Teacup Road from the lodge. The same road descends the other side, where it is

Nordic Way trail

now Screamer Hill. After the 1.2-kilometer descent, the road flattens and is called Hood River Road. It is easy to pick up a lot of speed going down Screamer. It is not for beginners, especially in icy conditions. In the other direction, Screamer Hill is a long, steady uphill trudge. Fortunately, Screamer can be avoided. Skiing away from the trailer, turn off of Teacup Road onto Lakeside to avoid the downhill on Screamer. Returning to the trailer, use Larch and the Meadow Trail to avoid the long climb up Screamer.

9 POCKET CREEK

Distance: 2–10 miles
Trails: Ungroomed ski trails
Track Quality: Good classic skiing, no skating
Skill Level: Novice to intermediate
Elevation: 3800 feet
Maximum Elevation Gain: 1080 feet; 680 feet excluding Road 640
Season: Mid-December to late March
Services and Facilities: None
Hours: NA
Fees: Sno-park permit
Information: Hood River Ranger District, Mount Hood National
    Forest, (541) 352-6002

A mix of beginner and intermediate trails contribute to Pocket Creek's popularity. Magnificent Mount Hood views that can be reached with minimal effort add to the allure. Options include out-and-back road tours with views and intermediate loops through the woods. Positioned in Mount Hood's rain shadow, the area enjoys relatively sunny weather, but, at 3800 feet, trails near the sno-park do not have good snow until well into December.

To get there from Portland, drive Interstate 84 to exit 64 in Hood River. Turn right off the exit and follow Highway 35 south 30 miles. The sno-park is a long strip along the highway shoulder on the left. If coming through Government Camp, drive east on Highway 26 for 2 miles to Highway 35. Follow Highway 35 for 12 miles to Pocket Creek Sno-Park, 2 miles beyond the Teacup Lake Sno-Park. From Portland, the longer trip through Hood River avoids the worst road conditions and traffic.

Pocket Creek Trail. Tours start at the north end of the sno-park on the Pocket Creek Trail. This trail follows Forest Road 3540, which many people call Pocket Creek Road. Beginners and novices can ski south on the road, easily reaching the East Fork Hood River and a view of Mount Hood in 0.6 mile. The trail crosses the East Fork Hood River after passing an entrance to the Meadows Creek Tie Trail on the right. The river is absolutely lovely in winter, and a stop to enjoy it is a must. Beyond the river, the road climbs, passing several clear-cuts on the right with excellent views. The first is just 0.3 mile after the bridge. When you have had enough uphill, turn around and return downhill the way you came. If the road is icy, the downhill can be difficult for beginners. In icy conditions, the flat Meadows Creek Tie Trail is a safer, but less scenic, out-and-back option for beginners.

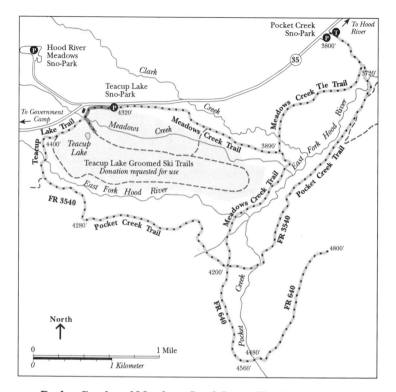

Pocket Creek and Meadows Creek Loop. The Pocket Creek Trail can be combined with the Meadows Creek Trail, which is a challenging and scenic venture through the woods, for an intermediate tour of nearly 6 miles. Skied counterclockwise starting from the Pocket Creek trailhead, the narrow Meadows Creek Trail is mostly uphill and the downhill return is on Forest Road 3540. (The loop is described in this direction.) More aggressive skiers can ski the loop clockwise for a downhill run on the woods trail. From the sno-park, ski 0.5 mile to Meadows Creek Tie Trail, which "ties" the Pocket Creek Trail to the Meadows Creek Trail. Turn right and follow a gentle route past small clearings and tall timber. Cross Clark Creek and turn left on the Meadows Creek Trail, which winds through the woods, crosses Meadows Creek, and passes near the groomed trails at Teacup Lake. In 0.8 mile, cross to the south side of the East Fork Hood River on a new bridge that replaced one swept away by torrential rains and flooding in 1999. Meadows Creek Trail climbs steeply here, enters a large clearcut, and meets Forest Road 3540 (Pocket Creek Trail) at the top of the clearing (4200 feet). Turn left onto Forest Road 3540 and descend to the river and the sno-park in 2.7 miles. The road crosses Pocket Creek just beyond the junction, one of the few places where the creek is visible.

Meadows Creek and Teacup Lake Loop. A challenging loop for intermediate skiers follows the Meadows Creek and Teacup Lake Trails. It features plenty of ups and downs and a couple of river crossings. The round trip from the sno-park is nearly 10 miles. From the sno-park, ski 0.5 mile on the Pocket Creek Trail and turn right onto the Meadows Creek Tie Trail. Continue 1 mile to the Meadows Creek Trail. Turn left onto Meadows Creek Trail, cross Meadows Creek and the river, and climb to a four-way junction with Forest Roads 3540 and 640. Turn right onto Forest Road 3540 and ski 2 miles, climbing a little. The Teacup Lake Trail drops steeply to the right a short distance before Pocket Creek Road ends. Turn right onto this challenging intermediate trail with sharp twists, descending to cross the East Fork Hood River on a second new bridge. The trail skirts the west edge of the Teacup Lake area (Chapter 8), passes north of tiny Teacup Lake, and meets a road that is part of the Teacup groomed trail system 100 feet from Meadows Creek. Turn left, cross the creek, and ski past the Oregon Nordic Club's warming trailer. The Teacup Lake Trail curves right at the trailer and parallels Highway 35 to the Teacup Lake Sno-Park. This 0.3-mile section to the sno-park is groomed. Pick up the ungroomed Meadows Creek Trail near the sno-park bulletin board. Parallel the highway for another 0.3 mile through thick trees. The trail turns southeast, skirts meadows, and follows a skid road back to the junction with the Meadows Creek Tie Trail. Turn left onto the trail for a flat, 1.5-mile return to Pocket Creek Sno-Park.

Road 640. The best views in the Pocket Creek ski area are earned by a steep climb on Forest Road 640. The road leads south from its junction with the Pocket Creek and Meadows Creek Trails. It ends on a logging landing after passing clear-cuts and slopes that beckon telemark skiers. The climb and the distance require stamina and good skills.

Bridge across the East Fork Hood River

10 COOPER SPUR

Distance: 6–14 miles
Trails: Ungroomed ski trails
Track Quality: Fair classic skiing, no skating
Skill Level: Novice to advanced
Elevation: 3810 feet
Maximum Elevation Gain: 2090 feet
Season: Early December to early April
Services and Facilities: Rustic cabins
Hours: NA
Fees: Sno-park permit
Information: Hood River Ranger District, Mount Hood National
   Forest, (541) 352-6002

Cross-country trails near the Cooper Spur Ski Area on the northeast side of Mount Hood are appreciated for generally clear weather and views of Mount Hood's north side. Well-known tours from the Tilly Jane Sno-Park are long uphill treks that require stamina. Destinations include historic Cloud Cap Inn for its great view and Tilly Jane Campground for an overnight stay in a rustic cabin. A less demanding tour

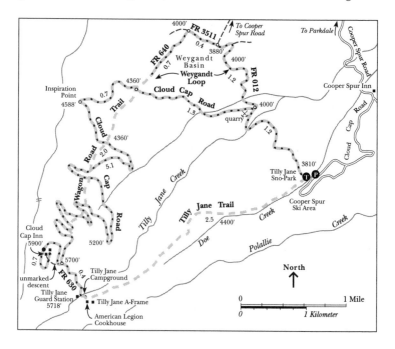

in the Weygandt Basin below Cloud Cap Road yields views of three volcanoes without a long uphill climb.

From Portland, drive east on Interstate 84 to Hood River. From exit 64 at Hood River, turn right and follow Highway 35 south for 13.5 miles to the tiny town of Mount Hood. Turn right onto Cooper Spur Road. A store at this intersection has a bakery that should be investigated before a hard day of skiing. Head uphill on Cooper Spur Road 10 miles to Cooper Spur Inn on the left. Turn right onto Cloud Cap Road, across from the inn. Continue uphill 1.5 miles to the sno-park on the right, just before the turn to the small Cooper Spur Ski Area. Cloud Cap Road is not plowed beyond the Tilly Jane Sno-Park.

Cloud Cap Road. Ski tours start on Cloud Cap Road, leading northwest from the sno-park. Cloud Cap Road climbs nearly 2100 feet in 9 miles to Cloud Cap Inn and views of Mount Hood and the volcanic peaks of southern Washington. The grade is not steep, but the long climb is physically demanding. In 2.5 miles from the sno-park, Cloud Cap Road passes the Wagon Road Trail on the left. At 3.2 miles, the road reaches a view of Mount Hood at the first of ten sharp switchbacks. This is Inspiration Point and a good turnaround point for novices. The seventh switchback, a sharp left at 7.2 miles, has a view of Mount Adams. At 8.3 miles, Forest Road 630 leads left to Tilly Jane Campground. Cloud Cap Road continues to the right and leads 0.7 mile to Cloud Cap Inn and views of Mount Hood.

Built in 1889, Cloud Cap Inn is the oldest building on Mount Hood. Scheduled for demolition in the early 1950s, it was saved by the Crag Rats, a local climbing and rescue group that now uses it as a base. A nearby building is owned and operated by the Snowshoe Club. Neither building is open to the public. Advanced skiers can start the return trip on a steep, unmarked shortcut through sparse trees that descends from the south side of the inn. It reaches Cloud Cap Road near the junction to Tilly Jane Campground. Less experienced skiers should follow the road back down to this junction.

Tilly Jane Campground has three cabins available for overnight use. The nicest is the Guard Station, built in 1924. The Columbia Gorge chapter of the Oregon Nordic Club maintains the building and manages reservations. There is usually a waiting list. The Tilly Jane A-Frame and the American Legion Cookhouse are across a ravine from the Guard Station. Contact the Hood River Ranger District for information.

Wagon Road Trail. The Wagon Road Trail, a narrow track that follows an early road to Cloud Cap Inn, provides an alternative to a long downhill return to the sno-park on Cloud Cap Road. It is a fun, 2-mile descent, cutting through the switchbacks of Cloud Cap Road

Cloud Cap Inn and Mount Hood

and trimming 4 miles from the trip. Ski down Cloud Cap Road 0.3 mile from the junction to Tilly Jane Campground to the first switchback. The sections through the first two switchbacks are short but steep. This stretch requires strong intermediate skills and should be avoided when icy. The last section of Wagon Road Trail meets Cloud Cap Road across from a trail to Weygandt Basin. Turn right on Cloud Cap Road and ski 2.5 miles to the sno-park. A round trip up Cloud Cap Road and returning on the Wagon Road Trail is 14 miles.

Tilly Jane Trail. Many skiers in a hurry to reach the Tilly Jane cabins ascend the Tilly Jane Trail. Its trailhead is to the left of Cloud Cap Road, a few yards west of the sno-park. This more direct route reaches the cabins in just 2.5 miles. It is another mile beyond the cabins to Cloud Cap Inn. This is less than half the distance to reach the same destination as via Cloud Cap Road, but the steep and narrow ascent is more of a trudge than a ski tour. Descending on the Tilly Jane Trail requires excellent skills, and only advanced skiers should attempt it.

Weygandt Loop. The Weygandt Basin is an area of clear-cuts and managed forest north of Cloud Cap Road. A little-known, 6-mile loop on roads through Weygandt Basin yields exceptional views without a long uphill trek. The loop is appropriate for strong beginners. From the Tilly Jane Sno-Park, ski 1.2 miles on Cloud Cap Road to a small rock quarry on the left. Just beyond, turn onto Forest Road 012, which angles to the right. This starts a loop that drops into the basin, passes numerous views, and climbs back to Cloud Cap Road. Follow Road 012 for 1.4 miles to a T at Forest Road 3511. Take a left to follow the loop, passing through clear-cuts with views of Mount Hood, Mount Adams, and Mount Rainier.

In 0.5 mile, turn left onto Forest Road 640 and ski south 0.7 mile, climbing back to Cloud Cap Road. The last few hundred yards before Cloud Cap Road are narrow and overgrown with brush. Turn left onto Cloud Cap Road and return 2.5 miles to the sno-park. Several logging roads branching off the loop can make routefinding confusing. Take a map.

The Future. In late 2001, the Mount Hood Meadows Ski Resort announced plans for developing resort facilities in the area east of the ski trails described here. It has purchased Cooper Spur Inn and Cooper Spur Ski Area and large tracts of land near the inn. Hood River County has granted the resort approval for commercial groomed cross-country trails near the inn. Other proposals may include a housing development, a golf course, and expansion of the existing ski area. Depending on the scale of the project, the housing development could disturb the tranquility currently enjoyed in Weygandt Basin. Likewise, extensive expansion of the tiny alpine ski area could alter the existing Tilly Jane Ski Trail.

11 BILLY BOB

Distance: 3–8 miles
Trails: Groomed snowmobile trails, ungroomed ski trails
Track Quality: Good classic skiing, fair skating
Skill Level: Novice to advanced
Elevation: 3960 feet
Maximum Elevation Gain: Up to 1100 feet
Season: Mid-December to late March
Services and Facilities: Outhouse, lookout cabin
Hours: NA
Fees: Northwest Forest Pass required
Information: Barlow Ranger District, Mount Hood National Forest, (541) 467-2291

The open forests east of Mount Hood lie in the mountain's rain shadow and often experience clear weather even when rain clouds shroud the mountain. Cross-country skiers are discovering an area in this region near Fivemile Butte long enjoyed by snowmobilers. You can choose between skiing on shared-use groomed trails and exploring new trails away from snowmobiles. All provide fine views. An overnight stay in a lookout tower on the butte is a unique way to spend a weekend exploring the area.

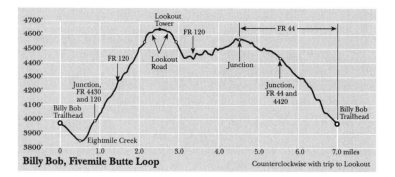

Billy Bob, Fivemile Butte Loop — Counterclockwise with trip to Lookout

The area is 120 miles from Portland. It is reached via Forest Road 44 leading west from Dufur. Most skiers reach Dufur by driving south from The Dalles. Dufur can also be reached from Highway 26 and then Highways 216 and 197. From Portland, drive Interstate 84 to exit 87, Highway 197, near The Dalles. Drive south 12 miles on Highway 197 to Dufur Road angling right to Dufur. Pass the Barlow Ranger Station and curve through town, following signs to Camp Baldwin. In 1.2 miles from Highway 197, turn right onto Dufur Valley Road toward Camp Baldwin and Highway 35. In another 5 miles, stay right at a fork. The road becomes Forest Road 44. The road is plowed for 17 miles, then ends at a gravel lot. The Forest Service plows the lot and a Northwest National Forest Pass must be displayed. Sno-park permits are not valid. The lot is shared with snowmobilers.

Fivemile Butte. Shared-use trails groomed weekly by a snowmobile club lead to the top of Fivemile Butte, 2.5 miles from the parking lot. The route requires intermediate skills. From the entrance to the parking lot, walk or ski across Forest Road 44, then ski north on Forest Road 4430. Pass Eightmile Creek and turn left onto Forest Road 120. Climb steadily for 1.5 miles, gaining 700 feet from Eightmile Creek, to a sharp left. Ski 0.4 mile on this spur to a lookout tower on the butte, with views of the high desert and Mount Hood. The lookout was built in 1934 and rebuilt in 1957. For information on overnight rentals, contact the Barlow Ranger District.

To complete a loop on snowmobile trails, return down the spur and continue to the left on Forest Road 120 past more views, reaching Forest Road 44 in 1.6 miles. Follow Forest Road 44 east back to the sno-park. The loop, including the side trip to the lookout, is 7 miles with a cumulative climb of 939 feet.

Bulo Point. Forest Road 4420, another groomed snowmobile trail, leads south off of Forest Road 44 and climbs continuously to overlooks of the eastern lowlands. The long climb and downhill return warrant an advanced rating. Ski north 50 feet through the trees from the parking lot and turn left onto Forest Road 44. Ski 1.5 miles west on Forest Road 44 to Forest Road 4420 on the left. For a stellar view of Mount Hood, before starting uphill on Forest Road 4420, ski a few yards farther to where Forest Road 44 curves right. Ski south on Forest Road 4420. Bear right at a fork in 0.9 mile and reach a viewpoint after 2.1 miles of climbing. Continue straight 0.3 mile to a better viewpoint above Bulo Point, just before the road starts to descend. This is nearly 4 miles from the sno-park and 1100 feet above it. The good news is that the return trip is all downhill.

Wolf Run. In summer 2001, volunteers from the Portland chapter of the Oregon Nordic Club helped the Forest Service mark ski trails in the Wolf Run area northeast of the sno-park. Wolf Run is the name of a local irrigation ditch. These ungroomed trails, suitable for beginner to advanced skiers, are mostly on forest roads and are closed to snowmobiles. They lead to excellent views of three major volcanoes. Some trails that are not shown on the map that accompanies this chapter have been marked, but the system is still under develop-

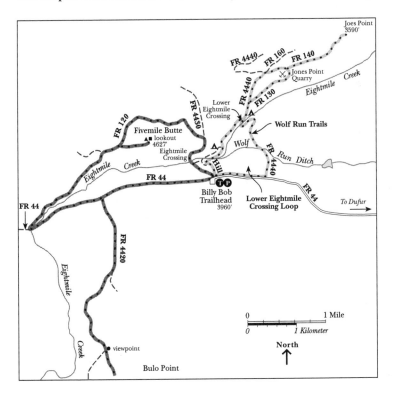

ment and early markers may be changed.

Lower Eightmile Crossing Loop. The 3-mile Lower Eightmile Crossing Loop is beginner level if skied counterclockwise. From the sno-park, cross Forest Road 44 and ski east, parallel to the plowed road. The marked trail is in the trees between the road and a clear-cut. In 0.7 mile, turn north onto Forest Road 4440. In another mile, cross Eightmile Creek and then reach the Lower Eightmile Crossing Campground. The loop leaves the road with a sharp left near an outhouse. It follows a summer wheelchair trail through a clearing and arrives at another campground. It leaves this campground on a steep, 0.3-mile trail uphill to the sno-park. If the loop is skied clockwise, this section is an advanced-level downhill run.

Jones Point Quarry. Jones Point Quarry is an easy beginner destination with views of Mount Hood, Mount Adams, and Mount Rainier. The quarry forms a shallow bowl that is a fun place to practice downhill

turns. Reach it by skiing east along Forest Road 44 to Forest Road 4440 and skiing north to Lower Eightmile Crossing Campground, 1.7 miles from the parking lot. Continue 0.2 mile north on Forest Road 4440 and bear right onto Forest Road 130. Ski 0.6 mile to the south side of the quarry and the volcano views. Cross to the north side of the small quarry and turn right onto Forest Road 140. This road leads northeast 0.8 mile to its end near Joes Point. As the trail system is developed, two or three trails will lead from here through the woods for loop routes back to Lower Eightmile Crossing Campground. Check with the Barlow Ranger District for up-to-date information.

Fivemile Butte lookout

View of Mount Hood from Fivemile Butte

12 SKYLINE

Distance: 8–13 miles
Trails: Groomed snowmobile trails
Track Quality: Good classic skiing, good skating
Skill Level: Intermediate
Elevation: 3640 feet
Maximum Elevation Gain: 1204 feet
Season: Mid-December to mid-April
Services and Facilities: Outhouse
Hours: NA
Fees: Sno-park permit
Information: Barlow Ranger District, Mount Hood National Forest,
(541) 467-2291

Two miles east of Government Camp, Highway 26 turns south and passes through 20 miles of national forest that many skiers have not explored. There are few designated ski trails and only two sno-parks. Both of these, Frog Lake and Skyline, are hubs for 90 miles of connecting roads groomed by the Mount Hood Snowmobile Club. The groomed roads from Skyline Sno-Park are fine ski trails, and it is easy to cover long distances on them.

The roads offer limited viewpoints. The finest is on Clear Lake Butte, less than 4 miles but a long climb from the Skyline Sno-Park. A Forest Service lookout tower at the top can be rented for an overnight stay. Little Crater Lake and its beautiful meadows make a fascinating destination for a long tour on easy terrain. This area is especially good in spring when lengthening daylight hours and waning snowmobile activity provide excellent skiing and relative solitude.

To reach Skyline Sno-Park, drive east on Highway 26 from Government Camp. After the junction with Highway 35, Highway 26 turns south toward Madras and crosses two 4000-foot passes. A gas station 2 miles from Highway 35 is the last chance for gas for 43 miles. Seven miles past Highway 35, turn right toward Timothy Lake onto Forest

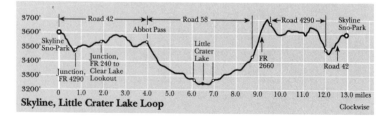

Skyline, Little Crater Lake Loop   Clockwise

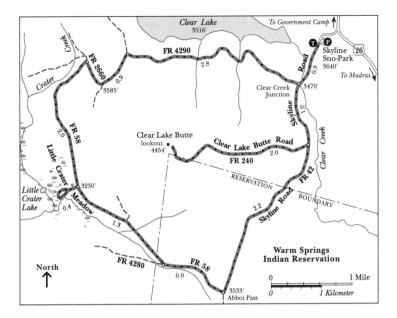

Road 42 (known as Skyline Road). Drive south 0.4 mile to the end of the plowed road and a large sno-park on the left. The sno-park has outhouses and a large log shelter.

The snowmobile club grooms midweek, packing a 10-foot-wide trail. A second overlapping pass on roads near the sno-park creates a surface of 15 to 18 feet that is fine for skating. On weekends, snowmobile traffic creates little moguls or bumps in the trails. These add to the fun of the area and most skiers easily adapt to them.

Tours start on Skyline Road, at the gate near the sno-park entrance. A short trail from the south side of the lot leads to the road. Head south on Skyline. If there is snowmobile traffic, ski to one side. The road is wide enough for them to pass easily, and most slow down near skiers.

The 1887 McQuinn Line defines the border of the Warm Springs Indian Reservation 2.5 miles south of the sno-park. Skyline Road passes through a corner of the reservation. The tribe restricts nontribal travel to Skyline and two smaller roads. Do not wander from these roads when skiing through the reservation.

Little Crater Lake. Barely 100 feet across, Little Crater Lake is an exceptionally clear pool fed by an artesian spring. There is no crater. It earned the name from the deep, clear water, reminiscent of the big Crater Lake in southern Oregon. The tour can be skied as a 13-mile out-and-back on easy terrain or as a slightly shorter loop with 1 mile along a steep, narrow road. The steep section is not always well groomed and can be difficult for skaters. The long distance makes this an intermediate tour.

Ski south on Skyline Road, descending steadily 0.9 mile to Clear Creek. Fifty feet farther on the right is a junction with Forest Road 4290, the return leg for the loop tour. Beyond the creek, Skyline climbs gradually, passing the road to the lookout. The Warm Springs Reservation boundary is 1.6 miles past the creek, but it is not clearly marked. The road continues through easy terrain to Abbot Pass, 4.1 miles from the sno-park. Turn right onto Forest Road 58 heading to Little Crater Lake Campground. The moderately steep downhill requires caution if icy. Bear right at a fork in 0.9 mile, staying on Forest Road 58. Shortly after the fork, the road leaves tribal land. From the fork, ski an easy 1.3 miles to the entrance to Little Crater Lake Campground. At the far end of the campground, a clearly marked trail leads to the lake, only 250 yards distant. Mount Hood can be seen to the north along this trail.

Explore the meadows adjacent to the campground, looking for signs of beaver and otter. As the meadows lose snow in spring, they attract wetland birds. In April, look for sandhill cranes and listen for the eerie winnowing of snipe in courtship flight.

Return to Forest Road 58 from the lake. Turn right onto the road to retrace your route, 6.3 miles. It is mostly a gradual climb to the sno-park. Turn left to continue the loop. The loop is a bit shorter than the out-and-back route, but has a steep hill. Ski 2 miles on Forest Road 58, to a sharp right onto Forest Road 2660. This narrow road climbs steeply 0.4 mile to a small road that may have snowmobile tracks. Stay on 2660, which turns north for 0.5 mile and drops to Forest Road 4290. Turn right and ski 2.8 miles west to Skyline Road near Clear Creek, completing the loop. The sno-park is to the left.

Clear Lake Butte. A panoramic view from Clear Lake Butte, elevation 4454 feet, is ample reward for the relentless climb to the top. Mount Hood towers to the north on a clear day and nearby Timothy and Clear Lakes seem just a stone's throw below. On rare cloudless days, 5600-foot Mount Wilson to the southeast, the volcanoes of central Oregon, and Mount Adams 60 miles to the north can be seen. Intermediate skills are needed, as the long climb and downhill return are difficult for beginners.

The butte's original lookout tower was built around 1930. It was rebuilt in the early 1960s. The 40-foot tower, still used in fire season, can be rented in winter for a stimulating overnight stay. Groups are limited to a maximum of four. Contact the Barlow Ranger District for information. The lookout has an outhouse, but a snow shovel may be needed to get the door open.

Little Crater Meadows

From the Skyline Sno-Park, ski south on Skyline Road 1.9 miles to Clear Lake Butte Road, which is also Forest Road 240. Ski west on Forest Road 240, which climbs steadily for 2 miles to the top of the butte, 954 feet above Skyline Road. This road is normally well packed, but skaters will have difficulty maintaining momentum on the continuous hill. Diagonal stride is the saner choice. Stay to the left at junctions with side roads. There are no memorable views before the summit.

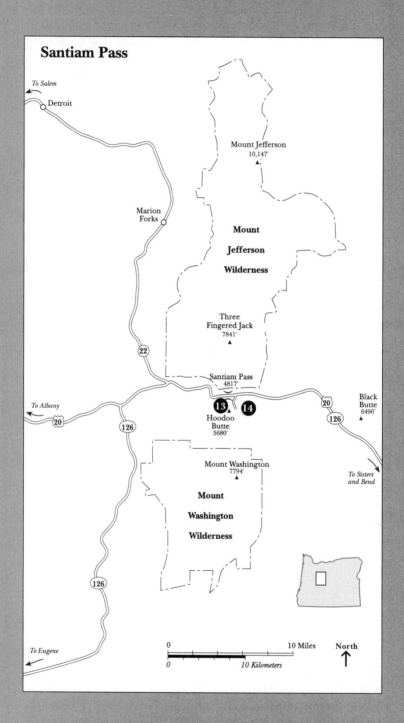

Santiam Pass

Highway 22 leading southeast from Salem climbs to more than 4800 feet at Santiam Pass. At this altitude, the plateau along the pass receives plenty of snow. The pass marks the divide between the Willamette National Forest on the west side and the Deschutes National Forest on the east side. A mile south of Santiam Pass, the dense forests give way to large clearings left by the 1967 Airstrip Burn. The open burn area provides many views of prominent peaks: Three Fingered Jack and Mount Jefferson to the north, sharp-toothed Mount Washington south of the pass, and Black Butte to the east. Santiam Pass is 88 miles from Salem and 40 miles from Bend. Skiers from Albany and Eugene reach the area via Highways 20 and 126, which merge with Highway 22 five miles west of the pass.

The region's best trails and best snow are close to the pass, especially near Ray Benson Sno-Park. The ungroomed trails here include a variety of loops designed for skiing and miles of groomed snowmobile trails. There is also a fine system of groomed ski trails at the commercial ski area next door. Other sno-parks in the Santiam region provide access to numerous ungroomed ski trails, but most are more than 1000 feet lower than Ray Benson Sno-Park and have less reliable snow conditions.

Skiers may also hear mention of other groomed ski trails at Black Butte and Blue Lake Resorts. Black Butte Resort, between Santiam Pass and Sisters, is a popular base for a weekend of skiing. The sports shop at the resort rents Nordic skis. The resort does not receive much snow, but when it does, groomed ski tracks are occasionally set on the golf course. These are beginner trails with spectacular views of central Oregon volcanoes, but they are only open to resort guests. Blue Lake Resort, just east of Santiam Pass, once had a fine system of groomed trails for classic skiing, but the resort closed in the late 1990s.

13 HOODOO

Distance: 2.2–8 kilometers (1.4–5 miles)
Trails: Groomed ski trails
Track Quality: Good classic skiing, good skating
Skill Level: Novice to advanced
Elevation: Lower trails, 4700 feet; upper trails, 5000 feet
Maximum Elevation Gain: Lower trails, 100 feet; upper trails, 340 feet
Season: Early December to late March
Services and Facilities: Ski rentals, lessons, meals
Hours: 9:00 A.M.–4:00 P.M., lower trails Wednesday–Sunday, upper trails weekends and holidays
Fees: $7
Information: Hoodoo Ski Area, (541) 822-3337; *www.hoodoo.com*

Groomed Nordic trails at Hoodoo Ski Area are a good option for Willamette Valley skiers reluctant to make the long drive to better-known ski areas. Hoodoo Ski Area's two trail systems are separated by a chairlift and a long downhill run. The lower trails are always groomed and have nice intermediate and novice terrain. The upper trails start 275 feet above the base and are primarily in open terrain. Their attraction is killer views of Three Fingered Jack, Mount Washington, and other volcanic peaks. Advanced ski skills are required to descend from the upper trails, which are only open on weekends and holidays.

From Salem, drive east on the Santiam Highway, State Route 22. In 86.4 miles turn right onto the Hoodoo Ski Area access road. From Albany, this is 5 miles east of the junction of Highways 20 and 22. From central Oregon, it is 20 miles west of Sisters. Drive 0.9 mile south on the access road to a fork and bear right to the Hoodoo Ski Area. The lot may fill on busy weekends. Parking on the access road is allowed only in a few marked spaces. In winter 2002, Hoodoo opted out of the state sno-park program and sno-park permits were not required. It remains to be seen if the area will continue to handle its own plowing expenses or rejoin the program.

A massive ski lodge completed in 2002 offers a restaurant, lounge areas, and a lunchroom. The former Nordic Center was razed during construction. It is unclear if a new Nordic Center will be built. Check at the ski shop in the new lodge for cross-country ski rentals and trail information.

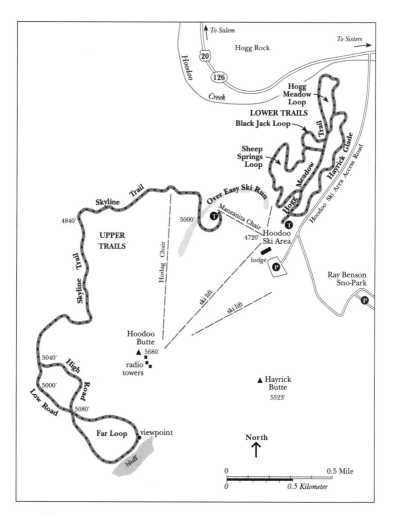

To Salem
Hogg Rock
To Sisters
Hoodoo
Creek
Hogg Meadow Loop
LOWER TRAILS
Black Jack Loop
Sheep Springs Loop
Skyline Trail
Over Easy Ski Run
Manzanita Chair
Hogg Meadow Trail
Hayrick Glade
4840'
5000'
Hoodoo Ski Area
Hoodoo Ski Area Acces Road
4720'
UPPER TRAILS
Hodag Chair
lodge
Ray Benson Sno-Park
Skyline Trail
ski lift
ski lift
Hoodoo Butte
▲ 5680'
radio towers
5040'
High Road
Hayrick Butte
5523'
5000'
Low Road
5080'
Far Loop
viewpoint
bluff
North
0   0.5 Mile
0   0.5 Kilometer

LOWER TRAILS

The lower trails have no outstanding views but are well designed and flow nicely through forests of mountain hemlock and fir. The forests provide protection from high winds. Though there are only 7 kilometers (4.4 miles) of trails, they include good beginner and intermediate terrain. Trails are groomed for skating and classic skiing. Snowshoes, if rented at Hoodoo, are allowed on the groomed shoulder outside the classic lane.

The one access to the lower trail system is not obvious to first-time visitors. From the parking lot, walk to the right of the new lodge. The trailhead is 150 feet to the right up a gentle hill that is used as a ski slope for children. It is easy to ascend the hill to the trailhead.

Hogg Meadow Trail. The sole trail from the trailhead is the Hogg Meadow Trail, the central thoroughfare that leads to all other trails. This is a good beginner trail when combined with Hogg Meadow Loop at its end, 2.2 kilometers round trip. The trail has short hills that most beginners will enjoy except in icy conditions. The area was surveyed for the Hogg Railroad in the 1890s. "Colonel" E.T. Hogg dreamt of a line from the Pacific Ocean to Boise, Idaho, but his railroad never reached farther east than Idanha, Oregon, 30 miles from Santiam Pass.

Three trails branch off the Hogg Meadow Trail and provide hills for intermediate level skiers and novices with spunk.

Hayrick Glade. Beginning to the right not far from the trailhead, Hayrick Glade rolls constantly as it parallels the Hogg Meadow Trail. It ends on the Hogg Meadow Loop in 1 kilometer.

Black Jack and Sheep Springs Loops. These two trails lead west of Hogg Meadow Trail. Black Jack Loop is a 0.5-kilometer route that connects to Sheep Springs Loop. The latter is a 2.5-kilometer trail with challenging uphill and downhill in either direction. It flows best counterclockwise, starting from the Black Jack Loop. Beginners should practice on other trails before trying Sheep Springs.

UPPER TRAILS

Hoodoo's 8-kilometer (5-mile) upper trail system starts 275 feet above the parking lot. A Nordic trail pass includes one ride on the Manzanita chairlift to the trails. It is possible to ski up the downhill ski slopes, but the climb is too steep to be enjoyable. Only advanced skiers should use the upper trails because the return to the lodge is via downhill ski slopes and requires strong skills.

The upper trails are in mostly open terrain on the west side of Hoodoo Butte, with severe wind exposure at times. Trails are hard to follow when visibility is low, and intersecting snowmobile trails can confuse the route. The trails have some steep pitches and lack the rolling hills that make the lower trails flow well. In spite of these drawbacks, the upper system merits a visit for what might be the best views of Three Fingered Jack and Mount Washington in the Santiam Pass area. Skiers using grip wax should remember the snow on the upper trails can be 10 degrees colder than below.

The chairlift ride takes eight to ten minutes. Clothing that is comfortable while skiing may be inadequate on the lift, so don an additional windproof layer before boarding.

Sand Mountain, from Hoodoo's upper trails

Skyline Trail. Bear left coming off the chair, passing down a short hill to a gentle downhill run. Look for a sign pointing uphill to Skyline Trail. Turn right and ski uphill 200 feet to another Skyline Trail sign. Turn right, climb a short hill, and cross the Over Easy downhill run. Look uphill for skiers before crossing. When returning to the lodge later, turn here and ski down Over Easy. Now, continue on Skyline Trail and descend to the bottom of the Hodag chairlift. The Nordic route is not obvious here. Ski behind the lift terminal, stay to the right, and herringbone 30 feet up a steep pitch. A hard right turn is the continuation of Skyline Trail. The rest of the route is away from alpine slopes.

The Skyline Trail reaches a sharp left turn as it emerges from forest into open clearings. Look back for a grand view of Three Fingered Jack. Round the turn for an equal view of Mount Washington to the south and Sand Mountain to the west. Beyond this point, the trail is difficult to follow in bad weather.

High Road, Low Road, and Far Loop. Continue 0.5 kilometer (0.3 mile) across the open hillside to an unmarked fork. Both trails lead to a junction with the Far Loop. The left fork takes the High Road, which climbs gradually. The Low Road on the right descends a steep pitch with a hard right turn, drops farther, and then climbs to the junction. The High Road is about 0.7 kilometer; the low road is about 0.5 kilometer. The Far Loop climbs to an overlook on a steep bluff with views of the north side of Mount Washington. It is a 1.5-kilometer loop.

Return via the Far Loop and High Road to Skyline Trail and follow it to the Over Easy alpine run. This run is rated easy for alpine skiers but is challenging on cross-country skis. Control your speed. Avoid steep slopes by staying to the left, following Over Easy or Hesitation down to the lodge and parking lot.

85

14 RAY BENSON

Distance: 4–9.7 miles
Trails: Ungroomed ski trails, groomed snowmobile trails
Track Quality: Good classic skiing, fair skating
Skill Level: Novice to advanced
Elevation: 4800 feet
Maximum Elevation Gain: 200 feet
Season: Early December to early April
Services and Facilities: Outhouse, trailside shelters
Hours: NA
Fees: Sno-park permit
Information: Sisters Ranger District, Deschutes National Forest,
    (541) 549-7700

Twelve miles of ungroomed ski trails create a variety of loops east of Ray Benson Sno-Park, which is just south of Santiam Pass. The trails are popular and a ski track is usually broken. They are mostly novice and intermediate trails in rolling terrain. Skaters can use the nearby groomed snowmobile trails. Cloudy days are common, but Mount Washington and Three Fingered Jack generally can be seen through breaks in the clouds. At nearly 5000 feet, the area gets plenty of snow and has good skiing when lower-elevation trails are marginal.

From Salem, drive southeast on the Santiam Highway, State Route 22. In 86.4 miles, turn right onto the Hoodoo Ski Area access road. This is 5 miles east of the junction with Highway 20 from Albany. From central Oregon, it is 20 miles west of Sisters. Bear left at the fork 0.9 mile from Highway 22 and continue 0.5 mile to the sno-park. The 700-foot north wall of Hayrick Butte dominates the scenery along the access road. The sno-park has four parking areas around a big oval. Outhouses and a log shelter maintained by the Mount Jefferson Snowmobile Club are in the center. The area is shared by skiers, snowmobilers, snowshoers, and even a few sled dog teams.

The southern half of the Ray Benson trail system is in the 1967 Airstrip Burn area. After thirty-five years, new trees are still small. The large clearings and open vistas created by the burn contrast with the dense forest and tall trees north of the fire line, marked by the Fireline Loop snowmobile trail. There are three day-use shelters along the trails. Island Junction Shelter, at the edge of the old burn, and Brandenburg Shelter have great views of the surrounding volcanic peaks. Oregon Nordic Club volunteers keep the shelters stocked with firewood. Two ski loops and two snowmobile trails start from the sno-park. These connect to other trails to form numerous routes. A few are described here, but there are other possibilities.

South Loop. The South Loop begins from the sno-park's southeast corner, near the second of the four parking areas. The mostly flat, 6-mile round trip passes through the old burn, providing memorable views of Mount Washington, Three Fingered Jack, and, weather permitting, Mount Jefferson. Ski south past Hayrick Butte to the South Loop junction in 1 mile. Continue straight for a counterclockwise loop that returns to the junction via the trail on the left. Ski 1.5 miles to a junction at the base of Brandenburg Butte. Bear left here to follow the South Loop 0.4 mile around the north side of the butte. Turn right for a 0.6-mile side trail that leads to the Brandenburg

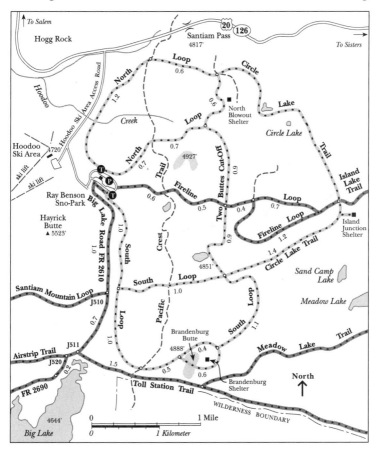

Shelter and then reconnects with the South Loop. This side trail has steep sections that are difficult for beginners. The shelter has a grand view of Mount Washington to the south. Skiers and snowmobilers alike play on the open hills east of the shelter. From the Brandenburg Shelter, continue 0.2 mile to reconnect to the South Loop and turn right. From here, ski north 1.1 miles through easy hills to a four-way intersection. The trails straight ahead and to the right are part of the Circle Lake–Two Buttes Loop. To complete the South Loop, turn left at the intersection for another mile on flat trail to the start of the South Loop. Turn right at the junction to return to the sno-park in another mile.

Sled dog team on a snowmobile trail

North Loop. The North Loop is a 4-mile tour through mixed forest north of the burn, a contrast to the open terrain of the South Loop. Because it is more protected than the South Loop, this is the trail to choose on windy days. The loop is rated intermediate because its south leg has short, difficult hills. The north leg is flatter. From the northwest corner of the sno-park, ski about 100 yards on a marked connector trail to the start of the north loop. The north leg of the loop is to the left and the south leg is to the right. The loop can be skied in either direction. Headed clockwise (left) it is 1.8 miles to a junction with the Circle Lake Trail, which leads to the left. The North Loop continues to the right and reaches the North Blowout Shelter in 0.3 mile. This stretch includes a difficult downhill. From the shelter, it is 0.3 mile to another junction. Bear right to ski the North Loop's hilly south leg, which is 1.4 miles back to the start of the loop. Turn left on the short connector to return to the sno-park.

Circle Lake Trail. Add the Circle Lake Trail to sections of the North and South Loops for a 9.7-mile intermediate tour. This long loop offers excellent views from open clearings and then passes through mature forest. To start, ski counterclockwise on the South Loop past the Brandenburg Shelter to the four-way intersection 1.3 miles beyond the shelter. Turn right onto Circle Lake Trail, which leads past the Island Junction Shelter. After passing a side trail on the right to the shelter, the route drops and crosses the Fireline Loop snowmobile trail. Be careful not to start downhill on the snowmobile trail, which may seem the natural route here. Continue north past lava fields and snow-covered ponds to a three-way junction with the North Loop. Just before this intersection there is a road on the left with a sign indicating Circle Lake. It may have tracks, but it is not part of the loop. Continue to the sno-park by turning either left or right onto the North Loop Trail, about 2 miles either way. Go left for hills and right for flatter terrain.

Two Buttes Cutoff. Combine Circle Lake Trail with Two Buttes Cutoff for a hilly 8.7-mile round trip that includes most of the North Loop. Strong downhill skills are required on the Two Buttes Cutoff in either direction. Downhill stretches on this trail are more thrilling from north to south. Less experienced skiers should ski south to north. For the more exciting direction, follow the hilly south leg of the North Loop 1.4 miles from the sno-park to a junction with the Two Buttes Cutoff. Turn right and follow this advanced-level trail south 1.8 miles to its end at a four-way junction. Turn left onto the Circle Lake Trail, which loops north and in another 3.7 miles reaches the north leg of the North Loop. Follow the North Loop 1.8 miles back to the sno-park.

Pacific Crest Trail. The Pacific Crest Trail (PCT) bisects both the North and South Loops. It is marked as a ski trail, but simply posting blue diamonds on a hiking trail does not create a ski trail. It is difficult to maintain rhythm on turns designed for walkers. The PCT is better suited to snowshoe travel.

Big Lake Road. Miles of snowmobile trails provide tour opportunities for skaters. Snowmobile traffic can be heavy, but there is little conflict. Move to the side when snowmobiles or sled dog teams pass. Snowmobile trails are marked with orange diamonds, and major intersections are numbered. Big Lake Road, which may be marked as Sand Mountain Loop, leads south from the sno-park past Hayrick Butte to the west. It is groomed weekly. Ski south past junction 510 to junction 511, 1.7 miles from the sno-park. Bear right a few yards to junction 520, then bear left on Forest Road 2690. The lake can be glimpsed through the trees on the left. In about 0.2 mile, it is easy to ski to its north shore for a better view. For a round trip of 3.8 miles, turn around here and return along the same route, climbing 200 feet to the sno-park. For longer out-and-back tours, ski west from junction 520 on the Airstrip Trail or east from junction 511 on the Toll Station Trail, which may be marked as the Cross District Trail.

Fireline Loop. From the sno-park, the Fireline Loop snowmobile trail runs east along the edge of the 1967 burn area and intersects the ungroomed cross-country loops. It is narrow for a snowmobile trail and has short, steep hills. It is not an easy trail to ski, and there are sections where it is difficult for snowmobilers to see skiers. It is best to use the other snowmobile trails already described.

Three Fingered Jack

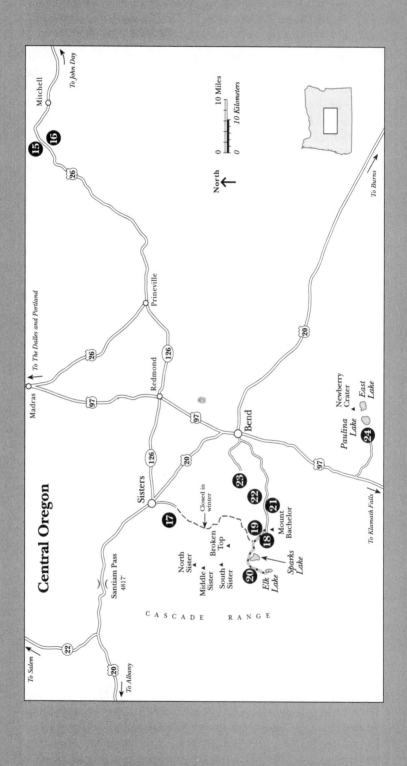

Central Oregon

Central Oregon, loosely defined here as the area on the east side of the Cascade Range, from the Ochoco Mountains in the north to Newberry Crater in the south, is blessed with plenty of sunshine. Open lodgepole pine forests are characteristic. High-elevation trails in Deschutes National Forest are easy to reach and provide a long ski season. Views of Cascade peaks, especially the Three Sisters and Broken Top, can be enjoyed throughout the area. The sunshine and relatively dry snow attract visitors from around the country and even from other corners of the world.

Mount Bachelor is the main attraction for groomed trail skiing, but the region also boasts hundreds of miles of excellent ungroomed marked ski trails. The town of Bend has a vibrant Nordic ski community and is home to a great many enthusiasts who live to ski. Local groups sponsor cross-country events and programs, including programs for children and a high school racing league. A local ski club grooms trails near Bend, and the Bend Parks and Recreation District occasionally grooms trails at two local parks. Check with the Central Oregon and Tumalo Langlauf chapters of the Oregon Nordic Club for information on skiing opportunities. Most ski trails north of the Cascade Lakes Highway are closed to dogs.

15 BANDIT SPRINGS

Distance: 1.5–5 miles
Trails: Ungroomed ski trails
Track Quality: Good classic skiing, no skating
Skill Level: Novice to advanced
Elevation: 4520 feet
Maximum Elevation Gain: 480 feet
Season: Late December to early March
Services and Facilities: Outhouse, trailside shelter
Hours: NA
Fees: Sno-park permit
Information: Ochoco National Forest, (541) 416-6500

The Ochoco Mountains northeast of Prineville are characterized by gentle slopes with open forests of ponderosa pine. Dry snow and cold sunny days make for delightful skiing. The Ochocos lack the prominent peaks of the Cascades, but they offer pretty views of rolling hills and valleys. The Bandit Springs ski loops are a mix of easy trails and challenging runs designed more for fun skiing than for reaching viewpoints. Volunteers developed the loops and the Ochoco chapter of the Oregon Nordic Club maintains them. The area gets less snow than similar elevations in the Cascades, and the snow disappears quickly in spring. The sno-park, a rest area on Highway 26, is easy to get to. This is important in a region where smaller roads are not plowed quickly. A newer sno-park at Walton Lake (Chapter 16) has more reliable snow, but it is shared with snowmobilers and can be difficult to drive to.

From Mount Hood, drive southeast on Highway 26 for 63 miles to Madras and continue another 29 miles on Highway 26 to Prineville. From Prineville, drive northeast on Highway 26 for 29 miles to Bandit Springs Sno-Park on the left. The summit of Ochoco Pass (4722 feet) is 1 mile farther on Highway 26. The parking area is limited. In the event that the lot is full, skiers can park at Marks Creek Sno-Park near a sledding hill 0.5 mile south and across the highway. From there, walk across the highway and ski 0.2 mile south to an unplowed road on the right that connects to McGinnis Creek Loop.

Bandit Springs has 12.5 miles of trails with enough loop possibilities to fill a day of skiing. All loops are best skied counterclockwise. Junctions are marked with letters. An astute observer might wonder what happened to the first half of the alphabet, as the junctions run from M to Z. Letters A through L are used at junctions on Walton Lake ski trails, which are described in the next chapter. Two trails

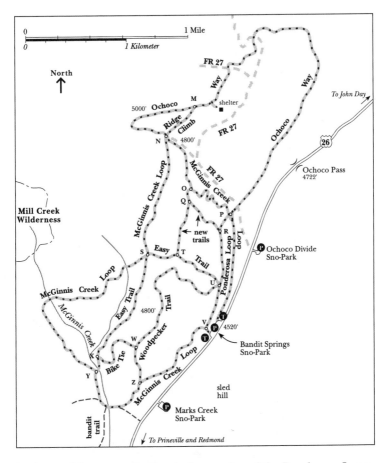

lead out of the sno-park. One is the east leg of the Ponderosa Loop, which starts to the right of the toilets, climbs a small hill next to the sno-park, and leads north. The other trailhead is a gated road that starts behind the toilets and runs north. This road is the start of the west leg of the Ponderosa Loop.

Ponderosa Loop. This 1.5-mile loop has a few short hills, but it is generally flat and a good beginner loop. It also provides access to all other trails. For a counterclockwise loop, climb the small hill next to the sno-park and ski north on the east leg, passing through pine forest. In 0.8 mile, the trail reaches junction P. Make a sharp left turn onto the west leg of Ponderosa Loop and ski south another 0.7 mile, returning to the sno-park on the gated road behind the toilets. This leg passes through forest and meadows and connects to other trails at junctions R, U, and V.

Ochoco Way. This hilly, 3.5-mile trail through junctions P, M, and N is part of a 6-mile round trip tour. Ski north from the sno-park on Ponderosa Loop to junction P and turn right onto the start of Ochoco Way. In 50 yards, Ochoco Way crosses Forest Road 27 on the first of several steep hills—this trail is for strong intermediate or advanced skiers only. After looping back south, it crosses Forest Road 27 a second time and reaches a shelter in another 0.3 mile on the left. The shelter is a three-sided lean-to 0.1 mile east of junction M. It is down a hill 200 feet from the trail. There is no trail sign and it can be overlooked. The lean-to faces south over an open slope. If playing on the slope, watch for barbed wire near the bottom. In 0.2 mile past the shelter, Ochoco Way angles right at junction M. The trail climbs, passes through a barbed wire fence, and descends. Be ready for an extra-sharp left turn on the moderate downhill. At junction N, turn right onto McGinnis Creek Loop. Ski south to junction S, turn left onto Easy, and ski east to junction U. Turn right on the Ponderosa Loop to return to the sno-park.

Ochoco Way shelter

McGinnis Creek Loop. This 5-mile intermediate loop has some distinct ups and downs as well as long gentle sections. It follows the Ponderosa Loop 0.8 mile to the P intersection. The McGinnis Creek Trail begins here. It leads west on a winding trail past junction O to junction N, where it turns sharply left onto a gated road and continues south. It passes through junctions S, Y, Z, and V before reaching the sno-park. The leg between S and Y visits forests scorched by the Mill Creek Fire in 2000. Signs of the burn are mostly covered by snow. The thin undergrowth burned, but the fire did not create heat intense enough to destroy many trees here. The last few hundred yards before junction V are through a meadow, where the trail is not obvious. Simply head east across the meadow to a road, which is the west leg of the Ponderosa Loop, and turn right toward the sno-park.

Blue diamonds mark a scenic trail leading from the south end of McGinnis Loop between junctions Y and Z. It travels about 0.5 mile along a lovely creek, then ends at private property. A local skier may have marked this route, as it is not an official Forest Service trail.

Easy Trail. The name describes this 1.3-mile trail through intersections U, T, S, X, and Y. It runs through old-growth ponderosa pine and connects to the McGinnis Loop at junctions S and Y. Follow the west leg of Ponderosa to Easy and return on McGinnis from junction Y for a 2.7-mile round trip.

Bike Tie and Woodpecker. The best views in the Bandit Springs trail system are from along a ridge on the Woodpecker Trail and from the top of the Bike Tie. Both look out over the Mill Creek Wilderness, including areas burned in a wildfire in 2000. Both trails are for advanced skiers. The Woodpecker Trail starts at junction U on the west leg of the Ponderosa Loop, climbs a ridge, and turns south along the ridge with views to the west. It passes junction W with the Bike Tie and drops to junction Z on the McGinnis Creek Loop. The Woodpecker Trail is a fun jaunt for advanced skiers. The Bike Tie is a 0.3-mile trail that climbs very steeply from junction X on the Easy Trail to junction W on the Woodpecker Trail. It is difficult to ski and hardly worth the effort. Trail signs at junction X can be confusing. A sign indicating that the Bike Tie leads to Woodpecker can be misread as indicating that Woodpecker Trail begins here.

Two new connector trails were not shown on Forest Service maps as of 2002. The first (O to T) descends south from the north leg of McGinnis to Easy. The descent is gentle except for a short, steep downhill just before reaching Easy. The second new trail (R to Q) runs east from the Ponderosa Loop. The junctions for both of these trails are not obvious but may be better marked in the future.

16 WALTON LAKE

Distance: 3.6–6.7 miles
Trails: Ungroomed ski trails
Track Quality: Good classic skiing, no skating
Skill Level: Novice to intermediate
Elevation: 5540 feet
Maximum Elevation Gain: 700 feet
Season: Early December to late March
Services and Facilities: Outhouse
Hours: NA
Fees: Sno-park permit
Information: Ochoco National Forest, (541) 416-6500

Thirteen miles of generally easy, ungroomed trails with moderate hills comprise a nice loop system at Walton Lake Sno-Park. The area is a thousand feet higher than Bandit Springs (Chapter 15) and receives considerably more snow. The more open terrain also allows for more scenic tours than at Bandit Springs. The downside to Walton Lake is that a steep access road can be difficult to drive in winter conditions and the sno-park is busy with snowmobile activity. Two Forest Service bunkhouses along the road to the sno-park offer an opportunity for an overnight visit in a secluded setting. For information, call (541) 416-6645.

From Prineville, drive northeast on Highway 26 for 16 miles to County Road 23, angling to the right. In 8.2 miles, pass the Ochoco Ranger Station, which is closed in winter. Turn left onto Forest Road 22 in another 0.3 mile (the bunkhouses are 100 yards west of this intersection on Forest Road 42). Forest Road 22 climbs steeply and may have loose snow. Be prepared with tire chains and a shovel. Drive 7.6 miles to a sharp right turn and another 0.1 mile to a small Nordic parking area on the right. The plowed road ends a little farther beyond at a large snowmobile parking lot. Several snowmobile trails leave this lot. Toilets are on a hill above the parking area. The ski trailhead is across the access road from the Nordic parking lot. The trail angles

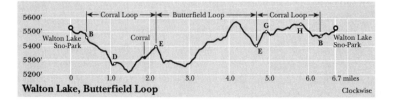

Walton Lake, Butterfield Loop   Clockwise

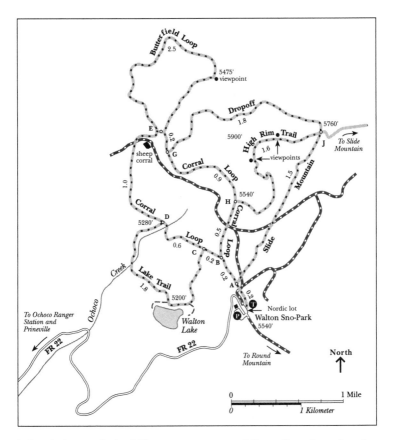

left as it descends the hill, crosses a snowmobile trail, and reaches the first trail junction in 0.2 mile.

As with Bandit Springs, trail junctions are marked with letters. Many junctions also have map boards. Still, there are places where the trail is not obvious. This should not be a serious problem if you check a map regularly and watch for trail markers. If necessary, backtrack to the last marked junction. Some Walton Lake brochures cite 20 miles of trails. These include out-and-back trails not described here. The brochures also indicate longer trail distances than those used here, which are based on a map by Don Wood, a local skier who planned the trails.

Corral Loop. This is the main loop providing access to all other trails. It is a beginner trail with only moderate hills. At the north end, it passes an old sheep corral and dilapidated outbuildings in a large clearing. From the trailhead, ski northwest, descending a hill and crossing a snowmobile trail. Pass junction A and reach junction B, the start of Corral Loop, at 0.4 mile. The loop can be skied in either direction. Continue straight at B for a clockwise loop that passes through pine forest and crosses Ochoco Creek. In 1.6 miles the trail crosses a large clearing with the sheep corral on the right. Beyond here, it reenters the woods and passes through junctions E, G, and H to complete the loop at junction B. It is 3.4 miles around the loop from the B intersection and 4.2 miles round trip from the sno-park.

Lake Trail. The trail to Walton Lake has short hills that will test beginners. Turn south from the Corral Loop at junction C and pass through open pine forest, descending to a road along the lake's north shore. The trail leaves the lakeshore heading north over a small hill. Bear left in a clearing, cross tiny Ochoco Creek, and ski north to the Corral Loop at junction D. The Lake Trail itself is 1.8 miles and round trip from the sno-park is 3.6 miles.

Butterfield Loop. Butterfield is an interesting 2.5-mile interme-diate loop branching off the north end of Corral Loop at junction E. Combined with Corral Loop, it is 6.7 miles round trip from the sno-park. It circles a large clearing where elk may be seen. The trail is not always obvious. Ski clockwise on Corral Loop to junction E and turn left. Ski near the left side of a clearing, descending to a road and turning right. Farther, at a split in the road, the trail follows a sharp, right curve uphill and climbs to a viewpoint of open hills. Look care-fully for blue diamonds here, continuing southwest to complete the loop at junction E. Take a left onto Corral Loop and ski through junctions G and H to complete the loop at junction B.

Sheep corral along the Walton Lake trails

High Rim. Intermediate skiers eager for some climbing can choose the High Rim Trail, which also starts on the Corral Loop, 0.9 mile from the sno-park. Head counterclockwise on Corral to reach junction H and turn right. High Rim starts in dense pines and climbs 300 feet to a plateau. At 1 mile, it skirts a large clearing on the left. Ski 200 yards west from the marked trail to the edge of the plateau for expansive views west and south. The trail reenters the woods, passes a viewpoint to the north, and descends to junction J. Turn right onto the Slide Mountain Trail for an easy descent to junction A. Turn left toward the sno-park to finish the 4.2-mile tour.

Dropoff. Dropoff is a 1.8-mile connector trail between junction J at the north end of the High Rim Trail and junction G on the Corral Loop. Most of the trail offers delightful intermediate-level skiing with moderate hills and a mix of forest and clear-cuts, but a 200-yard section near junction J is extremely difficult. From junction J, this section is a steep descent through closely spaced trees. Skiers will need to combine short traverses with sections of sidestepping down the hill. After reaching the bottom of the hill, look for blue diamonds leading to the left.

17 THREE CREEK LAKE

Distance: 3.1–12.2 miles
Trails: Groomed snowmobile trails, ungroomed ski trails
Track Quality: Fair classic skiing, fair skating
Skill Level: Intermediate to advanced
Elevation: 5150 feet
Maximum Elevation Gain: 1430 feet
Season: Late November to early April
Services and Facilities: Outhouse, lean-to shelter
Hours: NA
Fees: Sno-park permit
Information: Sisters Ranger District, Deschutes National Forest, (541) 549-7700

An inspiring view from an alpine lake at the base of Tam McArthur Rim is the reward for a long uphill ski trip from Three Creek Lake Sno-Park, south of Sisters. A groomed snowmobile trail can be followed most of the distance to the lake, or skiers can opt for an ungroomed trail to bypass much of the snowmobile route. A small system of ungroomed ski trails offers quieter opportunities near the Three Sisters Wilderness, with views of Mount Jefferson and North Sister.

The western-themed town of Sisters is 21 miles east of Santiam Pass and 22 miles northwest of Bend. Passing through Sisters, Highway 20 is a central thoroughfare for tourism and can be congested on sunny weekends. Follow the highway to the middle of town and turn south (right, coming from Santiam Pass) onto Elm Street, which becomes Forest Road 16 in the national forest. Follow the road 11 miles to Three Creek Lake Sno-Park, a paved lot where the snow plowing ends. An adjacent gravel lot a few yards before the paved lot is less congested on weekends. Forest Road 16 is not always well plowed. Carry chains and a shovel. Plowing occasionally stops 2 miles early at a lower sno-park. In this case, ski the 2 miles to the upper sno-park on Forest Road 16. Snowmobile traffic is not as heavy in this area as it is at nearby Santiam Pass or Dutchman Flat (Chapter 19).

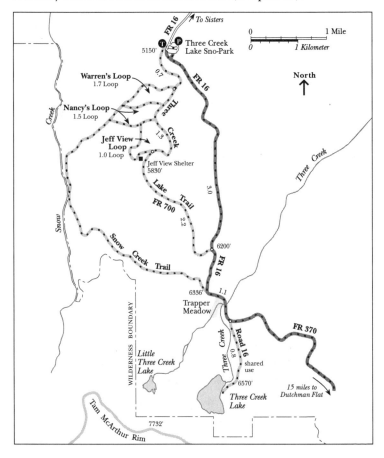

Forest Road 16. Forest Road 16 is the most direct route to Three Creek Lake. It heads south from the sno-park and climbs along most of the route, gaining over 1400 feet in 4.9 miles. Most of the route is a snowmobile trail, groomed weekly by the Sno-Go-Fers snowmobile club. The groomed trail is fine for skating, but the final 0.8 mile to the lake is an ungroomed snowmobile route. This section can be skated, but it should be considered adventure skating. Classic skiers will have no problem. Ski the last 0.8 mile even if the trail is rough. Awesome views across the lake to the cliffs and bowls of Tam McArthur Rim are worth the effort. En route to the lake, Forest Road 16 climbs past junctions with ungroomed ski trails at 3.0 and 3.5 miles. At 3.8 miles it reaches Trapper Meadow with its impressive view of Tam McArthur Rim. In another 0.3 mile, the groomed snowmobile trail turns left toward Dutchman Flat. Forest Road 16 continues straight for that last 0.8 mile to the lake.

Three Creek Lake Trail. Skiers with touring equipment and intermediate skills can enjoy marked, ungroomed trails west of Forest Road 16 that are closed to snowmobiles. The Three Creek Lake Trail roughly parallels Forest Road 16 and connects to the ungroomed loops. Walk to the northwest corner of the sno-park and ski a few feet to the start of the trail on the right. It starts up a moderate hill for 0.7 mile and then climbs more gradually. In another 3.5 miles it connects to Forest Road 16. Turn right on Road 16 and continue uphill 1.9 miles to Three Creek Lake, for a total one-way distance of 6.1 miles.

Warren's Loop and Nancy's Loop. Two short, intermediate-level trails with little ups and downs run west from the Three Creek Lake Trail. These trails are named for volunteers who helped develop them. The first, Warren's Loop, starts 0.7 mile from the sno-park and is 1.7 miles long. The second, Nancy's Loop, starts 1 mile from the sno-park and is 1.5 miles long. Its north leg is also the south leg of Warren's Loop. Nancy's Loop has a great view of Mount Jefferson from a clearing at its junction with Jeff View Loop.

Jeff View Loop. Jeff View Loop starts off Three Creek Lake Trail 2 miles from the sno-park and drops quickly to a shelter in a small clear-cut. The shelter faces northwest toward Mount Jefferson. The trail then descends a steep, but very skiable, section to a flat clearing with views of Mount Jefferson 1 mile from the shelter. Return to the sno-park via Nancy's Loop and Three Creek Lake Trail for a 4.3-mile tour.

Snow Creek Trail. The Snow Creek Trail is a challenging trail for advanced skiers. It can be combined with the Three Creek Lake Trail and Nancy's Loop for a tour of about 10 miles round-trip from the

Tam McArthur Rim above Three Creek Lake

sno-park. Skied clockwise, the loop has very challenging downhill turns on its Snow Creek section. The upper end of the Snow Creek Trail is on Forest Road 16, a half-mile south of the Three Creek Lake Trail junction. The trail, which is partly on an equestrian trail, starts fairly level, descends steep hills with some sharp turns, and continues through clearings with views of North Sister before dropping to the southwest corner of Nancy's Loop. Follow Nancy's Loop back to the Three Creek Lake Trail and go north to return to the sno-park.

Forest Road 370. Skiers interested in long tours can follow groomed snowmobile trails from Three Creek Lake Sno-Park to Dutchman Flat or Mount Bachelor. The 19-mile, one-way tour requires a car shuttle and is only for skiers in excellent physical condition. Use touring skis, as sections may be rough for skating. From Three Creek Lake Sno-Park, ski south on Forest Road 16 for 4.1 miles to where the groomed snowmobile trail turns left onto Forest Road 370 toward Dutchman Flat, which is another 15 miles. Carry a snowmobile trail map. (They are usually available in the sno-park.) The route is not always obvious, so be prepared to use a topographic map and compass. Carry emergency gear and plenty of water. The tour should be done in spring when the days are longer.

18 MOUNT BACHELOR

Distance: 1–12 kilometers (0.6–7.5 miles), 56 kilometers total
Trails: Groomed ski trails
Track Quality: Excellent classic skiing, excellent skating
Skill Level: Novice to advanced
Elevation: 6350 feet
Maximum Elevation Gain: 650 feet
Season: Late November to early May
Services and Facilities: Nordic lodge, cafeteria, ski shop, rentals, lessons, daycare
Hours: 8:00 A.M.–4:00 P.M., daily
Fees: $11, sno-park permit not required
Information: Mount Bachelor Ski Area; snow phone, (541) 382-7888; *www.mtbachelor.com*

Mount Bachelor is Oregon's premier resort destination for Nordic skiers. Skiers come from around the world to enjoy its reliable, relatively dry snow, sunshine, and long season. The trails have a few fine views of Mount Bachelor and South Sister, but views are not the main attraction. Cross-country skiers come here to ski on extremely varied terrain with excellent trail grooming. Quite simply, the Mount Bachelor Cross Country Center is the best groomed Nordic area in the state and one of the best in the country.

A less tangible but important attraction is the sense of community among Nordic enthusiasts. The Cross Country Center's lower-floor lunchroom is a gathering place for locals and visitors, from beginners to elite World Cup skiers. Two active ski clubs and a ski racing foundation work with the ski area to host a full calendar of clinics, races, and other Nordic events. Skiers from other areas envy this synergy within the Nordic community.

From Bend, drive 20 miles west on Century Drive, which becomes the Cascade Lakes Highway. At the end of the highway plowing, an access road curves left to the West Village parking lot. The approach

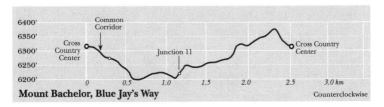

Mount Bachelor, Blue Jay's Way   Counterclockwise

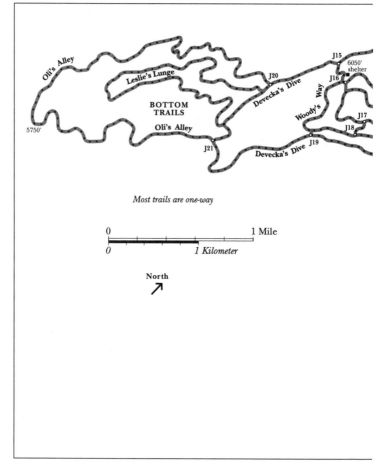

Most trails are one-way

North

has a view of Mount Bachelor straight ahead. Entering the huge lot, bear right toward the Cross Country Center. Sno-park permits are not required because, unlike most of Oregon's ski areas, Mount Bachelor elects not to use sno-park funds for plowing. Traffic on the Cascade Lakes Highway can be heavy on weekends. An alternative is to use shuttle buses that leave from a large commuter lot off Colorado Street at the south end of Bend.

Buy a trail pass at the Cross Country Center, a short walk from the parking lot. The upper floor has a fireplace, a snack bar with hot meals, and a ski shop. Rental equipment includes basic touring gear and lightweight high performance equipment. The ski school has excellent instructors for beginner to advanced skiers. The lower floor has

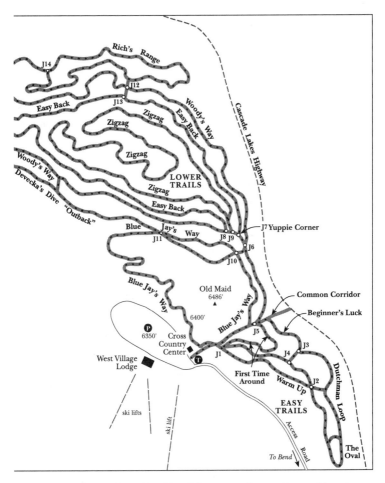

waxing benches and picnic tables. There are almost always skiers here, and it is easy to get sidetracked in conversation.

The Mount Bachelor Ski Area advertises 56 kilometers (35 miles) of groomed trails. As at most commercial areas, the calculation recounts trail sections that are used in multiple loops. The result is an exaggeration, but it matters little. There are enough trails to keep most skiers happy for days.

Several trail names honor local celebrities. Woody's Way remembers a colorful ski instructor, noted for his polyester ski slacks. Others are named for successful racers who also served cross-country skiing through coaching and program development. Even Blue Jay's Way is indirectly named after a well-known skier.

There are too many trails to describe them all in this book. Take a trail map and enjoy the many possibilities. Trail names and junction numbers are posted and easy to find. Most trails are one-way. Remember that the trails are lower than the Cross Country Center and you face an uphill return at the end of the day. Also, do not forget about the altitude—most trails are above 6000 feet. At this elevation less oxygen is available for muscle activity, and strenuous exercise can quickly lead to fatigue. Tailor your exertion level if you are used to skiing at lower elevations.

From the parking lot, start your tour next to the Cross Country Center by descending the short hill to a wide bowl, using the obvious slope or a less steep slope on the right. A corridor leading north provides access to the groomed trails and to backcountry trails near Dutchman Flat (Chapter 19). A trail pass is not required to ski down the corridor to the unplowed Cascade Lakes Highway (a snowmobile route) and many miles of ungroomed trails. The fee trail system includes easy trails near the lodge, intermediate lower trails, and very challenging bottom trails, as well as a single challenging trail near the Cross Country Center.

Easy trails. Three easy trails leave the bowl to the right of the Common Corridor. These trails return to the Nordic center along the Common Corridor, which has a moderate 80-foot climb. The left trail, First Time Around, is a great warm-up loop with short ups and downs. The others lead to Dutchman Loop and The Oval near Dutchman Flat. Experienced racers and novices use this flat 400-meter loop to practice technique drills. It boasts views of Mount Bachelor and South Sister.

Skiing near the training oval, Mount Bachelor

Blue Jay's Way. Stellar jays are common in Oregon, but blue jays are rare. Anyway, the bird had little to do with the trail name. The trail was first named Jay's Way after one of Bend's former Olympic skiers. It is a fun, but challenging, 2.5-kilometer loop that descends the Common Corridor to the first left turn and a long, fast downhill. It rolls easily and then climbs the back of the Old Maid, a cone north of the Cross Country Center. The long climb culminates in a twisting descent to the bowl near the center.

Lower trails. Woody's Way, Zigzag, Easy Back, and Rich's Range form the meat of the Mount Bachelor trail system. Many experienced skiers spend most of their time on these trails. The intermediate terrain is varied and can easily fill a ski day. From the Cross Country Center, ski down the Common Corridor, left down a long hill, and then up a short rise to junction 7, 150 feet lower than the Cross Country Center. This junction, often called Yuppie Corner, is the starting point for these trails. Trails converge here, and so do skiers, who often stop here for a chat. Woody's Way, the longest of the lower trails, is close to 7 kilometers. It is skied clockwise, dropping more than 150 feet in its first half and then climbing past a trailside shelter and back to Yuppie Corner. Easy Back and Zigzag branch to the right off of Woody's Way shortly after its start. Easy Back is the easiest of these three trails. Zigzag rolls up and down and is the "best flowing" of all these trails. Rich's Range, a biathlon course, branches off the return leg of Woody's Way and passes through open terrain with some views.

Bottom trails. The three lowest-elevation trails have the area's most exciting downhill sections. These require strong downhill turning skills and are not for novice skiers. The downhill fun is in the first half of each trail and is followed by a long climb out that can be grueling, especially at the end of the day. To reach these advanced trails, ski on Devecka's Dive from junction 6, a few yards southeast of Yuppie Corner. The first 1.5 kilometers to junction 19 are easy. Some skiers call this section the Outback. At junction 19, a right leads to Woody's Way in the lower trail system and a left leads to the challenging downhill section of Devecka's Dive. Oli's Alley and then Leslie's Lunge start with sharp left turns off this downhill section. Oli's Alley has the most drop, descending to 600 feet lower than the Cross Country Center. Both trails climb back to Devecka's Dive near junction 20. Devecka's Dive climbs back to Woody's Way near the shelter.

19 DUTCHMAN FLAT

Distance: 2.5–6.5 miles
Trails: Ungroomed ski trails
Track Quality: Good classic skiing, fair skating
Skill Level: Novice to intermediate
Elevation: 6300 feet
Maximum Elevation Gain: 490 feet
Season: Mid-November to early May
Services and Facilities: Outhouse at sno-park
Hours: NA
Fees: Sno-park permit
Information: Bend–Fort Rock Ranger District, Deschutes National
  Forest, (541) 383-4000

Dutchman Flat, in the high Cascades southwest of Bend, offers eye-popping views of Mount Bachelor, the Three Sisters, and Broken Top. Skiers from around the state come for the mix of marked ski trails, along with early and reliable snow. Miles of ungroomed ski trails and groomed snowmobile trails near timberline north of Mount Bachelor provide a bounty of ski opportunities for novice to advanced skiers. Add the groomed cross-country trails at adjacent Mount Bachelor Ski Area, extensive unmarked backcountry routes, and a few runs on the alpine slopes, and it is understandable why many skiers from nearby Bend seldom stray far from home.

Tours start from Dutchman Flat Sno-Park. The Cross Country Center at Mount Bachelor West Village is an alternate starting point. From Bend, drive south and west on Century Drive, which becomes Cascade Lakes Highway. In 21 miles, Dutchman Flat Sno-Park is on the right. Not plowed beyond the sno-park, the highway becomes a snowmobile trail from this point.

Plowing continues on an access road curving to the left and climbing 0.5 mile to the Mount Bachelor West Village lot. Bear right and park near the Cross Country Center. From here, a common corridor trail provides access to the Dutchman Flat trails. No fee is charged to ski the groomed Common Corridor between Mount Bachelor's Cross Country Center and the Cascade Lakes Highway.

The network of ungroomed Forest Service trails northeast of the unplowed Cascade Lakes Highway creates a variety of ski loops, especially if combined with groomed snowmobile trails. Four tours are described here. Use a trail map and modify tours to suit your interests. Dogs are not allowed on any ski trails north of the Cascade Lakes Highway.

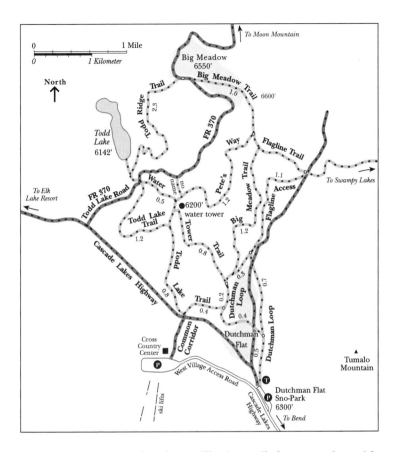

Dutchman Loop. Dutchman Flat is a mile-long meadow with wide-open views of Mount Bachelor, the Three Sisters, and Broken Top. Just a few inches of snow coverage make it skiable, making it one of Oregon's best early-season ski venues. A loop around the edge of the meadow is part of an excellent 2.5-mile novice tour. From Dutchman Flat Sno-Park, follow blue diamonds 0.5 mile north to the edge of the open area. Stay to the right, climbing slightly and following the Dutchman Loop through the trees on the east side of Dutchman Flat. At the north end, the trail crosses the flat and turns left. It enters the trees again, climbs a little, and passes junctions with the Big Meadow and Water Tower Trails on the right. Skiers have the option of not following the trail and just skiing south along the edge of Dutchman Flat. At a junction with the Todd Lake Trail, the Dutchman Loop heads east and crosses the meadow, following blue diamonds on bamboo or plastic poles and returning to Dutchman Flat Sno-Park.

Water Tower and Todd Lake Trails. For a 6-mile, round-trip tour from the sno-park, ski north to Dutchman Flat and west across the flat to the Water Tower Trail. Ski north through the sparce trees west of Dutchman Flat. The Water Tower Trail turns northwest and continues through forest and over short hills. The trail descends a steep hill to a small clearing 2 miles from the sno-park. The small water tower at the end of the clearing is part of the water system for the Mount Bachelor Ski Area. A few yards past the tower, the trail crosses a stream to a small clearing. Look back for a view of Mount Bachelor. Both the stream and the water tower may be obscured in heavy snow years. From the clearing, the Water Tower Trail turns left and descends to Forest Road 370. Ski across the road and climb 0.2 mile to the south shore of Todd Lake, nestled in a glacial basin. The top of Broken Top can be seen beyond the north side of the basin. It is possible to ski along the lakeshore, but the best views are from this shore. To return to the sno-park, ski back to Forest Road 370 and cross the road. Then bear right into a meadow and follow the Todd Lake Trail south. This trail has some steep uphill sections. It touches the Cascade Lakes Highway across from the Common Corridor and then continues to Dutchman Flat and the sno-park. Intermediate-level skiers who enjoy fast downhills can use this trail as the route to Todd Lake. Another return option from Todd Lake is to descend Forest Road 370 to the Cascade Lakes Highway, turn left, and ski 1.9 miles to Dutchman Flat Sno-Park. Both roads are groomed snowmobile trails. The mile on the Cascade Lakes Highway from Road 370 to Mount Bachelor's Common Corridor is a tough uphill climb.

Pete's Way and Flagline Access. This 5.7-mile loop mixes open meadows and forest trails. It is rated intermediate, but it is on the difficult end of that rating. In icy conditions, it is only for advanced skiers. From Dutchman Flat Sno-Park, ski across Dutchman Flat to the Water Tower Trail and continue north to the Water Tower, 2 miles from the sno-park. Turn north from the Water Tower and cross a small clearing with a view of Mount Bachelor to the Pete's Way Trail. This trail climbs, steeply at times, winding northeast 1.2 miles to the Big Meadow Trail. Big Meadow is to the left, but the loop turns right. In 0.1 mile, continue straight on Flagline Trail when Big Meadow Trail turns right. Turn right in another 0.5 mile onto Flagline Access Trail for a mile of challenging, winding descent through old-growth hemlock to the north end of Dutchman Flat. Continue south along the flat to Dutchman Flat Sno-Park.

Broken Top

Big Meadow. Big Meadow is just what the name implies. It is a large alpine meadow surrounded by ridges, with views of Mount Bachelor, Tumalo Mountain, and Broken Top. From Dutchman Flat Sno-Park, ski north to Dutchman Flat, west across the flat, and then turn north onto the Water Tower Trail. Continue a short distance to the northwest corner of Dutchman Flat and the start of the Big Meadow Trail, 1.2 miles from the sno-park. Big Meadow leads north, climbing steadily through stands of mountain hemlock. After a little more than 1 mile, it descends to a junction with the Flagline Trail. Big Meadow Trail bears left, passes Pete's Way Trail on the left, and cuts through a small clearing where the top of Broken Top can be seen. It continues north to the east edge of Big Meadow, about 3 miles from the sno-park. Forest Road 370, the Todd Lake Road, enters the meadow on the left. After a break to enjoy the meadow, return to Dutchman Flat by skiing downhill on Forest Road 370. In 1 mile, turn left on a short connector to the Water Tower Trail and continue to the sno-park for a round-trip distance of 6.5 miles. The Todd Ridge Trail, starting near the west end of Big Meadow, looks like an alternate return route on a map, but most skiers should avoid it. It is a narrow trail with sharp switchbacks and is only for advanced skiers.

20 ELK LAKE

Distance: 22 miles
Trails: Groomed snowmobile trails
Track Quality: Good classic skiing, good skating
Skill Level: Intermediate to advanced
Elevation: 6300 feet
Maximum Elevation Gain: 1400 feet
Season: Late November to mid-April
Services and Facilities: Restaurant, cabins
Hours: Lodge open daily
Fees: Sno-park permit
Information: Elk Lake Resort, (541) 480-7228, *www.elklakeresort.com*

The Cascade Lakes Highway runs south and west from Bend through the Deschutes National Forest, passing a dozen alpine lakes. In winter, the highway is closed at Dutchman Flat near Mount Bachelor Ski Area for use as a ski and snowmobile route. A scenic but difficult tour along the highway leads to two of the alpine lakes, Sparks Lake and Elk Lake. The tour is 22 miles round trip and is only for strong skiers in good weather. The best plan is to spend a night at Elk Lake Resort, 11 miles along the unplowed highway from Dutchman Flat. The lodge rents cabins and its restaurant is open during winter.

The tour starts at Dutchman Flat Sno-Park. From Bend, drive south and west on Century Drive, which becomes the Cascade Lakes Highway. In 21 miles, turn right into Dutchman Flat Sno-Park. The highway is not plowed beyond this point, but plowing continues on an access road that curves left and climbs to the Mount Bachelor West Village parking lot. If you are spending a night at Elk Lake Resort, check the sno-park signs for overnight parking rules. The spaces designated for overnight parking alternate during the week to aid plowing. The resort can advise you on the parking regulations. After an overnight stay, be

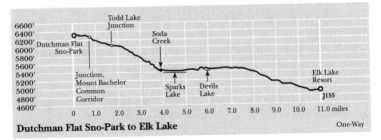

Dutchman Flat Sno-Park to Elk Lake   One-Way

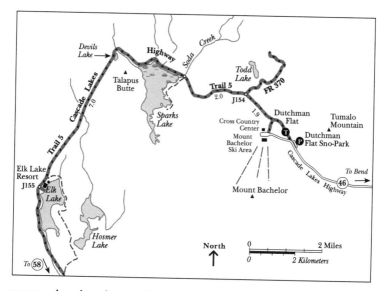

prepared to shovel snow piled by plows before freeing your vehicle to drive out of the lot.

The route to Elk Lake along the Cascade Lakes Highway is a wide snowmobile trail groomed by the Moon Country Snowmobile Club. The wide trail has plenty of room, but stay to the right to make it easy for snowmobilers to pass. The snowmobile trail is marked with orange diamonds and junction numbers. Skating conditions are usually good, but skaters may have trouble maintaining momentum on the long uphill return to the sno-park.

From the north end of the sno-park, ski northwest a few yards to reach snowmobile Trail 5, which is the trail that follows the highway. Ski northwest on the snowmobile trail, with views of Broken Top and South Sister. The highway passes the Common Corridor connector trail from the Mount Bachelor Cross Country Center on the left in 0.8 mile. From here, the road descends a moderate hill to snowmobile junction 154, 1.9 miles from the sno-park. Forest Road 370 to Todd Lake is on the right. The Cascade Lakes Highway continues straight from junction 154, descending steeply for 2 miles. This is the most difficult part of the route. It can be an intimidating downhill stretch on the way to Elk Lake and a laborious climb on the return.

The road levels off near Soda Creek before entering the wide, flat expanse of Sparks Lake and surrounding meadows. Sparks Lake is nearly 2 miles long from north to south. An old lake, it has been filling with sediment for centuries and much of it is now marsh. The

flats closest to the highway are marsh and meadow; the open part of the lake is nearly 1 mile south. If time permits, ski south on an access road that starts just east of Soda Creek. In 1 mile, it leads to the east shore of the lake and a view of Mount Bachelor. Sparks Lake is a good destination for a day tour. The return to Dutchman Flat Sno-Park from the lake is 4 miles with an 890-foot climb.

To continue to Elk Lake, follow the highway beyond Sparks Lake and past Talapus Butte on the left. The road is flat and skiing is fast here. Nearly 2 miles from Soda Creek, the road climbs a short hill and turns south as it passes tiny Devils Lake. The Devils Hill lava flow north of here played a part in Apollo missions to the moon. Astronauts trained on the lava rocks and James Irwin carried a rock from the flow to the moon, leaving it behind as a monument.

From Devils Lake, the highway continues south through gentle hills for 2 miles and then descends a long moderate grade to snowmobile junction 155. Turn left onto the entrance road to Elk Lake Resort and ski 0.2 mile to the resort. The resort is 11 miles from the Dutchman Flat Sno-Park and 1400 feet lower (7 miles from Soda Creek/Sparks Lake and 510 feet lower). The picture-postcard beauty of this lake in winter is enhanced by views of Mount Bachelor and South Sister from its shores.

The lodge caters to skiers and snowmobilers. Accommodations are in simple but nicely renovated cabins. Advance reservations are an absolute requirement. The lodge restaurant is reliably good. It is open almost daily, but check ahead for the winter schedule. For a fee, the lodge can haul overnight gear or guests to or from the sno-park in its funky snow van. Arrangements should be made in advance.

The return to Dutchman Flat Sno-Park is along the same route, with a long, steep climb from Sparks Lake to junction 154. After an overnight stay at the lodge, get an early start for the return trip to the sno-park. Check weather conditions, and do not start out if a storm is expected. Whiteout conditions on the Cascade Lakes Highway can be deadly. Carry overnight survival equipment.

Skiers in excellent physical condition can make the 22-mile round trip as a day tour, stopping at Elk Lake Resort for lunch in the restaurant. This is best done in March or April to take advantage of longer daylight hours. Get an early start in the morning and carry food, plenty of water, and overnight survival gear. This is a very strenuous tour and should only be attempted by advanced skiers.

Soda Creek

21 WANOGA

Distance: 1–8.5 miles
Trails: Groomed snowmobile trails
Track Quality: Fair classic skiing, good skating
Skill Level: Intermediate to advanced
Elevation: 5480 feet
Maximum Elevation Gain: 250 feet
Season: Early December to early April
Services and Facilities: Outhouse, log shelter
Hours: NA
Fees: Sno-park permit
Information: Bend–Fort Rock Ranger District, Deschutes National Forest, (541) 480-7228

Wanoga Sno-Park is snowmobile country. Groomed snowmobile routes lead to Edison Butte, Lava Lake, and Dutchman Flat, and connect to miles of ungroomed trails. On busy weekends, leave Wanoga to the snowmobiles and opt for groomed ski trails at nearby Virginia Meissner (Chapter 22) or ungroomed trails at Swampy Lakes Sno-Park, 1 mile to the west. But do not ignore this area entirely. It offers nice ski opportunities close to Bend and unusual views of Mount Bachelor. It is generally quiet on weekdays and late-season weekends. The wide trails are particularly good for skating, especially on Fridays as grooming is often done on Thursday nights. Dog owners enjoy Wanoga because its trails are the closest to Bend, where dogs are allowed.

From Bend, drive southwest on Century Drive, which becomes Highway 46/the Cascade Lakes Highway. In 14 miles, the entrance to Wanoga

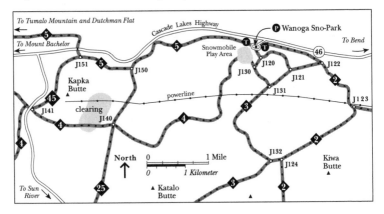

Mount Bachelor's east side

is on the left 1 mile beyond Virginia Meissner Sno-Park. Drive around the parking oval to the south side of the lot. Outhouses and a log shelter are located in the oval. Maps of the snowmobile trails may be available at the shelter, but the scale is deceptive. Most loops are too long for skiers.

Snowmobile routes are marked with orange diamonds. Tracks wander off marked routes in many directions, as snowmobiles are not restricted to specific trails. Junctions are numbered and many have directional signs. There is a snowmobile play area in the little hills just west of the sno-park. It is hard to predict which way a snowmobile will turn here, so ski through the area with caution and do not linger.

Trail 5. From the west end of the sno-park, Trail 5 heads north and west, running close to the Cascade Lakes Highway. It is used for fast access to a tunnel under the highway and trails near Tumalo Mountain. Snowplows may throw gravel along this trail. There are better trails.

Trails 2 and 3. A trail from the south side of the lot leads quickly to two short loops. Both are best skied counterclockwise. The closer loop is only 0.7 mile in circumference. Unnamed, it connects junctions 120, 130, 131, and 121. It has short steep sections and sharp turns. The outer loop, incorporating Trails 2 and 3, is 2.1 miles and includes most of the closer loop. Ski this route from junction 120 through junctions 120, 130, 131, 132, 124, 123, 122, 121, and back to 120.

Trail 4. Trail 4, starting at the west end of the sno-park, is the most interesting route for a long tour. It passes through the snowmobile play area, climbs a steep hill, and leads south, passing under powerlines. There are often snowmobile tracks on the powerline right-of-way, which is an option for a return route on this 7.4-mile, out-and-back tour. In 1.3 miles, the trail turns west and climbs gradually, with glimpses of Mount Bachelor and Tumalo Mountain. Look for tracks and other signs of coyote. Bobcat sign is occasionally seen as well.

In 3.5 miles, Trail 4 reaches Trail 25 at junction 140. For excellent views of Mount Bachelor's east side, continue straight 0.2 mile to a short descent to an open area. Here is a brilliant view of Mount Bachelor (9065 feet). The minor peak jutting from Mount Bachelor's south flank is Tot Mountain and the snow-covered butte 2 miles south of Bachelor is Kwolh Butte (7358 feet). A little bushwhacking through the trees to the right leads to a large clearing and more views of Bachelor and Tumalo Mountain.

Return to Trail 4. A long option is to continue west to junction 141 and complete a 3-mile tour around Kapka Butte to junction 150. Then ski 2 miles on Trail 5 to the sno-park for an 8.5-mile round trip. Otherwise, return to junction 140. For an easy return, stay on Trail 4, reversing the earlier route. Be alert for approaching traffic on downhill sections. For more adventure, turn left onto Trail 25 and ski 0.2 mile to the powerlines. Turn right and follow the powerlines 1.5 miles through rolling hills. It may be necessary to break trail. Turn left on Trail 4 and return to the sno-park for a round trip of about 7.2 miles.

22 VIRGINIA MEISSNER

Distance: 3–10 miles
Trails: Groomed ski trails
Track Quality: Very good classic skiing, fair skating
Skill Level: Novice to advanced
Elevation: 5350 feet
Maximum Elevation Gain: 500 feet
Season: Early December to late March
Services and Facilities: Outhouse, trailside shelters
Hours: NA
Fees: $3 per person suggested donation, sno-park permit
Information: Tumalo Langlauf Chapter, Oregon Nordic Club,
www.tumalolanglauf.com

Virginia Meissner Sno-Park is an easy 20-minute drive west of Bend. Ski club volunteers groom more than 10 miles of track and maintain shelters along ski trails mostly suited to beginners. The terrain is mostly gentle, but there is a hilly loop that rewards skiers with tremendous views of Tumalo Mountain, Mount Bachelor, and the Three Sisters. The trails connect to popular ungroomed trails in the Swampy Lakes system to the west. The sno-park, opened in 1990, is named in memory of Virginia Meissner, an energetic ski instructor and tour leader. One of her passions, wildflowers, inspired many of the area's trail names.

The Central Oregon chapter of the Oregon Nordic Club helped develop the ski trails and initiated occasional trail grooming. The new Tumalo Langlauf ONC chapter expanded the grooming program. Trails are usually groomed on Tuesday, Thursday, and Saturday. Tracks set for classic skiing are excellent. Four miles are groomed double-wide for skating. If conditions permit, other trails are groomed as well. This program is dependent upon volunteers and donations. Look for the donation box at the trailhead.

From Bend, drive south and west on Century Drive, which becomes Highway 46/the Cascade Lakes Highway. In 13 miles, turn right into Virginia Meissner Sno-Park. Two groomed trails leave the trailhead near the middle of the north side of the sno-park. Tangent Loop runs to the left for a few yards and then turns north on a forest road. Wednesdays Trail turns right from the trailhead and heads northeast. Dogs are not allowed on Meissner trails or any other ski trails north of Cascade Lakes Highway.

Several trails follow forest roads and are connected by narrower trails to form loops. Regularly groomed routes include trails to two shelters that are popular lunch stops. A third shelter on an ungroomed loop is close to the sno-park. Nordic club members maintain all three shelters and keep them stocked with firewood. Use the firewood sparingly.

Meissner Shelter. The 3-mile out-and-back trip to Meissner Shelter is good for beginners. The route is groomed regularly, has small hills, and only climbs 100 feet from the sno-park. Ski north on Tangent Loop. In 0.8 mile, pass a junction with Pine Drops and continue on Tangent Loop, climbing gently 0.2 mile to a right turn onto the Manzanita Trail. Follow this narrow road 0.5 mile to the shelter, which is 50 feet to the left of the trail. The shelter sits on a low ridge. Views from the shelter are limited, but the open slope a few yards north provides vistas of Cascade peaks and surrounding forests. Manzanita continues east from the shelter, but this section is not groomed and has a difficult downhill stretch. It is best to return to the sno-park the way you came. On the return, bypass the last 0.5 mile of Tangent Loop by turning right onto Knotweed. Little ups and downs on Knotweed make it more interesting than Tangent Loop. Knotweed ends on another section of Tangent Loop. Turn left and ski 0.1 mile east, turn right, and ski south a short distance to the sno-park.

Pine Drops–Wednesdays Loop. A 4.3-mile loop along Pine Drops and Wednesdays Trail is a fine beginner tour with just enough hills to be interesting. The loop can be combined with a trip to Meissner Shelter for a 5.7-mile round trip. Ski north on Tangent Loop. In 0.8 mile, the junction with Pine Drops is on the right. Ski east onto Pine Drops, easily descending 1 mile to Snowbush Trail. Turn right onto Snowbush and descend a moderate hill to Wednesdays Trail in 0.3 mile. Watch for signs of wildlife tracks in this area. Coyote tracks are common and cougar tracks are seen occasionally. Turn right onto Wednesdays Trail and follow it 2.2 miles through meadows and thin Ponderosa stands to the sno-park. Before the sno-park, bear left at a four-way junction to stay on Wednesdays Trail. Going straight at the intersection onto Penstemon also leads to the sno-park, but the track is often in rough condition.

Wednesdays. Wednesdays Trail is named for a midweek touring group that Virginia Meissner led for many years. Combined with the Tangent Loop, it forms a 7-mile, mostly groomed loop. Most of the loop is easy, but a downhill section of Wednesdays earns an intermediate rating. Touring skis work well on this loop. Ski north on the Tangent Loop 1.8 miles to a junction with both Wednesdays and Snowbush Trails. Tangent Loop turns left. Go straight and follow a regularly groomed, 1.7-mile section of Wednesdays Trail, curving east and drop-

Shooting Star Shelter

ping gently to a junction with the Paintbrush Trail. The groomed route continues straight on Paintbrush. Turn right to ski down a steep, 1.2-mile, ungroomed section of Wednesdays to a junction with the eastern end of Snowbush. Continue on Wednesdays to the sno-park.

Shooting Star. The best views in the Meissner trail system are at the north end along a hilly loop to Shooting Star Shelter. The round-trip distance from the sno-park is 9.4 miles. This includes a 4-mile out-and-back section on a road that is groomed double-wide for skaters. The 1.4-mile Shooting Star Loop has steep hills and is best suited to advanced skiers.

Ski north on Tangent Loop. In 1.8 miles, Tangent Loop turns left. Go straight here on Wednesdays, which follows the groomed road. The road curves east and then turns north. The groomed road becomes Paintbrush where Wednesdays turns right on an ungroomed section. Ski north 0.7 mile on Paintbrush to Shooting Star Loop on the left. Old signs may call it Paintbrush Loop. The loop can be skied in either direction, but the north leg may not be groomed. At the intersection, continue straight to a second junction with Shooting Star Loop. Beyond this point, the Paintbrush Trail, occasionally groomed, leads 0.5 mile to a cinder pit. Turn left at this intersection toward Shooting Star Shelter and climb steeply to the west leg of the loop and the shelter. Tumalo Mountain, Mount Bachelor, and the Three Sisters loom to the west from several places along the loop. The rest of the loop is a fast, challenging run back to the first junction with Paintbrush.

Snowbush. The Snowbush Trail starts on Tangent Loop, 1.8 miles from the sno-park. It leads east on an old road, passing below the low ridge that Meissner Shelter is on. Near its east end, it connects to Manzanita and Pine Drops before ending at Wednesdays Trail. The short section between Pine Drops and Wednesdays is groomed regularly. The rest of the trail is groomed when snow conditions permit. Drifting snow sometimes makes part of the trail difficult to ski and impossible to groom.

Wild Strawberry Run. Volunteers have flagged a new trail running east from the Lupine Trail and connecting to Pine Drops. The Forest Service has tentatively named the trail Wild Strawberry Run. If the trail is approved as planned, it will be a roller-coaster run for advanced skiers. The trail shown on the map is just a best guess of the future trail.

23 TUMALO FALLS

Distance: 1–5.8 miles
Trails: Ungroomed ski trails
Track Quality: Good classic skiing, no skating
Skill Level: Novice to intermediate
Elevation: 4740 feet
Maximum Elevation Gain: 212 feet
Season: Mid-December to mid-March
Services and Facilities: Outhouse, nearby group lodge
Hours: NA
Fees: Sno-park permit not required
Information: Bend–Fort Rock Ranger District, Deschutes National Forest, (541) 383-4000

Only 10 miles west of Bend, the Tumalo Creek area offers easy beginner trails, unique scenery, and relative solitude. An easy road tour follows Tumalo Creek through a broad, open valley, culminating at the base of 97-foot-high Tumalo Falls. The route to the falls passes a large burn area. In 1979, the Bridge Creek Fire, started by a campfire, destroyed more than 4000 acres of old-growth forest in the Bridge Creek Watershed. The area has been replanted with ponderosa pine, but growth is slow and the new trees are still small. Unfortunately, snow conditions are unreliable here. This valley does not get a lot of snow, and the snow melts quickly in warm weather. Try to visit after a recent snowfall.

From downtown Bend, drive 10 miles west on Galveston, which becomes Skyliners Road. Skyliner Sno-Park, a small gravel parking area, is on the left just before the entrance to Skyliners Lodge. A sno-park permit is not required because, despite the name, it is not part of

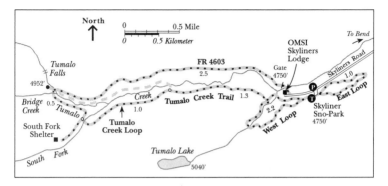

Oregon's sno-park program. The road is not plowed beyond the lodge.

Oregon's first downhill ski area was at the snow-play area next to the parking lot. The current sledding hill was the site of a rope tow. Skyliners Lodge, the old ski lodge, is just west of this area. The Oregon Museum of Science and Industry (OMSI) maintains the lodge as an outdoor education camp. Groups can rent the lodge in the winter, with sleeping accommodations in yurts and small bunkhouses. For information, call OMSI at (503) 795-4547.

A private landowner near the lodge uses an ATV to set tracks in his large back yard, primarily for use by children's groups. The tracks are simple, but the wooded setting is pretty. The tracks are not open to the public, but dozens of children ski here each year through ski club programs. Check with the Tumalo Langlauf Ski Club for information about these programs.

East Loop and West Loop. Two short beginner loops start at the sno-park. East Loop is a flat, 1-mile trail through the woods. Ski 100 feet north from the sno-park and turn left to start the loop. The West Loop is a little more challenging. Skied clockwise, it leads west from the sno-park, climbs on a narrow road for a mile, and then passes through part of the Bridge Creek Burn area. It loops back to the east, passes Skyliner Lodge, and returns to the sno-park for a 2.2-mile loop.

Road 4603. A 5-mile, out-and-back round trip along Tumalo Creek passes through the old burn and ends at the base of Tumalo Falls. This easy beginner tour follows Forest Road 4603, climbing gently to the falls with no difficult hills. To start, walk across Skyliners Road and ski along a powerline route 0.1 mile to the unplowed end of the road. Follow the road across Tumalo Creek, ski up a short hill, and bear left past a gate on Forest Road 4603. Ski west through open terrain on the road, with Tumalo Creek always on the left. In 2.5 miles, Road 4603 crosses Tumalo Creek. The upper part of Tumalo

Falls can be seen from the far side of the bridge. For a better view of the falls, ski up a hill next to the Bend water treatment facilities.

Tumalo Creek Trail and Loop. The Tumalo Creek Trail is an alternate route to Tumalo Falls. Many skiers will prefer the narrow, rolling trail over the wide, gentle route on Road 4603. The first half of the Tumalo Creek Trail follows the south side of Tumalo Creek to the Tumalo Creek Loop. One leg of the loop continues on the south side of the creek to Tumalo Falls, and the other leg crosses the creek before continuing to the falls.

From the sno-park, ski counterclockwise on the West Loop past Skyliners Lodge. The start of Tumalo Creek Trail is on the right 0.5 mile from the sno-park. It follows the ridge south of the creek, passing through second-growth ponderosa pine in the Bridge Creek Burn area. In 1.3 miles from the West Loop, Tumalo Creek Trail reaches the Tumalo Creek Loop, which offers two routes to Tumalo Falls.

The north leg of the loop is to the right. It descends a steep hill, turns upstream for 30 yards, and crosses the creek on a sturdy bridge. It then meanders west along the north bank of the creek, between the creek and Road 4603. At least 3 feet of snow are needed to cross little creeks and brushy areas in this section. It climbs a short steep hill to reach Road 4603 just before Tumalo Falls. After visiting the falls, return to the sno-park via Road 4603 for a 5.5-mile round-trip tour.

The south leg of the Tumalo Creek Loop is a continuation of the Tumalo Creek Trail along the south side of the creek. It is a little more challenging than the north leg and is the better choice when the snow depth is low. In 1 mile from the start of the loop, the trail crosses a new bridge over the South Fork of Tumalo Creek to a junction with the South Fork Trail. A left turn leads 0.2 mile to the South Fork Shelter. Tumalo Creek Loop continues straight, following the South Fork Trail 0.5 mile to Tumalo Falls. Return to the sno-park via Road 4603 for a 5.8-mile round-trip tour.

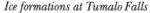
Ice formations at Tumalo Falls

24 PAULINA LAKES

Distance: 6–10.6 miles
Trails: Groomed snowmobile trails
Track Quality: Good classic skiing, good skating
Skill Level: Novice to advanced
Elevation: 5600 feet
Maximum Elevation Gain: 2297 feet
Season: Early December to early April
Services and Facilities: Outhouse, 3-mile ski to resort and restaurant
Hours: Lodge open daily, restaurant open weekends
Fees: Sno-park permit
Information: Paulina Lake Resort, (541) 536-2240

Paulina Lake Resort, in the basin of the Newberry Crater, is base camp for exploring the caldera of an old volcano. Like Crater Lake 75 miles to the south, Newberry's 5-mile-wide crater was formed when the top of a volcano collapsed. Newberry National Volcanic Monument was established in 1990 to protect the area's unique geological formations. Paulina Lake and East Lake lie in the crater's basin surrounded by the 1000-foot rim on three sides. Day trips include the two lakes, peaks along the rim, and an obsidian lava flow. A snowmobile club grooms roads in the crater and the area sees heavy snowmobile use.

From Bend, drive 23 miles south on Highway 97. Turn left onto Paulina Lake Road and drive east 10 miles to the appropriately named 10 Mile Sno-Park. The road is plowed, but the sno-park may have loose

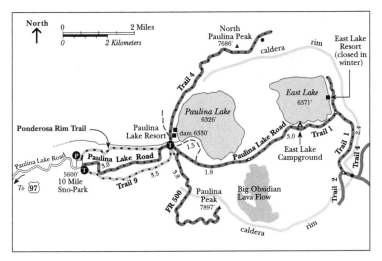

snow. The road is not plowed beyond the sno-park, where it becomes the major ski route to the caldera.

Popular ski routes are on snowmobile trails groomed weekly by the Lodgepole Dodgers snowmobile club. A few quiet-use trails exist, but the snowmobile routes provide enjoyable skiing for those who do not mind the machines. The wide trails allow snowmobilers to give skiers a wide berth when passing, and the snowmobile club has long promoted courteous riding. Skiers, appreciating that the best tours in the crater would be long slogs without the groomed trails, stay to one side when snowmobiles approach and even greet the drivers with a smile. The efforts of both groups allow mixed-use enjoyment of the area with little conflict. The snowmobile club usually grooms on Thursday night. The surface is excellent for skating on Friday.

The Paulina Lake Resort on the west end of Paulina Lake is popular with snowmobilers and skiers—with just fourteen rustic cabins, it is full most weekends. The resort restaurant serves lunch and dinner on weekends only. Cabins include kitchen facilities. Reach the resort by skiing 3 miles on Paulina Lake Road from the sno-park.

Some of the following trail descriptions begin near the resort. For day trips on these trails from the sno-park, add 6 miles for the round trip to the trailhead. Long day trips from the sno-park are best

planned for late winter and spring when daylight is more plentiful.

Paulina Lake. This 6-mile, out-and-back tour on a groomed road is suitable for novices. It begins at the southeast corner of the sno-park. Ski up Paulina Lake Road for 3 miles, climbing 730 feet to the west end of Paulina Lake at 6330 feet. A road to the left crosses a small dam and leads 0.25 mile to the resort. Along the way from the sno-park, there are views of Paulina Peak and the surrounding countryside, but the best views are from Paulina Lake and beyond. The lake is a good destination for an easy day trip from the sno-park. The lake, the small falls below the dam, and views of the crater rim justify the effort.

Trail to Paulina Peak

Trail 9. Trail 9 is an alternate, ungroomed route away from snow-mobiles. It starts on the east side of the sno-park, immediately turns south, and crosses Paulina Lake Road. It continues south of the road, climbing to the dam in 3.5 miles. The route is in trees but has views of the crater rim and the Cascades. Ponderosa Rim Trail, another ungroomed route to the dam, begins at the north side of the sno-park and heads uphill along Paulina Creek.

Paulina Peak. The views from Paulina Peak make this the first-choice tour for skiers in Newberry Crater. From the dam at the lake's west end, look up to the southeast. Paulina Peak, at 7897 feet, stands out against the crater rim. If it's hidden by clouds, choose another trip and save the peak for a day with better visibility. From the dam next to the resort, ski up Paulina Lake Road 0.3 mile to Forest Road 500 on the right. Follow this wide, groomed road 3.8 miles to the summit. This intermediate trail includes a 1570-foot climb. Spectacular views begin after about 1.5 miles of skiing. Views from the summit include the Cascade Mountains from Mount Hood to Mount Shasta, the crater rim, the lakes in the caldera, and the Ochoco Mountains. Ski back down Forest Road 500 to return to the lake.

East Lake. A tour from Paulina Lake to East Lake is a good choice for an easy day trip or when bad weather precludes a climb to the rim. Several spots along East Lake's shore are good turnaround points, making the tour length variable from 7.4 to 10.6 miles. From the dam by the resort, follow Paulina Lake Road east toward East Lake. The best views of Paulina Lake are at the start of the tour, as the road quickly angles away from the lake. For variety, start on a marked ski and snowshoe trail from the south end of the dam. Follow the narrow trail 1.5 miles through a campground, into the woods, and back to the road. This adds 0.5 mile to the tour. At 3.7 miles, the road passes East Lake Campground. Take a short detour here for good views of the lake. From the campground, follow the road or the lakeshore to the east side of the lake and East Lake Resort, which is closed in winter. All of East Lake and the crater's north rim can be seen from the shore. Return the way you came.

A snowmobile route climbs the caldera's East Rim from the east side of East Lake and leads to many miles of groomed snowmobile trails. However, venturing past the East Rim requires good maps, ample daylight, plenty of water, and a lot of stamina.

North Caldera Rim. A trip to the north rim of the caldera provides different views of the caldera than those from Paulina Peak. Skiers get a nice look at Paulina Lake on the way up, but this is a difficult route and the tracks are often rough. Follow snowmobile Trail 4, which starts by climbing a steep, narrow road on the north side of the dam.

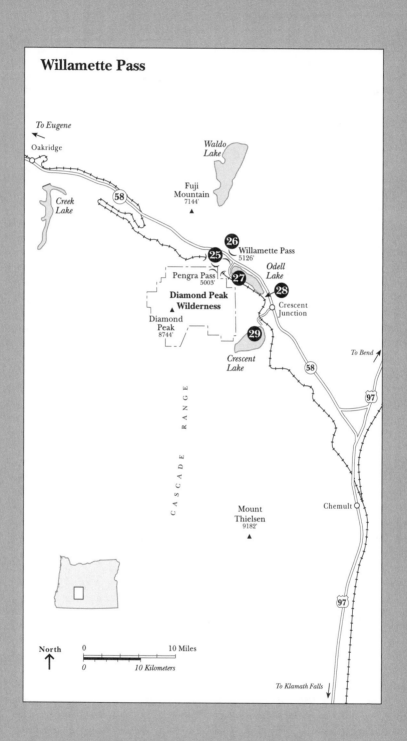

Willamette Pass

To Eugene

Oakridge

58

Creek
Lake

Waldo
Lake

Fuji
Mountain
7144'

26
25 Willamette Pass
5126'

Pengra Pass
5003'

27

Odell
Lake

28
Crescent
Junction

**Diamond Peak
Wilderness**

Diamond
Peak
8744'

29

Crescent
Lake

To Bend

58

97

C A S C A D E   R A N G E

Mount
Thielsen
9182'

Chemult

97

North

0   10 Miles

0   10 Kilometers

To Klamath Falls

Willamette Pass

The rugged, heavily forested Willamette Pass area straddles the crest of the Cascade Mountains southeast of Eugene. The crest marks the divide between two national forests, with the Willamette National Forest on the west and the Deschutes National Forest on the east. The area is easily accessible from Eugene and central Oregon. The pass is about 70 miles from both Eugene and Bend.

Skiers coming from farther away will not be disappointed by what the area has to offer. At more than 5100 feet, the pass gets plenty of snow. Breaks in the heavy forest offer views of Diamond Peak and Mount Thielsen south of the pass. Excellent views are easily reached at Odell and Crescent Lakes, large lakes with mountain backdrops. A commercial ski area at the pass has impeccably groomed trails open on weekends. Two cozy lakeside resorts offer simple groomed trails with good scenery and a low-key atmosphere. The forests north and south of the pass have many miles of marked ungroomed trails and unmarked backcountry trails. East of the pass, ample sunshine and snowmobile trails provide more ski opportunities. A weekend of exploring, with an overnight stay at one of the picturesque resorts, is well worth a long drive from Portland (185 miles) or Medford (145 miles via Chemult).

25 PENGRA PASS

Distance: 2.4–8.4 miles
Trails: Ungroomed ski trails
Track Quality: Good classic skiing, no skating
Skill Level: Novice to intermediate
Elevation: 5000 feet
Maximum Elevation Gain: 346 feet
Season: Late November to mid-April
Services and Facilities: Nordic Patrol warming hut, outhouse, trailside shelters
Hours: NA
Fees: Sno-park permit
Information: Oakridge Ranger District, Willamette National Forest, (541) 782-2291

The best combination of novice and intermediate trails in the Willamette Pass area are near Pengra Pass, starting from Gold Lake Sno-Park. The trails are not groomed, but usually tracks have been set by other skiers. An interesting variety of routes include short loops through heavy timber and trails following gentle roads. A few excellent views are within easy reach for intermediate skiers. Two shelters along the trails can be used for overnight visits.

The Willamette Backcountry Ski Patrol warming hut at Gold Lake Sno-Park is staffed and open to the public most weekends. Patrol volunteers are active in trail maintenance, public information, and rescue operations. Trail conditions are posted on weekends. The patrol usually hosts a winter safety open house in mid-January.

From Interstate 5 south of Eugene, drive southeast on Highway 58 for 63 miles. At the summit of Willamette Pass, Gold Lake Sno-Park is on the right 0.6 mile before the Willamette Pass Ski Area. Drive 0.2 mile on the access road to parking, outhouses, and the ski patrol cabin. The sno-park is 72 miles from Bend via Highways 97 and 58. Trails start at the south end of the parking lot and lead south on Forest

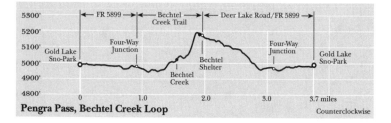

Pengra Pass, Bechtel Creek Loop   Counterclockwise

Road 5899. The area has more trails in the Diamond Peak Wilderness and across the highway than those described here. Check with the ski patrol for information.

Pengra Pass. This 2.4-mile beginner tour with just a 40-foot elevation gain follows gentle roads and connects to more interesting trails. Head south on Forest Road 5899, with views of Salt Creek Valley to the right. After passing the Westview Trail on the left, the road passes over a mile-long railroad tunnel hidden 200 feet below the surface. Another easy 0.8 mile leads to the first corner of the Triangle, a loop with three 0.2-mile legs. For Pengra Pass, bear left and ski uphill on the Pengra Pass Road. In 0.2 mile, pass the Triangle's south junction and continue to Pengra Pass, 1.1 miles from the sno-park. The pass is named after Oregon's first surveyor general, who explored the area in the 1860s. It marks the Cascade Divide and the border between the Willamette and Deschutes National Forests. The Pacific Crest Trail (PCT) crosses the Pengra Pass Road a few feet beyond the pass. A right turn onto the PCT leads immediately into the Diamond Peak Wilderness. A left onto the PCT leads to Willamette Pass. Pengra Pass Road continues straight, with a narrow and steep descent to railroad tracks, West Odell Road, and Shelter Cove (Chapter 27). From Pengra Pass, return to the south junction of the Triangle. Follow the Triangle's west and north legs to complete the loop before returning to the sno-park.

Westview Loops. Several short, beginner-to-intermediate loops with varied terrain straddle the Cascade Divide between Forest Road 5899 and Odell Lake. There are three main loops: north (N), middle (M), and south (S). The middle loop, the easiest of the three, is split by a short marked trail that does not appear on most maps. A three-sided shelter along the middle loop has a sleeping loft and woodstove, as well as an open view to the west. The north and south loops have short downhill sections that will challenge beginners.

The most direct access to the loops is the Westview Trail, 0.4 mile from the sno-park. The trail angles to the right from Forest Road 5899, traversing the hillside. It climbs 100 feet to a junction with the north loop that may not be obvious. It is 50 feet before an obvious junction with the middle loop. Bear right to ski the north loop, the most challenging of the three, counterclockwise. Bear left at this junction for the quickest route to the shelter.

The loops also can be reached from Pengra Pass Road on a wide connector to the south loop. This second option is a good route for beginners. There is also a connector trail from the PCT to the south loop, but it is very steep. The PCT is primarily a hiking trail and has narrow turns that are difficult to ski.

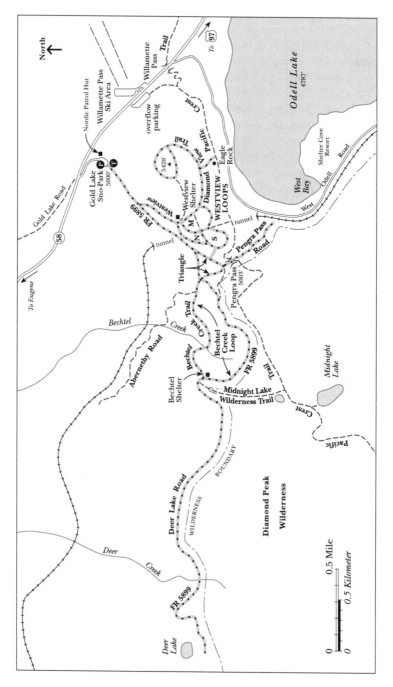

From the east side of the middle loop, the Diamond View Trail climbs a small butte (5428 feet) to a limited view through the trees of Diamond Peak to the southwest. A loop around the peak has sections of difficult sidehill skiing.

The most stunning viewpoint in the Westview system is at Eagle Rock, high above Odell Lake. From the east side of the middle loop, ski 0.2 mile on Diamond View Trail to a trail on the right. Ski down this trail 0.1 mile to the PCT, turn right, and carefully ski 150 yards to the overlook. This is a tricky downhill section that approaches the edge of a steep bluff. Ski cautiously, especially if the trail is icy. Eagle Rock sits nearly 400 feet above the west end of Odell Lake. Diamond Peak and Lakeview Mountain are across the lake. Deep snow may form cornices over the bluff. Stay away from the edge.

Bechtel Creek Loop. This intermediate loop climbs easy roads and a more challenging forest trail to the Bechtel Shelter. The shelter has a woodstove, firewood, and a sleeping loft. The loop portion of the route is best skied counterclockwise. The entire tour is 3.7 miles round trip from the sno-park, with an elevation gain of 240 feet. Ski to the Triangle on Forest Road 5899, as described previously, and follow the Triangle's north leg west 0.2 mile to a four-way junction. The road continuing straight is the return leg of the Bechtel Creek Loop. Turn right onto the Bechtel Creek Trail, which follows Forest Road 409, and ski past a junction with Abernethy Road and through clearings with views. When the road ends in 0.3 mile, the loop continues on a well-marked trail. After crossing Bechtel Creek, it climbs through clearings and then descends a short, steep hill to the shelter. The return trip is along Deer Lake Road (Forest Road 5899), which passes just above the shelter. Reach the road by climbing the steep pitch behind the shelter or via a fairly level, narrow trail starting near the southwest corner of the shelter. Turn left onto Deer Lake Road and ski down a moderate grade to the Triangle to return to the sno-park the way you came.

Deer Lake. This 8.4-mile round-trip tour on a road with gentle grades merits an intermediate rating for its distance. The terrain is good for long, easy-paced skiing. Ski to the Bechtel Shelter, as described above, and continue west on Deer Lake Road (Forest Road 5899). In 0.1 mile, the Midnight Lake Wilderness Trail is on the left. Beyond here, Deer Lake Road is not heavily used and tracks may not be broken. The road turns sharply left and follows rolling terrain, descending gradually for more than a mile. Enjoy broad vistas to the right. The prominent peak to the north is Fuji Mountain. At 1.7 miles from the Bechtel Shelter, the road crosses Deer Creek and starts climbing to more views and the end of the road. Deer Lake is 120 feet below the road. Return along the road, descending 300 feet to the sno-park.

Eagle Rock overlook of Odell Lake

26 WILLAMETTE PASS SKI AREA

Distance: 2.7–8 kilometers (1.7–5 miles); 22 kilometers total
Trails: Groomed ski trails
Track Quality: Fair classic skiing, excellent skating
Skill Level: Novice to advanced
Elevation: 5100 feet
Maximum Elevation Gain: 780 feet
Season: Late November to early April
Services and Facilities: Ski rentals, outhouse, snacks, meals at
   alpine lodge
Hours: 9:00 A.M.–4:00 P.M., weekends and holidays
Fees: $6, sno-park permit
Information: Willamette Pass Ski Area, (541) 345-7669,
   www.willamettepass.com

The alpine ski area at the summit of Willamette Pass grooms 22 kilometers of cross-country trails through thick forests that include stands of old-growth fir. Sitting above 5000 feet, the area gets plenty of snow, mostly of the wet Cascades variety. The trails are groomed on weekends and holidays. Bill Koch, an Olympic skier and World Cup champion, designed these trails with long hills and manageable turns. The wide, well-groomed trails are particularly suited to skating.

From Interstate 5 south of Eugene, drive south on Highway 58 for 63 miles. Willamette Pass Ski Area is 0.6 mile past the Gold Lake Sno-Park (Chapter 25), near the summit of Willamette Pass. The ski trails, lodge, and main parking lot are north of the highway and a large overflow lot is on the south side. Bear left as you enter the main parking lot. The Nordic Center is at the far end, in front of the tubing hill.

The Nordic Center sells trail passes and snacks and has a small lunchroom. Warm meals are served at the alpine lodge. Touring skis can be rented here. The hectic activity of the tubing hill can be overwhelming and is a reminder that Nordic skiing is only a small part of the area's business. Alpine grooming machines are used to create wide, smooth trails that are excellent for skating. Tracks for classic skiing are not set regularly, but non-skaters will enjoy the trails anyway.

The cross-country loops wind through the forest on the lower slope of West Peak (6594 feet). Four primary loops branch off of the Outback Trail, a maintenance road that loops around the peak to the backside of the ski area. Three loops are on the downhill slope from the Outback and the fourth is uphill. Several short connector and cutoff trails make a number of loops possible. Trail names are not posted.

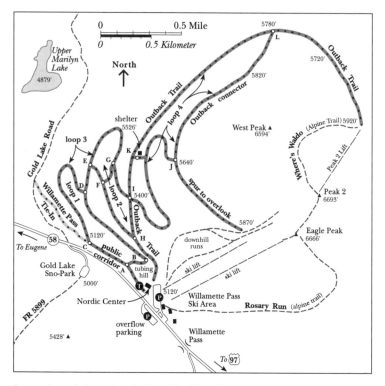

Instead, each junction is identified by a letter. All trails can be skied in either direction, but the loops are described clockwise here.

Loop 1. The lowest of the four main loops offers the area's gentlest terrain and is the best novice loop. The 2.7-kilometer (1.7-mile) route starts behind the Nordic Center and leads northwest to junction A and then continues to junctions C, D, B, and back to the Nordic Center. The 0.7-kilometer (0.4-mile) section from the Nordic Center to junction C is a public corridor. A trail pass is not required to ski this section, which provides access to backcountry trails. At junction C, the Willamette Pass Tie-In drops sharply to the left. This is a narrow, ungroomed trail with sharp turns. In 1 mile, it reaches Gold Lake Road, which is part of several backcountry trips.

Loop 2. The second of the loops—junctions H, F, E, G, I, and H—has long uphill sections and some steep downhill runs. From the front of the Nordic Center, ski up the right side of the tubing hill and follow the trail as it curves above the tubing hill to the Outback Trail. This trail climbs to junction H. Bear left here and follow the trail through junction F and continue to E. The loop continues to the right with 0.4 kilometer of steep uphill and a fast downhill through junctions G and I and back to H and the Nordic Center. The round-trip tour from the Nordic Center is 3.8 kilometers (2.4 miles).

Loop 3. A third loop that uses sections of both lower loops starts with gentle ups and downs, followed by a long climb with steep sections and then some fast downhill. From the Nordic Center, it passes through junctions A, C, D, E, G, I, and H to return to the Nordic Center for a total distance of 4.5 kilometers (2.8 miles).

Loop 4. The upper loop starts at junction I and follows the Outback Trail as it climbs northeast for 2.4 kilometers to junction L, where it makes a sharp uphill turn to the right. After a short section of more climbing, it drops to junction J. Straight ahead is a spur trail to an overlook next to the downhill ski runs. A hard right at J starts a section with exciting downhill turns that returns to junction I. A short cutoff, connector K, along the J–I section connects to the Outback Trail. Connector K can be used to avoid some of the difficult downhill stretches. There is a small shelter along the connector, but it is dreary and not an appealing spot for a break.

Outback Trail. The Outback Trail starts at the top of the tubing hill and loops around West Peak to the base of the ski lift on the peak's back side. The out-and-back route from the Nordic Center is 8 kilometers (5 miles) round trip. The trail has long hills, but skiing them requires more endurance than skill.

Skating on groomed trail

An exciting loop incorporating the Outback Trail is possible with the purchase of a one-ride lift pass. Skiers with strong cross-country downhill skills can ride the ski lift to the summit, descend alpine runs on the peak's back side, and return on the Outback Trail, which starts at the base of the Peak 2 lift. Even the easiest route from the summit is extremely challenging on cross-country skis. This loop is also possible in reverse by skiing generally uphill on Outback to the backside ski lift and returning downhill on Rosary Run to the alpine lodge. Backcountry skiers can also use the lift to access the Rosary Lakes area east of the ski area.

27 SHELTER COVE

Distance: 1–4 miles
Trails: Groomed ski trails
Track Quality: Good classic skiing, no skating
Skill Level: Novice
Elevation: 4750 feet
Maximum Elevation Gain: 40 feet
Season: Early December to late March
Services and Facilities: Store, ski rentals, cabins
Hours: NA
Fees: None
Information: Shelter Cove Resort, (800) 647-2729,
www.sheltercoveresort.com

A relaxed, friendly atmosphere and heart-stopping views are the hallmarks of this small resort tucked between Odell Lake and the Diamond Peak Wilderness. The resort grooms 4 miles, more or less, of tracks on novice-level terrain. Tracks are primarily for guests renting cabins, but anyone is welcome. There is no trail fee.

From Eugene, drive southeast 63 miles on Highway 58 to Willamette Pass. Continue 0.3 mile past the alpine ski area and turn right onto West Odell Road. Follow the access road 2 miles, descending 250 feet. The road may have packed snow. Turn left and continue 0.2 mile to a general store and the parking area. A sno-park permit is not required.

The store is open until 5:00 P.M. and rents touring skis. Eight rental cabins are often booked a year in advance. Skiers who are not guests can make a purchase in the store to show appreciation for the free trail use, but the resort does not expect this.

Trails are groomed with a homemade track-setter and are not

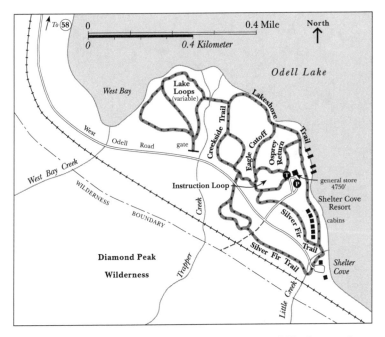

wide enough for skating. The area is small and it is difficult to get lost. There are three linked areas: the main trails near the store, the Lake Loops in Trapper Creek Campground, and Silver Fir Trail south of the access road. Pengra Pass (Chapter 25) and wilderness trails are accessible from the resort.

Main Trails. The main trails include the Lakeshore Trail and loops through the resort's summer campground. Lakeshore starts near the cabins, passes the store, and follows the convoluted shore of Odell Lake's West Bay Peninsula. Awesome views across Odell Lake to bluffs on the north shore are the attraction. Lakeside connects to Osprey, Eagle, and Creekside Trails. These create flat loops, all less than 1 mile, back to the store.

Lake Loops. Trapper Creek separates the Lake Loops from the main trails. From Lakeshore Trail, follow Creekside Trail to the left 100 feet and turn right on a connector to a wooden bridge. Look for dippers along the creek, especially in late winter. These black sandpiper-like birds feed underwater, grasping rocks to stay submerged. On the other side of the bridge, groomed loops within the Trapper Creek Campground are unmarked and vary with the whim of the track-setter. Don't worry about getting lost. Just enjoy views of the lake and creek while you follow the trails, which all loop back to the bridge.

Look for dippers at Trapper Creek

Silver Fir Trail. The resort's only intermediate-level hills are on the 0.5-mile Silver Fir Trail. Starting from the south side of the main trail system, ski south on Silver Fir and cross the access road. Climb a short distance and turn east. Continue through short, steep dips and climbs, crossing a trail leading to Diamond Peak Wilderness, and then the appropriately named Little Creek. Silver Fir recrosses the access road near maintenance buildings and follows a flat route to the main trails.

A partially tame half-wolf dog has lived around the resort since the mid-1990s. It is not a pet. The animal has stayed in the vicinity for years without incident. It is called Loner, an apt description. It stays to itself and should be treated as a wild animal. Do not approach it. Do not consider feeding it. It fends for itself, feeding on fish or small animals in the surrounding woods.

28 ODELL LAKE

Distance: 1–6 miles
Trails: Groomed ski trails
Track Quality: Good classic skiing, no skating
Skill Level: Novice to intermediate
Elevation: 4800 feet
Maximum Elevation Gain: 100 feet
Season: Early December to early April
Services and Facilities: Ski rentals, restaurant, lodging
Hours: 8:00 A.M.–5:00 P.M., daily
Fees: $5, sno-park permit not required
Information: Odell Lake Lodge, (541) 433-2540,
www.odelllakeresort.com

Odell Lake Lodge is Oregon's only winter resort catering almost exclusively to cross-country skiers. Sunshine, spectacular lake views just out the door, a restaurant noted for excellent food, and a comfortable, homey atmosphere are ample attractions. More than 5 miles of trails particularly suitable for beginners are groomed for classic skiing. For skiers interested in backcountry skiing, the Diamond Peak Wilderness is half a mile away. The Lycra-clad racing crowd is seldom found here, but Odell Lake Lodge is popular with families and couples enjoying a quiet winter getaway.

From Interstate 5 south of Eugene, drive southeast on Highway 58 for 63 miles to the summit of Willamette Pass and continue 5 miles to East Odell Lake Road. Turn right and drive 0.5 mile to the end of the road and the lodge's small parking lot. Purchase a trail pass in the lodge.

The lodge, built in the 1940s, is at the southeast corner of 5-mile-long Odell Lake. Odell Creek flows from the lake in front of the lodge. There are seven rooms with private baths in the lodge, plus twelve cabins with kitchen facilities. Rooms are often booked a year in advance. The community Lodge Room has a huge fireplace and beam ceiling. The restaurant is consistently good and reasonably priced. The varied menu always includes a vegetarian entrée, homemade soups, and excellent pies. In winter, the restaurant is open Friday through Sunday, holidays, and during spring break. Reservations are recommended for dinner.

The groomed trails are open seven days a week. Trail use is free for lodge guests. Other skiers pay a small fee. Skis with old-fashioned but functional three-pin bindings are available for rent. Dogs are allowed

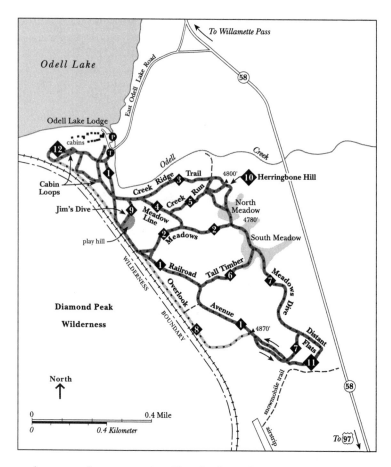

at the resort, but not on the ski trails. Snowshoes are not allowed on groomed trails, but there is plenty of ungroomed terrain where they can be used. Snowmobiles won't be encountered and, except for an occasional train on nearby tracks, there is little to disturb the peace and quiet.

Trails are groomed 6 feet wide with two sets of classic ski tracks. They are too narrow for skating. The trails are designed more for skiing than for reaching spectacular viewpoints. This is fine, as the view of the lake from the lodge is enough to satisfy most people. Trails are both named and numbered 1 through 12. Trail numbers are posted at junctions.

Reach the trails from the south end of the parking lot by walking up a short, steep hill to Railroad Avenue (Trail 1) or Creek Ridge (Trail 3). Guests can ski from their cabin on Cabin Loops to reach Creek Ridge.

Railroad Avenue. Railroad Avenue leads south and is mostly flat to its junction with Trail 6. Along the way, it passes a kid-sized hill near the junction with Trail 9. This open hill is a fun spot to play and practice basic downhill skills. After passing Trail 6, Railroad Avenue has a long uphill section and an intermediate-level downhill run on a one-way section.

Creek Ridge and Herringbone Hill. Creek Ridge Trail, running east toward Herringbone Hill, crosses three little hills that are fun for most beginners. An ungroomed trail on the left just before Herringbone Hill leads to within 100 feet of Odell Creek and, with a little bushwhacking, the creek can be glimpsed. Be cautious following the trail marked "Most Difficult" up Herringbone Hill. It has tight turns and there may be skiers coming downhill. From the top of Herringbone Hill, an easy downhill run leads to North Meadow.

Meadows and Tall Timber. An easy loop suited for beginners and families with small children passes through open meadows and old-growth timber. From Creek Ridge Trail, follow Meadow Line (Trail 4) and Creek Run (Trail 5) to the North Meadow and then south to South Meadow. From the latter, turn west on the aptly named Tall Timber (Trail 6), which passes through a stand of 200-foot-tall old-growth trees. Complete the loop by turning north on Railroad Avenue and following it back to the trailhead.

Overlook. Overlook (Trail 8) runs along the east side of the Southern Pacific Railroad tracks. It generally is not groomed. It is fun to watch trains pass, but be cautious when railroad plows are on the tracks, as they can throw hunks of ice onto the ski trail.

Distant Flats. At the south end of the groomed trails, the Distant Flats Trail passes 50 feet from an unplowed road that can be followed 0.2 mile to the Crescent Lake airstrip. Groomed snowmobile trails from here lead to Crescent Lake. The Distant Flats Trail is best reached by skiing uphill from South Meadow on the Meadows Dive Trail. If skied in the opposite direction, Meadows Dive is a challenging but fun downhill run to South Meadow.

Ski tracks along the Overlook Trail

29 CRESCENT LAKE

Distance: 14.8 miles
Trails: Groomed snowmobile trails
Track Quality: Fair classic skiing, good skating
Skill Level: Intermediate
Elevation: 4820 feet
Maximum Elevation Gain: 256 feet
Season: Early December to early April
Services and Facilities: Outhouse, cabins and store at nearby resort
Hours: NA
Fees: Sno-park permit
Information: Deschutes National Forest, (541) 383-5300

Skaters looking for an alternative to the groomed trails at Willamette Pass Ski Area can take advantage of miles of forest roads groomed for snowmobile use near Crescent Junction, 7 miles southeast of Willamette Pass. For skiers with good stamina, the most interesting tour on these groomed roads is a nearly 15-mile loop around Crescent Lake. Less athletic skiers can reach the best views by skiing the first 4 miles of the loop along the north shore and returning by the same route. Conditions for skating are often good. Classic technique skiing is slower but is enjoyable regardless of trail conditions. Crescent Lake enjoys the sunny clime that is common on the east side of the Cascades.

From Interstate 5 south of Eugene, drive 70 miles southeast on Highway 58 to Crescent Junction. If approaching from the east, it is 17 miles on Highway 58 from Highway 97 to Crescent Junction. Gas and groceries can be bought here. Coming from Willamette Pass, turn right onto Crescent Lake Road. Pass Junction Sno-Park on the right 0.2 mile from the highway. After crossing railroad tracks 1.9 miles from the highway, the road turns sharply left. Continue 0.3 mile to Crescent Lake Sno-Park on the right. The entrance to Crescent Lake Resort is another 0.2 mile. The resort has rustic cabins and caters mostly to snowmobilers.

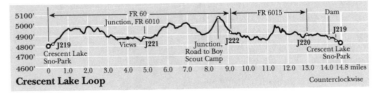

Crescent Lake Loop

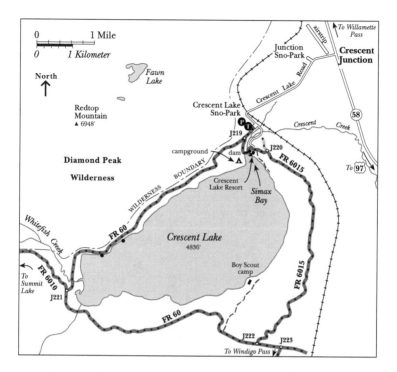

Volunteers from the Walker Rim Riders snowmobile club groom nearby roads with a large snow machine. Grooming is typically done twice a week. Friday and early Saturday are good bets for smooth trails. Snowmobile traffic can make the trails bumpy by Sunday. Stay to the side of the trail when encountering snowmobiles, and be friendly. Remember that snowmobile gas taxes and fees pay grooming expenses.

Crescent Lake Loop is on generally easy terrain, but the 14.8-mile distance makes this a tough intermediate-level tour. Start on groomed Forest Road 60 at the south side of the sno-park, opposite the plowed road. Snowmobile routes are marked with orange diamonds. Junction numbers are posted and are key for following the loop. Forest Road 60 heads southwest and then parallels the lake's northwest shore. The Diamond Peak Wilderness boundary is just to the right of the road.

The road reaches junction 219 in 0.2 mile. Turning left leads to Crescent Lake Resort and a clockwise tour around the lake. Go straight for a counterclockwise tour, as described here, or for an 8-mile, out-and-back trip to views of nearby peaks. Continue straight at junction 219, climbing and then dropping gently to just above lake level. Four

miles from the sno-park, the road hugs the west shore, with clear views of Mount Thielsen to the south and Odell Butte to the east. One mile farther, the road crosses Whitefish Creek and reaches junction 221. A hard right leads uphill to Summit Lake. Instead, continue on Forest Road 60, which climbs steeply after junction 221. On the uphill, look back for a view of Diamond Peak.

After a long, gradual hill, the road crests at an unnumbered junction with a road that leads to a Boy Scout camp. Continue straight 0.4 mile, descending to junction 222. Turn left onto Forest Road 6015. Missing this turn leads 0.1 mile to junction 223, a fork to Windigo Pass. From junction 222, Forest Road 6015 leads 4 miles north to junction 220 near the north end of the lake. There are no major views along this stretch. Turn left at junction 220 and ski a snowmobile trail with short ups and downs 0.1 mile to the Crescent Lake Resort, a collection of rough-looking cabins. Follow orange diamonds around the resort. Remove your skis to cross plowed driveways. The trail crosses a dam across Crescent Creek west of the resort. Stop and enjoy the view south across the lake. Turn right immediately after the dam and ski straight on the road, past the campground entrance. In 0.2 mile from the dam, finish the loop at junction 219. The sno-park is 0.1 mile to the right.

Springtime view from shore of Crescent Lake

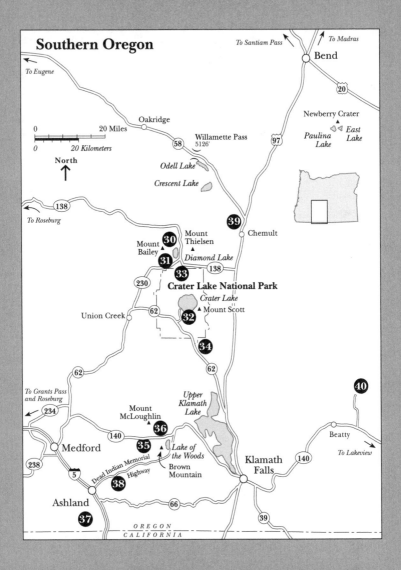

Southern Oregon

Crater Lake National Park is the best-known cross-country ski destination in southern Oregon. Spectacular views and an annual snowfall of over 40 feet at Crater Lake Rim account for the park's popularity. Reliable snow makes the rim a good bet for early- and late-season ski tours. But southern Oregon, which extends from Diamond Lake and Chemult south to the California border, has much more to offer skiers. Many miles of ski trails in the Cascade Range and Siskiyou Mountains provide opportunities for a wide variety of tours and exceptional views. These include trails in the Umpqua, Winema, and Rogue River National Forests, as well as some on land managed by the Bureau of Land Management. Prominent peaks, especially Mount Thielsen, Mount McLoughlin, Mount Bailey, and Brown Mountain serve as landmarks on many ski tours. Most skiing in the region is at relatively high elevation, from 4800 to 7000 feet.

Southern Oregon is also home to the Oregon Shakespeare Festival. This Ashland theater company produces some of the nation's best live theater. The theater season begins in mid-February. A few days of ski tours combined with some fine theater make an excellent mini-vacation.

30 DIAMOND LAKE

Distance: 5–9.5 miles
Trails: Groomed and ungroomed ski trails
Track Quality: Good classic skiing, good skating
Skill Level: Novice to intermediate
Elevation: 5200 feet
Maximum Elevation Gain: 100 feet
Season: Early December to late March
Services and Facilities: Restaurant, store, lodging, ski rentals
Hours: Daily
Fees: None
Information: Diamond Lake Resort, (800) 733-7593,
www.diamond lake.net

Incredible views of Mount Thielsen and Mount Bailey are just outside the door at Diamond Lake Resort, which features a comfortable lodge and fine dining. The resort grooms a small number of easy ski trails and does not charge a fee for their use. Additional trails are groomed for special events such as Senior Week, when spirited skiers age fifty and older take over the resort. Miles of nearby ungroomed ski trails and groomed snowmobile trails add almost unlimited opportunities for ski tours.

From Interstate 5 at Roseburg, head east on Highway 138. In 79 miles, turn right at a sign for North Diamond Lake. Follow the Diamond Lake Resort access road 1 mile to the lodge. If not a guest, use the parking area south of the cabins. From Medford, take exit 30 off Interstate 5 and follow signs to Highway 62 and Crater Lake. Drive north on Highway 62. In 60 miles, where Highway 62 turns east, continue north on Highway 230. Reach Highway 138 in 24 miles, turn left, and drive north 4.4 miles to the turn to North Diamond Lake. The resort is 250 miles from Portland by way of Interstate 5 and Highway 138. A shuttle to the resort is available from the Amtrak station in Chemult (30 miles).

Accommodations include motel rooms, studios with a kitchenette, and two-bedroom cabins. The restaurant is excellent. The resort has a gas station and a small grocery store that rents cross-country skis. The lodge is popular with snowmobilers—they outnumber skiers except during Senior Week and other ski events. The lodge can arrange snow cat tours to Crater Lake's north rim.

Cross-country skiing at Diamond Lake is at its best during Senior Week, a four-day get-together of skiers from around the West. There is no age requirement, but most participants are age fifty and older.

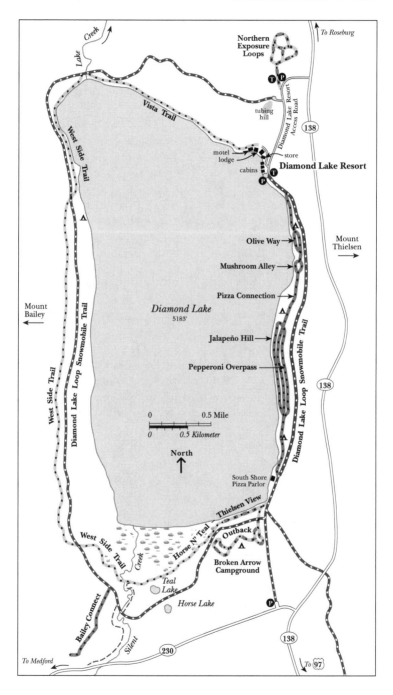

Senior Week is in early January and, because of its popularity, is repeated in early February. Tours and lessons are organized for all abilities. Skiers enjoy good food, wine, snow cat tours, ski football, music, and friends. Participants have been described as, "not seniors, but recycled teenagers." Trail grooming is expanded during Senior Week.

Pizza Connection. Pizza Connection is the one ski trail that is groomed weekly. It starts at the parking lot south of the lodge and cabins. Pizza Connection leads 2.5 miles south along the east shore of Diamond Lake to the South Shore Pizza Parlor (closed in winter). The trail is groomed with double ski tracks and for skating. It is easy skiing through a campground with views of Diamond Lake and Mount Bailey. Four short side loops branch from the Pizza Connection. Often, at least one of these is groomed. The side loops are Olive Way, Mushroom Alley, Pepperoni Overpass, and Jalapeño Hill. The Diamond Lake Loop snowmobile trail parallels the Pizza Connection 100 yards to the east.

Horse N' Teal Trail. The Horse N' Teal Trail, which is normally not groomed, is an easy trail along the south shore of Diamond Lake. It is 3.2 miles round trip from the South Shore Pizza Parlor and 8.2 miles round trip from Diamond Lake Resort. From the pizza parlor, ski 0.1 mile south on the Diamond Lake Loop snowmobile trail, past buildings and across a creek, and turn right onto the Outback ski trail. In another 0.1 mile, Outback turns left. Outback is an uninteresting trail in the Broken Arrow Campground, so continue along the shore on Horse N' Teal, which rewards skiers with views of a broad

Mount Bailey and Diamond Lake

mountain across Diamond Lake. This is Mount Bailey. Look behind you to see sharp-peaked Mount Thielsen. This view earns the trail its second name, Thielsen View (the resort prefers this name, but the official Forest Service name is Horse N' Teal). After a boat ramp, Horse N' Teal follows marshes at the south end of Diamond Lake. It enters the woods, skirts Teal Lake, and reaches Silent Creek (Chapter 31) 1.6 miles from the pizza parlor. Return to the pizza parlor along the same route. During Senior Week, parts of Horse N' Teal, Outback, and extra loops in Broken Arrow Campground are groomed.

Northern Exposure Loops. Several road loops through thick ponderosa pine north of the resort are groomed for special events. The trails are open any time but are not particularly interesting unless they are groomed. When they are groomed, the track conditions are excellent for skating and classic skiing. January and February are the best months to check out these trails, as they are groomed then for several races and two sessions of Senior Week. To reach the trailhead, turn off of Highway 138 on the Diamond Lake Resort access road and drive 0.3 mile to a small parking area on the right. One road leads north from this parking area for 0.2 miles, where it connects to the loops. The loops are unnamed. Up to 3 miles of connecting loops are groomed, but the specific loops can vary with each special event.

Diamond Ski Loop. The Diamond Ski Loop is a scenic, 9.5-mile loop around Diamond Lake. It follows easy terrain, but its distance earns an intermediate rating. The Pizza Connection is the east side of the loop and is the only groomed portion. From Diamond Lake Resort, follow the Pizza Connection south 2.5 miles to the South Shore Pizza Parlor and then follow Horse N' Teal Trail west 1.6 miles to Silent Creek. Cross the creek on an arched bridge and continue on the West Side Trail, turning north and following the lakeshore. In about 1 mile from Silent Creek, the West Side trail turns uphill and continues north above summer homes along the shore. It passes through forests on the lower slope of Mount Bailey, drops back to the lake, and reaches Lake Creek 3.6 miles from Silent Creek. Cross the creek and turn right onto the Vista Trail, which follows the creek a short distance to the lakeshore and then curves east, passing stands of large Douglas fir and ponderosa pine. Vista Trail ends next to the motel rooms at Diamond Lake Resort, 1.8 miles from Lake Creek.

The Diamond Lake Loop groomed snowmobile trail also circles the lake, following a loop road. It can be used in lieu of ungroomed sections of the Diamond Ski Loop. The two loops intersect near the South Shore Pizza Parlor, north and south of the west side summer homes, and at Lake Creek flowing from the lake's northwest corner.

31 THREE LAKES

Distance: 4.6–7.6 miles
Trails: Groomed snowmobile trails, ungroomed ski trails
Track Quality: Good classic skiing, fair skating
Skill Level: Novice to intermediate
Elevation: 5390 feet
Maximum Elevation Gain: 850 feet
Season: Early December to late March
Services and Facilities: Cabin along trail
Hours: NA
Fees: Sno-park permit
Information: Diamond Lake Ranger Station, Umpqua National Forest, (541) 498-2531

A delightful tour along the banks of beautiful Silent Creek and a climb to an overnight skiers' cabin are the attractions at tiny Three Lakes Sno-Park. The trails are on the south flank of Mount Bailey, a volcano that has been inactive for one million years. From here, skaters can travel well-groomed snowmobile trails to connect to trails at Diamond Lake (Chapter 30).

From Interstate 5 at Roseburg, drive east on Highway 138 for 83 miles to Highway 230. Turn right onto Highway 230, and drive southwest 3 miles to the sno-park on the right. There is room for fifteen cars. From Medford, take exit 30 off Interstate 5 and follow signs to Highway 62 and Crater Lake. Drive north on Highway 62. In 60 miles where Highway 62 turns east, continue north on Highway 230. Reach the sno-park on the left in 21 miles. A guide service runs a snow cat from the sno-park, carrying downhill skiers up Mount Bailey for exciting backcountry runs.

Silent Creek Trail. This is one of the most delightful streamside ski trails in the Cascade Mountains. The winding trail has a lot of little ups and downs and offers many opportunities to enjoy the creek's wild beauty. Along the route, Silent Creek appears seemingly from nowhere, starting from springs a few yards off the trail. The out-and-back trip is rated beginner and is 4.6 miles round trip.

The Silent Creek trailhead is a few yards from the sno-park to the right of the signboard. The trail meanders through the woods with no sign of the creek it is named after. In 1.1 miles at a hard left turn, it reaches a junction with the Silent Creek East Trail on the right. The junction is not obvious and can be missed. Silent Creek Trail continues left along Silent Creek's west side, though there is still no sign of the creek. It springs up in the gully just past the junction.

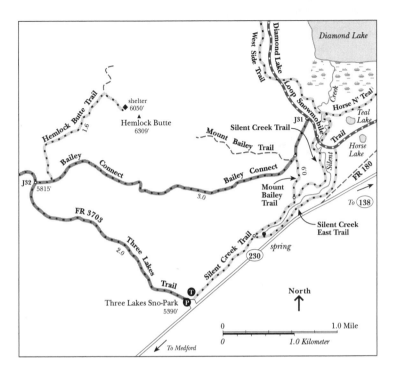

From the junction, Silent Creek Trail drops down a short steep pitch and leads northeast, with the gully on the right. In 100 yards, a noticeable creek appears in the gully, though in winter it is hard to see exactly where the creek begins. Silent Creek grows quickly and the trail runs close to it. In 1.5 miles from the sno-park, the Mount Bailey Trail is on the left. After crossing a bridge over a tributary of Silent Creek, the trail reaches the Diamond Lake Loop Road 2 miles from the sno-park. Turn right onto the road. Cross Silent Creek and immediately turn left onto the continuation of Silent Creek Trail. Ski 0.3 mile north with the creek now on the left. The trail ends at Horse N' Teal Trail near a beautiful wooden bridge. Look for signs of beaver activity. Return along the same route, 2.3 miles to the sno-park. Horse N' Teal leads east to the south shore of Diamond Lake.

Silent Creek East Trail. The Silent Creek East Trail follows the east side of Silent Creek from its headwaters north to Diamond Lake Loop Road. Silent Creek East is not an official trail name. The Forest Service sign at the trailhead describes it simply as the trail on the east side of Silent Creek. It is an intermediate trail that can be difficult to follow in places. It is easier to find your way when headed from south to north, so a loop along this section should head north on the Silent

Silent Creek

Creek East Trail and return on the Silent Creek Trail. From the sno-park, ski 1.1 miles on Silent Creek Trail and turn right onto the Silent Creek East Trail at the head of a gully. If you notice the creek on your right, you have missed the junction and need to backtrack. The Silent Creek East Trail starts with the gully on the left, quickly reaching the start of the creek. The trail markers may be difficult to find in places. When in doubt, simply keep Silent Creek close on the left. To cross a tributary creek, bear left down a steep bank. This trail reaches the Diamond Lake Loop Road 200 yards east of the Silent Creek bridge, at a big curve in the road. Ski west on the road to rejoin Silent Creek Trail, heading north just before the bridge.

Hemlock Butte Shelter. Hemlock Butte (6309 feet) is a parasitic cinder cone on the flank of Mount Bailey. A log cabin on a timbered ridge northwest of the summit is used for lunch stops or by reservation for overnight stays. The climb to the cabin is nearly 700 feet. Most of the climb is in the first 2 miles on a groomed snowmobile trail. Strong novice skiers who make the climb might have trouble with the downhill return. From the sno-park, ski 2 miles uphill on Three Lakes Trail, a groomed shared-use road to junction 32. Turn right onto the Bailey Connect and ski 0.2 mile to a left turn onto the Hemlock Butte Trail. Follow blue diamonds on this narrow, ungroomed trail as it climbs through hemlock and fir. In 1.4 miles a spur to the cabin veers sharply right. Hemlock Butte Trail continues uphill, but the spur is usually the obvious trail here. The spur rolls along for 0.2 mile to the cabin. The first visitors on cold weekends should start a fire in the stove. The cabin is in the trees, sheltered from the wind, but without views. It was built and is maintained by Edelweiss Ski Club of Roseburg. Contact the Diamond Lake Ranger Station for overnight reservations. Return along the same route to the sno-park for a 7.6-mile round trip.

Bailey Connect. The 3-mile Bailey Connect is a groomed snow-mobile road, not to be confused with the Mount Bailey Trail for backcountry skiing. It starts at snowmobile junction 32, 2 miles uphill from the sno-park and 425 feet higher. Ski on the Three Lakes Trail to junction 32 and turn right onto the Bailey Connect. The Connect descends 3 miles east to the Diamond Lake Loop Road at junction 31, a drop of 600 feet. The Silent Creek Trail is 0.1 mile to the right of junction 31. Three Lakes Trail, the Bailey Connect, and the Silent Creek Trail can be combined for a 7.1-mile loop.

32 CRATER LAKE, SOUTH ENTRANCE

Distance: 2–15.3 miles
Trails: Ungroomed ski trails
Track Quality: Fair classic skiing, no skating
Skill Level: Novice to advanced
Elevation: 7100 feet
Maximum Elevation Gain: 650 feet
Season: Mid-November to early May
Services and Facilities: Cafeteria, information center, post office
Hours: Cafeteria, 10:00 A.M. to 4:30 P.M., daily
Fees: Sno-park permit not required
Information: Crater Lake National Park, (541) 594-3000,
www.nps.gov/crla

Winter at Crater Lake National Park is a time of extreme weather and extreme beauty. The average annual snowfall is more than 44 feet. Snowstorms frequently create whiteout conditions, but a sunny day yields breathtaking views of the pristine lake, steep caldera walls, and snow-covered rim. Most winter visitors simply view the lake from the parking lot. Skiers can explore farther along the rim or choose nearby trails through trees that provide shelter from foul weather. There are no groomed trails and skiers often have to break track, but the effort seems trivial in exchange for the experience of skiing while surrounded by such beauty.

Crater Lake is Oregon's only national park. The lake sits in the caldera formed by the collapse of a gigantic volcano 7700 years ago. Wizard Island, at the lake's west end, was a small volcano that formed in the caldera after the collapse of the original peak. Nearly 2000 feet deep in places, Crater Lake is the world's seventh deepest lake. Water circulating from the depths prevents the lake from freezing except in the coldest winters. The last year it froze completely was 1949—though rangers walking on the lake that year found, to their consternation, that the ice was only 2 inches thick in places. Most years, visitors will see clear blue water ringed with ice.

Only the south entrance road from Highway 62 to Park Headquarters and Rim Village is plowed during winter. The rim road and the north entrance road are usually closed until June or July. The south entrance road is plowed regularly, but heavy snowstorms can close the road. In severe storms, it may be closed for days. Be prepared and carry a shovel and chains. Deep snow on the rim forms cornices that could break loose at any time. Stay well back from the edge. If the weather is bad at the rim, be flexible and ski at a lower elevation.

From Medford, drive north on Highway 62. In 60 miles, continue on 62 as it turns east at a junction with Highway 230. In another 16 miles, turn left onto the south entrance road leading to Park Headquarters and Rim Village. Reach this entrance from Portland by driving Interstate 5 to Roseburg and then traveling Highways 138, 230, and 62. Crater Lake is 300 miles from Portland, 130 miles from Roseburg, 80 miles from Medford, and 60 miles from Klamath Falls. The nearest gas station is 40 miles from the south entrance road. Drive 4 miles north on the south entrance road to Park Headquarters on the left. This is a good place for trail and weather information. It is open daily from 10:00 A.M. to 4:00 P.M. A post office in the headquarters building is open Monday through Saturday.

From Park Headquarters, continue on the rim road another 3 miles to a large parking lot at Rim Village. To help keep the lake pristine, the National Park Service plans to move parking away from the rim to south of the Rim Village cafeteria. This means the lake will no longer be visible from the parking lot, but the rim still will be only a short distance away. This move is expected to be complete by 2005.

Rim Village has fine overlooks of the lake nearly 1000 feet below. A day lodge with restrooms, a cafeteria, and a gift shop are open during the winter, but historic Crater Lake Lodge is closed and the park has no overnight accommodations. Winter months also mean there is no park entrance fee and a sno-park permit is not required. The unplowed road around the crater from Rim Village to Park Headquarters is 30 miles. It can be skied as a long backcountry tour, generally with one or two nights of winter camping. Check with Park Headquarters for information on this and other trails not described here.

West Rim Drive. In fair weather, most skiers choose West Rim Drive for outstanding overlooks of the crater and Wizard Island. The road starts at the west end of the parking lot near the entrance road. A snow ramp usually leads up the snowbank here. The route follows Rim Drive and is generally easy to find, but the entire 6.1-mile distance to the North Junction is exposed, and high winds and whiteouts can create dangerous conditions during storms. With at least three crater

Wizard Island

overlooks in the first 2 miles, this stretch is good for beginners. After 2 miles, the road pulls away from the rim to skirt around The Watchman, a prominent peak on the rim. Here the route traverses a steep hill where the downhill slope on the left can be intimidating in icy conditions. Use extreme caution or turn around here. After The Watchman, skiers reach the rim's best Wizard Island overlook at 4 miles from Rim Village. From here, the road again pulls away from the rim until it nears North Junction. North Junction connects the road with the park's unplowed, 9.2-mile-long north entrance road, a popular snowmobile trail and the only route in the park open to snowmobiles.

Hemlock. This 2-mile loop is a fun, rolling trail through the trees west of Rim Village. More sheltered than Rim Drive, Hemlock is the park's best trail for a mix of ups and downs, twists and turns, and pure skiing pleasure. It has views of the crater and Mount Scott, though not as spectacular as those from the Rim Road. For a place with so much snowfall, skiers will find a track set by other skiers surprisingly often. The trail starts and ends at the east end of the Rim Village parking lot, opposite the entrance road.

East Rim Drive. The south end of the unplowed East Rim Drive meets the south entrance road across from Park Headquarters. This route is a protected alternative when the west rim has high winds or blowing snow. It is also the course for a popular cross-country ski race every February. From Park Headquarters, the road stays far from the crater and has few views as it climbs 500 feet in 5 miles to Sun Notch on the rim. Sun Notch overlooks Phantom Ship, a rock island close to the crater wall. On a clear day, it has spectacular views of the crater. Beyond Sun Notch, the road drops away from the rim and climbs to Kerr Notch in 4 miles.

Rim Village to North Entrance. A 15.3-mile, one-way tour from Rim Village to the park's north entrance combines a scenic tour along the rim with a long gradual downhill on a groomed snowmobile trail. This route requires a car shuttle to the North Crater Lake Sno-Park, described in the next chapter. As with any tour along the rim, this one should be skied only in good weather. The first 6.1 miles follow the West Rim Drive from Rim Village to North Junction. This is the most scenic part of the tour. The junction connects the north entrance road to Rim Drive. The north entrance road is the only trail in Crater Lake National Park where snowmobiles are allowed. Ski north on the north entrance road, dropping 1175 feet in 9.2 miles to the North Crater Lake Sno-Park. The north entrance road portion of the trail is further described in the next chapter.

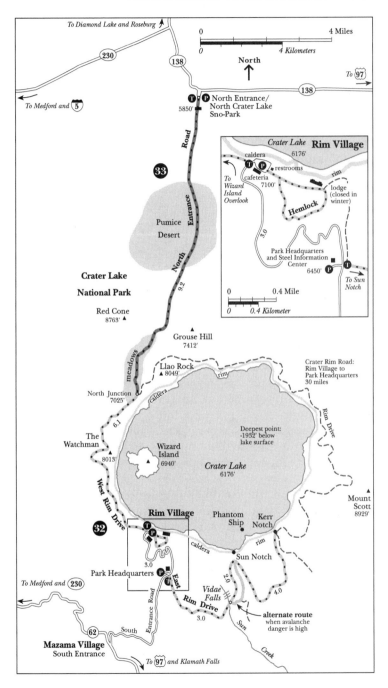

To Diamond Lake and Roseburg

230

138

North Entrance/
North Crater Lake
Sno-Park
5850'

To Medford and 5

North ↑

0   4 Miles
0   4 Kilometers

138

To 97

Rim Village

Crater Lake
6176'

caldera

restrooms

cafeteria
7100'

To
Wizard
Island
Overlook

rim

lodge
(closed in
winter)

Hemlock

3.0

Park Headquarters
and Steel Information
Center
6450'

To Sun
Notch

0   0.4 Mile
0   0.4 Kilometer

33

Road

Pumice
Desert

North Entrance

9.2

Crater Lake
National Park

Red Cone
8763' ▲

Grouse Hill
7412' ▲

Llao Rock
▲ 8049'

rim

Crater Rim Road:
Rim Village to
Park Headquarters
30 miles

meadows

North Junction
7025'

caldera

6.1

The
Watchman

8013'

Wizard
Island
6940'

Deepest point:
-1932' below
lake surface

Rim Drive

Crater Lake
6176'

Mount
Scott
8929' ▲

West Rim Drive

Rim Village

Phantom
Ship

Kerr
Notch

32

caldera

rim

Sun Notch

3.0

Park Headquarters

East

Entrance Road

2.0

4.0

To Medford and 230

Rim Drive

Vidae
Falls

← alternate route
when avalanche
danger is high

3.0

Sun

Creek

62

South

Mazama Village
South Entrance

To 97 and Klamath Falls

33 CRATER LAKE, NORTH ENTRANCE

Distance: 5.4–18.4 miles
Trails: Groomed snowmobile trail
Track Quality: Good classic skiing, fair skating
Skill Level: Novice to intermediate
Elevation: 5794 feet
Maximum Elevation Gain: 1516 feet
Season: Late November to late April
Services and Facilities: None
Hours: NA
Fees: Sno-park permit
Information: Crater Lake National Park, (541) 594-3000,
   www.nps.gov/crla
See previous page for map of Crater Lake National Park.

A different view of the Crater Lake caldera is reached via the unplowed north entrance road. Skiers earn spectacular views from the north rim by skiing more than 9 miles one-way and climbing more than 1500 feet. The road is a groomed snowmobile route. In spite of the presence of snowmobiles, the north rim is less hectic than busy Rim Village on the south rim. The Pumice Desert, a third of the distance to the rim, is an easy and rewarding tour for novice skiers. The huge plain of volcanic rock offers views of the Cascade Range to the north.

From Interstate 5 at Roseburg, take Highway 138 eastbound. In 83 miles, pass the Highway 230 junction. Continue on Highway 138 for 3 more miles. Right after the highway turns east again, North Crater Lake Sno-Park is on the right. It is the plowed end of the summer park entrance road. The sno-park is 16 miles west of Highway 97. Via Highway 97, it is 80 miles from Klamath Falls and 92 miles from Bend. It is 125 miles from Eugene via Highway 58 and 97. Lodging, food, and gas are available at nearby Diamond Lake Resort and about 20

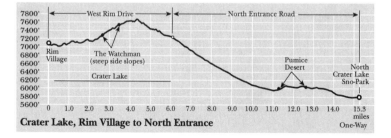

Crater Lake, Rim Village to North Entrance

Crater Rim Road in cloudy weather

miles east in Beaver Marsh and Chemult. The sno-park is outside the national park, and a sno-park permit is required.

The tour to the rim follows the north Crater Lake entrance road. The 9.2-mile road is groomed for snowmobiles by Diamond Lake Resort. This entrance road is the only place in Crater Lake National Park where snowmobiles are allowed. They must stay on the road and cannot wander in adjacent meadows. Stay to one side when snowmobiles are passing. Dogs are not allowed on the trail.

From the sno-park, the road passes the park entrance booth, often buried under snow, in a mile. After 2.7 miles of easy climbing, the road reaches the Pumice Desert. Novices who are not continuing to the rim can enjoy views to the north before starting the return trip. The road drops slightly through the desert and then begins to climb steeply. At 7 miles from the sno-park, open meadows on the right invite skiers to wander off the road. Here, the road passes between Red Cone on the right and Grouse Hill on the left. The road continues along the edge of the meadows to the rim, 1516 feet above the sno-park and 1000 feet above the lake surface. Llao Rock is the peak on the rim to the northeast. Wizard Island is 2 miles away. The views of the lake and peaks of the Cascade Range are excellent. Return to the sno-park along the same route.

34 ANNIE CREEK

Distance: 2.9–6.5 miles
Trails: Groomed snowmobile trails
Track Quality: Fair classic skiing, good skating
Skill Level: Novice to intermediate
Elevation: 4358 feet
Maximum Elevation Gain: 160 feet
Season: Early December to early March
Services and Facilities: Outhouse
Hours: NA
Fees: Sno-park permit
Information: Klamath Ranger District, Winema National Forest,
(541) 885-3400

Annie Creek rises from springs on the flank of Crater Lake and flows 10 miles through the national park. The final 2.5 miles are in a narrow peninsula where the park's boundary stretches out to shelter more of the creek in the park's protection. Annie Creek Sno-Park is just south of this protrusion. The area provides opportunities for long-distance skating and short tours near Annie Creek. Major trails are marked snowmobile routes, but miles of unmarked forest roads offer invitations to explore. These trails on forest roads are a sheltered alternative when the Crater Lake rim has severe weather.

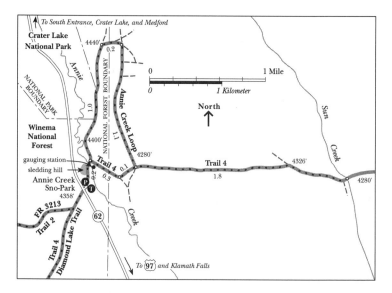

Annie Creek

The sno-park is on the north side of Highway 62, 5.5 miles north of Fort Klamath. This is 17.6 miles from Highway 97 and 47 miles from Klamath Falls. From the west, the sno-park is 10.4 miles on Highway 62 past the entrance road to Rim Village at Crater Lake.

Many miles of groomed snowmobile trails lie south of the highway. Most of those near the sno-park pass through a pine plantation and are not particularly scenic, but they do promise long skating tours. Trails on the sno-park (north) side of the highway are more interesting, but they are rougher and sometimes difficult to skate on. Generally, orange diamonds on these trails are posted so that they are on the left going away from the sno-park and on the right going toward the sno-park.

To reach the north-side trails, follow a short trail that starts near the sno-park outhouses, descends a short, steep hill, and continues past a sledding hill in a gravel pit. In 0.2 mile, the trail crosses Annie Creek. Most skiers will want to pause a few minutes to watch the creek. A USGS water-flow gauging station is downstream of the bridge.

Annie Creek Loop. The road forks immediately after crossing the creek. The two roads are the beginning and end of a 2.7-mile loop, best skied clockwise. The loop may not be groomed, but it is easy to follow. Bear left up a short hill. In 0.5 mile, the creek is visible 50 feet below on the left. The trail climbs again, levels off, and continues north. At times, the well-marked boundary of Crater Lake National Park is just a few feet to the left. One mile from the bridge, the road enters a lovely meadow. Bear right across the south edge of the meadow, passing quickly from the Winema National Forest into state forest land. In 0.2 mile, turn right to leave the meadow and continue through second-growth timber, descending gradually for 1.1 miles to a four-way junction. Turn right and continue 0.4 mile back to the bridge over Annie Creek.

Sun Creek. For a longer tour, instead of turning right at the four-way junction, turn left and ski east on snowmobile Trail 4. This trail is on a generally flat road that is easy to follow and normally groomed wide enough for skaters. It passes through a managed forest on state land. Several small roads through the timberland connect to Trail 4, offering exploring opportunities for those with touring skis. Trail 4 reaches Sun Creek 1.8 miles from the four-way junction. Sun Creek drains out of Sun Meadows 9 miles to the north in Crater Lake National Park. From Trail 4, it flows another 3 miles south before emptying into Annie Creek. This is a good turnaround point. The out-and-back to Sun Creek and the previously described loop tour combine for a 6.5-mile round trip. Skiers who want more can ski much farther on Trail 4, but it turns very steeply uphill in another 0.5 mile.

35 LOLLIPOP LOOPS

Distance: 5.7–7.2 miles
Trails: Ungroomed ski trails
Track Quality: Good classic skiing, no skating
Skill Level: Novice to intermediate
Elevation: 4645 feet
Maximum Elevation Gain: 469 feet
Season: Mid-December to mid-March
Services and Facilities: Outhouse, rustic resort
Hours: NA
Fees: Sno-park permit
Information: Ashland Ranger District, Rogue River National Forest, (541) 482-3333

Along Highway 140 between Medford and Klamath Falls, the crest of the Cascade Range marks the border of the Rogue River National Forest on the west and the Winema National Forest on the east. Long and narrow Fish Lake sits just 2 miles west of this crest. Fish Lake Sno-Park on its north shore is the starting point for a small system of ski trails mostly on forest roads. Highlights along the trails include views of Mount McLoughlin 4 miles to the north and Brown Mountain 3 miles to the southeast. The core of the trail system is Lollipop Loop, which on a map resembles a misshapen sucker. Three other trails—Peppermint, Sucker's Alley, and Candy Cain—expand on the sweet tooth theme. Trails near the area's south end may be confusing. Usually, a little searching for blue diamonds is all that is needed, but be ready to check your compass.

Drive Interstate 5 to exit 30 in Medford and follow Highway 62, the Crater Lake Highway, 5.5 miles to Highway 140. Turn right and drive east 31 miles. Turn right onto the Fish Lake access road and wind 0.7 mile to the sno-park by a boat ramp. Fish Lake Resort, which is along the access road, has rental cabins and a café and grocery store that is normally open on weekends. There is a stunning view of

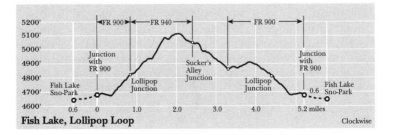

Fish Lake, Lollipop Loop   Clockwise

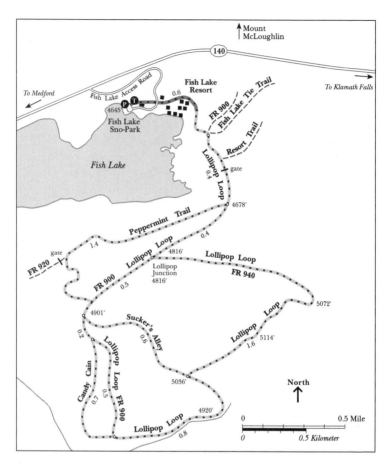

Brown Mountain (7311 feet) from the lakeshore. Dogs are not allowed on these trails or any other designated ski trails in the Rogue River National Forest.

Lollipop Loop. All tours start with an awkward 0.6-mile trail to Forest Road 900, the stem of the lollipop. Head east from the sno-park, skiing behind the bathrooms and through the campground. Walk across the access road and ski past the resort, paying heed to private property signs. The trail is shared with snowmobiles and can be rough. In 0.6 mile, drop to a junction with Forest Road 900, across from the Fish Lake Tie Trail to Summit Sno-Park. Turn right onto Forest Road 900. Consider this the start of the real tour and the previous 0.6 mile "just getting there." From this point, Lollipop Loop is 5.2 miles round trip, making a 6.4-mile trip from the sno-park.

In less than 0.1 mile, the Resort Trail, a snowmobile route to the Lake of the Woods Resort, bears left. Snowmobiles are not allowed on Forest Road 900 beyond this point. Stay on the road. Ski around a gate and reach a fork with Peppermint Trail at 0.4 mile. Stay left and climb gradually to Lollipop Junction, the start of the lollipop's sucker. The loop can be skied in either direction, but the downhill is more gradual when skied in a clockwise direction. Bear left and climb 200 yards to an excellent view of Mount McLoughlin to the north. Continue climbing and enjoying views as the road narrows. After turning sharply west, follow a ridge southwest through a pine plantation to the high point 469 feet above the sno-park. None of the climbing is steep.

As the trail drops, bear right through the plantation, looking carefully for blue diamonds that may be obscured as the young trees grow. Sucker's Alley, a cutoff trail to the right, leaves from a corner of the plantation. It descends easily for 0.6 mile to Forest Road 900, the west side of Lollipop Loop. Sucker's Alley is narrow in places but is a good choice for novices. It shortens the loop tour by 0.9 mile. To ski the full Lollipop Loop, look carefully for blue diamonds leading southeast from the plantation. The trail curves west again and rejoins Forest Road 900 at a junction with Candy Cain. Lollipop turns north on Forest Road 900, climbs until it passes Sucker's Alley, and then descends to Lollipop Junction before continuing back to the trailhead.

Candy Cain. Candy Cain and Peppermint Trail are interesting, intermediate-level alternatives to the easy western leg on Lollipop Loop. Candy Cain, named for a ski club leader, is a rolling 0.7-mile trail through more pine plantation. It starts in the plantation at the south end of Lollipop Loop, descending to the west and then curving

Pine plantation with Brown Mountain in background

north to rejoin the Lollipop Loop. Its north end is difficult to follow because young trees have obscured some trail markers. If in doubt, ski east to reconnect to Forest Road 900. Hopefully, trail markers will be added to ease routefinding.

Peppermint Trail. Peppermint is best skied clockwise from its southern junction with Lollipop. A short distance west of its start off of Lollipop, Peppermint takes a hard right into the woods and winds quickly downhill for 0.5 mile to Forest Road 920. Strong intermediate downhill skills are required for this tricky section. Turn right onto Forest Road 920 and follow the easy road to its northern junction with Lollipop. If skied the other way, the uphill section through the woods is not particularly fun and the turn from Forest Road 920 onto this section is easy to miss.

36 HIGH LAKES

Distance: 3.6–6.6 miles
Trails: Ungroomed ski trails
Track Quality: Very good classic skiing, no skating
Skill Level: Novice to advanced
Elevation: 5050 feet
Maximum Elevation Gain: 630 feet
Season: Early December to late March
Services and Facilities: Outhouse
Hours: NA
Fees: Sno-park permit
Information: Klamath Ranger District, Winema National Forest,
    (541) 885-3400

Summit Sno-Park near the Cascade Divide on Highway 140 provides access to numerous ski trails with a mix of difficulty levels. The Forest Service name for the area is High Lakes Nordic Trails, but most skiers call it Summit Trails after the sno-park. Along with a good mix of terrain, the system offers easy-to-reach views and the best snow along Highway 140. The trails also can be reached after a long ski on Fourmile Lake Road from just north of Lake of the Woods.

Drive Interstate 5 to exit 30 in Medford and follow Highway 62, the Crater Lake Highway, 5.5 miles to Highway 140. Turn right and drive east 33 miles to the crest of the Cascades. Just after entering the Winema National Forest, turn left at the sign for Summit Sno-Park and follow a short access road to the parking area. A short connector trail starts between the sno-park entrance and the outhouses and runs

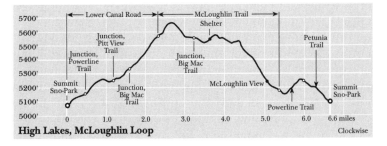

High Lakes, McLoughlin Loop — Clockwise

east to the Lower Canal Road. Other trails start from the Lower Canal Road, which climbs steadily 2.6 miles to Fourmile Lake Road, a groomed snowmobile route.

Pitt View Loop. This gentle beginner trail passes through a ponderosa pine plantation and skirts a large open area with mountain views. A round trip from the sno-park is 3.6 miles. Clockwise is the best direction for beginners to travel. Ski 1.2 miles up Lower Canal Road and turn right onto Pitt View Trail. Ski through a lodgepole plantation, pass an intersection with Petunia Trail, and arrive at a clearing with a view of "Mount Pitt," an early name for Mount McLoughlin. In 0.4 mile farther, turn right at a junction with the Powerline Trail, and continue west 1 mile back to the Lower Canal Road, 0.5 mile from the sno-park.

Petunia. This rolling, 2-mile, intermediate trail provides the most direct access to Summit Shelter. It starts from the Lower Canal Road near the sno-park and runs east a short distance following powerlines. It turns northeast, crosses the Powerline Trail, and in another 0.1 mile enters a large clearing with a rustic wood fence and views of Mount McLoughlin and Brown Mountain. Petunia continues through open forest to its end on Big Mac Trail. Turn right to reach Summit Shelter in less than 1 mile via Big Mac and then McLoughlin. Turn left onto Big Mac to complete a 4.4-mile counterclockwise loop of Petunia, Big Mac, and a return down Lower Canal Road.

McLoughlin Loop. The area's most exciting trail for intermediate to advanced skiers features an in-your-face view of Mount McLoughlin near the trail's southern end. The trail passes through varied forest on roads and narrower trails, with a good lunch spot at a lean-to shelter. Combined with the Lower Canal Road and Petunia, the McLoughlin Trail forms a fun 6.6-mile loop. This loop is generally skied clockwise, with some sections rated as advanced. Though less enjoyable, the route is easier to ski counterclockwise because most of the downhill skiing is on the wide Lower Canal Road instead of on the narrower trails.

The loop is described here in the more interesting clockwise direction. Ski 2.3 miles northeast on the Lower Canal Road to a right turn onto the McLoughlin Trail. The long climb on the road can be tedious, but the rest of the loop is worth the effort. Turn right and ski 0.3 mile through open trees, climbing another 75 feet. Descend a rolling trail through dense forest, passing through a four-way junction with Big Mac. The trail levels off and narrows as it passes through ponderosa pine plantations and then reaches Summit Shelter 1.2 miles from the turn off Lower Canal Road. The shelter was built in 1994 through the combined efforts of the Oregon Nordic Club and the Sierra Club. The Oregon Nordic Club keeps it stocked with firewood. The shelter faces east, but the best view is from the north side, where Mount McLoughlin is visible.

From the shelter, the trail continues south, descending gently and becoming very narrow at times. It drops to a road and a hard right turn, which puts Mount McLoughlin straight ahead. In 0.2 mile, it reaches a junction with Pitt View and the Powerline Trail at the corner of a clear-cut, with more views of McLoughlin. Continue straight on the road, which is now part of the Powerline Trail. Climb to the

Opening cut through a fallen tree on the McLoughlin Trail

next junction, turn left onto Petunia, and descend to the start of Lower Canal Road near the sno-park.

37 GROUSE GAP

Distance: 4.4–6.7 miles
Trails: Groomed ski area road, ungroomed ski trails
Track Quality: Good classic skiing, good skating
Skill Level: Novice to intermediate
Elevation: 6630 feet
Maximum Elevation Gain: 900 feet
Season: Early December to late March
Services and Facilities: None
Hours: NA
Fees: Sno-park permit
Information: Ashland Ranger District, Rogue River National Forest, (541) 482-3333

Mount Ashland, Oregon's highest peak west of the Cascades, sits in the eastern Siskiyou Mountains, 4 miles north of the California border. The Siskiyou Crest across Ashland's summit divides two national forests. The Rogue River National Forest on the north slope hosts an alpine ski area, while the Klamath National Forest on its open south side features Nordic trails with expansive views that include peaks in California.

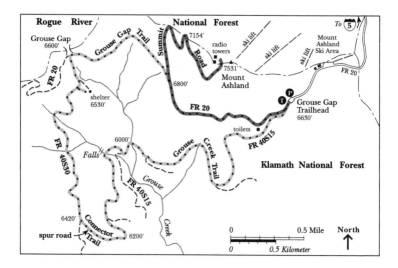

Strong beginner skiers will enjoy a 4.4-mile round-trip tour to the Grouse Gap Shelter. The Mount Ashland Ski Area periodically grooms the first mile of the route, as well as a road that continues to the summit (7531 feet). Local racers use the groomed section for training workouts. A new trail beyond the shelter completes a 6.7-mile loop tour. Mostly open terrain makes for scenic skiing, but on windy days blowing snow can hamper visibility and make the roads difficult to follow.

From Ashland, drive south on Interstate 5 to exit 6. Follow Mount Ashland signs 0.7 mile to Mount Ashland Road on the right. In 9 miles, bear left through the Mount Ashland Ski Area parking lot and continue 0.2 mile to the end of the plowed road at the Grouse Gap trailhead. On a clear day, Mount Shasta can be seen from here. Tours start on Forest Road 20, which is unplowed from here. Toilets 0.3 mile from the trailhead may be accessible, depending on snow depth. Dogs are allowed on the ski trails only as far as the toilets and on Forest Road 40S15 to Grouse Creek.

After new snow, the commercial ski area grooms the first mile of Forest Road 20 and Summit Road. The roads serve as the catch line for the few snowboarders who descend the mountain's south side, guiding them back to the ski area. When recently groomed, the trail is wide, smooth, and fun for skating. It gets rough after a few days. A snow cat traveling to communication towers on the summit sometimes leaves deep ruts. This stops skating, but touring is still good on the road.

Grouse Loop. From the parking area, ski southwest on Forest Road 20. In 0.1 mile, Forest Road 40S15 angles left. This is the Grouse Creek Trail and the return leg of the loop. Continue on Forest Road 20 toward Grouse Gap, passing the toilets at 0.3 mile and climbing gently to a junction with the Summit Road at 1 mile. Forest Road 20, ungroomed beyond this junction, bears left and descends past a nearly treeless bowl. The descent will challenge novices in icy conditions.

At 1.9 miles from the sno-park, the trail reaches a saddle at a junction with Forest Road 40S30. Grouse Gap crosses the Siskiyou Crest to the right. The trail turns left on Forest Road 40S30, which descends south 0.2 mile along an open ridge and makes a sharp right turn. Blowing snow can obscure the turn. In 100 yards, there is a trail on the left through the trees to Grouse Gap Shelter. An alternate route to the shelter is to continue straight at the sharp right turn, descending the open ridge 0.1 mile. The shelter is on the right, at the edge of the trees. The shelter has a picnic table, a fireplace with a hanging chimney, and two charming stone walls. The other walls are plywood and plastic and are ugly, but practical. Open, gentle slopes around the shelter invite skiers to play and practice turns. Beginners should turn around here to return to the sno-park the same way, for 4.4 miles round trip.

To continue on the loop, from the shelter climb back to Forest Road 40S30. Turn left and follow the road south, descending gradually through forest and meadows. In a little more than a mile, the Connector Trail descends a spur road on the left. It soon drops steeply. In 0.4 mile, turn left and descend a challenging section through the trees. Watch for blue diamonds. There are sharp left turns that are not obvious. After a clearing, drop to a narrow road and turn left (north). Pass a small waterfall and reach an intersection with Forest

Grouse Creek Trail

Road 40S15, the Grouse Creek Trail. Turn left on the wide road and cross Grouse Creek, which is not especially impressive. The rest of the loop is uphill, climbing more than 600 feet. Stay left at another intersection and climb Forest Road 40S15, even though the downhill to the right looks more inviting.

Summit Road. From its junction with Forest Road 20, described above, Summit Road climbs an 8-percent grade. Later sections of the 1.4-mile climb to the summit of Mount Ashland are even steeper. The views from the top are spectacular on clear days, but winds can be life threatening in bad weather. The return descent through the top section resembles a luge run more than a ski tour.

38 BUCK PRAIRIE

Distance: 4.6–5.4 miles
Trails: Ungroomed ski trails
Track Quality: Fair classic skiing, no skating
Skill Level: Novice to intermediate
Elevation: 5180 feet
Maximum Elevation Gain: 580 feet
Season: Late December to mid-March
Services and Facilities: Outhouse
Hours: NA
Fees: Sno-park permit
Information: Hyatt Lake Recreation Complex, Bureau of Land
  Management, (541) 482-2031

Ashland skiers can head in two directions to reach trails within 20 miles of town. South of town, the Grouse Gap area on Mount Ashland (Chapter 37) has better snow and southern views. East of town, the Buck Prairie loops are more protected from wind and blowing snow. When the valley is blanketed with low clouds, these ungroomed loops near the summit of Dead Indian Memorial Highway are often above the clouds and under clear skies. The trails include easy road tours and a couple of intermediate trails through the trees.

From Interstate 5 in south Ashland, drive east 0.6 mile on Highway 66 to Dead Indian Memorial Highway. Turn left and drive 13 miles to the Buck Prairie Sno-Park on the right. The road climbs through many twists, which can be hairy in icy conditions. Beyond the sno-park, the highway drops from its summit and continues 23 miles to Highway 140 at Lake of the Woods. The sno-park has room for 15 cars. There are no facilities here, but toilets 1 mile along the trail are maintained in winter.

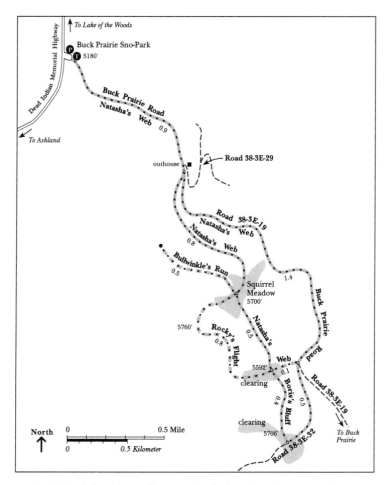

To Lake of the Woods

Buck Prairie Sno-Park
5180'

Dead Indian Memorial Highway

To Ashland

Buck Prairie Road
Natasha's Web
0.9

outhouse

Road 38-3E-29

Road 38-3E-19
Natasha's Web
Natasha's Web
0.8

Bullwinkle's Run
0.5

Squirrel Meadow
5700'

1.4

Buck Prairie Road

5760'

Rocky's Flight
0.8

Natasha's
0.5

5592'

Web
0.1

clearing

Boris's Bluff
0.4

Road 38-3E-19
0.5

clearing
5706'

Road 38-3E-32

To Buck Prairie

North

0   0.5 Mile

0   0.5 Kilometer

The Buck Prairie trail system includes three loops and an out-and-back trail to a viewpoint. Trail names such as Bullwinkle's Run and Natasha's Web will remind baby boomers of the Rocky and Bullwinkle television cartoon that was popular in their youth. Mileages posted at the trailhead may differ from those noted here. Trails are on Bureau of Land Management (BLM) acreage and private land and are administered by the BLM. Ski the loops counterclockwise, as blue diamonds are only visible from that direction on some sections.

Natasha's Web. From the sno-park, ski southeast on the unplowed Buck Prairie Road, which is part of the Natasha's Web trail. The first 0.9 mile climbs slightly to an outhouse at an intersection of three roads. The left fork, the lowest of the three roads, is not part of the ski loops. The middle fork, Buck Prairie Road, is the return leg of Natasha's

Natasha's Web

Web. Take the right fork and ski uphill. Natasha's Web is 2.8 miles around the loop back to this junction. The route is 4.6 miles round trip from the sno-park.

After the intersection, the next 0.8 mile of Nastasha's Web is a moderately steep climb to a large clearing often called Squirrel Meadow. There are junctions here with Bullwinkle's Run and Rocky's Flight. Natasha's Web turns left and continues on the road across the clearing and into the woods. The road drops to an east–west hillside meadow. Natasha's Web turns left and leaves the road, descending steeply through open trees 0.1 mile to the Buck Prairie Road. This short section will challenge novices. If skiing Natasha's Web in the opposite direction, this section is difficult to find, as the blue diamond signs are not visible from Buck Prairie Road. Turn left onto the road and descend gradually back to the junction by the outhouse and the sno-park.

Bullwinkle's Run. On a clear day, a side trip from Squirrel Meadow leads to the best views from Buck Prairie trails. After entering the meadow, as described above, turn right at a well-marked junction for Bullwinkle's Run. Follow a skid road past a large mound and descend gently along a ridge. In 0.5 mile the trail reaches an overlook with views of Ashland, Medford, and Mount Ashland. This is the normal turnaround point, but it is possible to descend farther along the ridge.

Rocky's Flight. The most challenging trail, an intermediate loop with narrow sections, also starts at Squirrel Meadow. The start of Rocky's Flight is not obvious. Look for blue diamonds in the trees southwest of the Bullwinkle junction. From there, climb to a small skid road and follow this to the east–west meadow uphill from Natasha's Web. Descend through the meadow to the road, at a junction of Natasha's Web and Boris's Bluff. Rocky's Flight is hard to ski in the opposite direction, as trail markers cannot be seen above the second junction with Natasha's Web.

Boris's Bluff. A loop off the south end of Natasha's Web can add nearly a mile to your tour. Boris's Bluff starts at the east–west meadow described above and follows a road heading south through the woods. The road continues 0.4 mile, climbing to another clearing. Descend to Road 38-3E-32, which traverses the clearing, and turn left. Road 38-3E-32 leads north, ending with a steep downhill to Natasha's Web where that trail joins Buck Prairie Road.

39 WALT HARING

Distance: 2.1–8.8 miles
Trails: Occasionally groomed ski trails
Track Quality: Good classic skiing
Skill Level: Novice to advanced
Elevation: 4820 feet
Maximum Elevation Gain: 285 feet
Season: Mid-December to mid-March
Services and Facilities: Outhouse, shelter
Hours: NA
Fees: Sno-park permit
Information: Chemult Ranger District, Winema National Forest, (541) 365-7001

Better known for annual sled dog races, Walt Haring Sno-Park near the tiny town of Chemult is also the trailhead for several interesting cross-country ski loops. The trails sit on the eastern edge of the Cascade Range, 30 miles southeast of Willamette Pass in an area known for cold, dry snow and sunny days. Volunteers occasionally set groomed tracks for classic skiing. From Christmas through February, tracks might be set a half dozen times, but there is no schedule. Groomed or ungroomed, these generally easy trails through pine plantation and mature ponderosa are a delight to ski. Two hilltops, one easy to reach

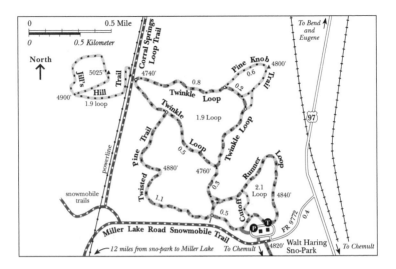

and the other requiring some effort, provide views of Mount Thielsen and surrounding hills.

Chemult is on Highway 97. It is 65 miles from Bend, 72 miles from Klamath Falls, and 100 miles from Eugene. The sno-park is 0.5 mile north of Chemult. From Bend, drive south on Highway 97 to the Walt Haring Sno-Park access road on the right 7.4 miles beyond the junction with Highway 58. This is Forest Road 9772. Drive 0.4 mile to the sno-park, which has outhouses and a log shelter maintained by a local snowmobile club.

Amtrak is a fun travel alternative. A train from the Willamette Valley arrives in Chemult every evening and leaves mid-morning. The trip through the Cascades is gorgeous and exciting, passing through a 1-mile tunnel and seventeen smaller ones. The Amtrak station is one block from the Dawson Hotel, a beautifully renovated structure built in 1929. The hotel may provide its Amtrak guests with transportation to the sno-park. Skiers can also use a short snowmobile trail between Chemult and the sno-park. Hotels fill for the sled dog races on the last weekend in January.

The sno-park access road enters the oval shaped sno-park near its east end. The main trailhead is near the middle of the north side and a less obvious marked trail starts on the west end. A loop around the perimeter of all the trails described here, with the exception of Jill's Hill, is 5 miles.

Runner Loop. From the main trailhead on the north side of the sno-park, follow a short trail 50 feet to a T on the Runner Loop, a wide,

2.1-mile trail. There are no one-way trails, but Runner Loop is usually skied counterclockwise. Turn right and ski over easy hills, passing through a young lodgepole pine plantation. The 25-feet-tall pines form a dense forest that will have to be thinned as the trees mature. A narrow marked trail on the left, halfway around the loop, is a shortcut back to the sno-park. In another 0.2 mile, Runner Loop reaches a junction with Twinkle Loop. Turn left and ski a short distance south to a junction with Twisted Pine Trail. Turn left again and ski 0.5 mile east to the sno-park.

Twinkle Loop with sun on the trees

Twinkle Loop. Twinkle Loop is another gentle, easy trail passing through a pine plantation. From the main trailhead, ski counterclockwise on Runner Loop for about 1.5 miles. Turn right and ski north. In 0.3 mile, the trail splits and continues in either direction, making a 1.9-mile loop that connects to Pine Knob, Jill's Hill, and Twisted Pine Trails. Return south 0.3 mile to Runner Loop and complete that loop for a total of 4.6 miles.

Pine Knob. Pine Knob Trail, a 0.6-mile trail off the northeast corner of Twinkle Loop, climbs an easy grade to a rocky knoll. Though not very high at 4800 feet, there are views in all directions, especially of the forests to the north and open country to the east. Ski Pine Knob counterclockwise for the easier uphill grade.

Twisted Pine. Twisted Pine Trail is a 1.1-mile, intermediate-level connector from the west end of Runner Loop to Twinkle Loop. From the main trailhead, follow Runner Loop clockwise to the Twisted Pine Trail, 0.5 mile west of the trailhead. Head west on Twisted Pine, passing through mature stands of ponderosa and lodgepole pine. The trail climbs moderately from Runner Loop, crests 60 feet above the snopark, and ends with a fun downhill run to Twinkle Loop. The climb is steeper and the downhill mellower if skied from Twinkle Loop to Runner Loop.

Jill's Hill. Jill's Hill is the most challenging of the Walt Haring Nordic trails, but it also provides the best views. It starts and ends at the northwest corner of Twinkle Loop, 100 feet east of the Corral Springs Loop snowmobile trail and powerlines. The Jill's Hill Trail heads west and crosses under the powerlines and climbs steeply along an old road. Groomed tracks are not set, but bandit snowmobile tracks may be encountered. The climb and the downhill return on Jill's Hill are difficult and not good for beginners. Near the top of the hill, the trail makes a small loop through mature sugar pine and ponderosa. Skiing counterclockwise (right) on the loop leads up steeply. A left follows an easy grade up. The loop reaches the top of a steep cliff (5025 feet) with excellent views of Mount Thielsen and other peaks. Round trip from Twinkle Loop is 1.9 miles.

Miller Lake Road. Skating is not possible on the marked ski trails, but skaters can use the groomed snowmobile trails. Miller Lake Road is good for out-and-back skating tours. To reach it, follow a short connector trail 75 feet from the south side of the sno-park. Turn right on Miller Lake Road and head west. The 24-mile round trip to Miller Lake, gaining 800 feet in elevation, is an opportunity for testosterone skiers. For other route possibilities along the snowmobile trails, check a snowmobile trail map.

40 WOODS LINE LINEAR STATE PARK

Distance: 6–17.6 miles
Trails: Ungroomed ski trails
Track Quality: Fair classic skiing, no skating
Skill Level: Novice to intermediate
Elevation: 5220 feet
Maximum Elevation Gain: 250 feet
Season: Late December to early March
Services and Facilities: None
Hours: NA
Fees: Sno-park permit not required
Information: Fremont National Forest, (541) 947-2151,
www.fs.fed.us/r6/fremont/trails

Two old railroads, the O.C. & E. and the Woods Line, have been combined into a "linear" state park of bike trails extending 80 miles northeast from Klamath Falls. The O.C. & E. portion of the bike trail follows the old Oregon California & Eastern railroad line northeast from Klamath Falls. In 52 miles, east of the town of Beatty, the Woods Line splits from the O.C. & E. and runs north 31 miles to Sycan Marsh. The north half of the old Woods Line is snow covered much of the winter, creating a unique skiing experience in the Fremont National Forest. Only a few skiers visit this remote trail, so the chance of finding a broken ski track is slim. Instead, skiers can anticipate solitude, possible wildlife sightings, and the charm of skiing on an old rail line. Beginners will have no trouble with the grade, but previous outdoor winter experience is needed because of the trail's remoteness. Strong skiers who want a long, slow-paced tour can ski 17.6 miles round trip to a rebuilt railroad trestle high over Merritt Creek.

From Klamath Falls, follow Highway 140 east 44 miles to Beatty, where gas and groceries are available. Continue 9.6 miles on Highway 140 to Ivory Pine Road on the left (called Camp Six Road on some maps). From the east, this turn is 46 miles from Lakeview, and 3 miles west of Bly. Drive north on Ivory Pine, which becomes Forest Road 30. In 12.6 miles, reach Forest Road 27 on the left, where the plowing stops. A sign points left to the Horseglade Trailhead. There is usually space for a few cars, but carry a shovel to clear a spot if necessary. This is not a sno-park and a permit is not required.

The trailhead is at 5220 feet. Despite the elevation, the area gets only a few feet of dry snow. Ski 1.3 miles northwest on Forest Road 27, an uninteresting stretch, to the Woods Line crossing. At times, it may

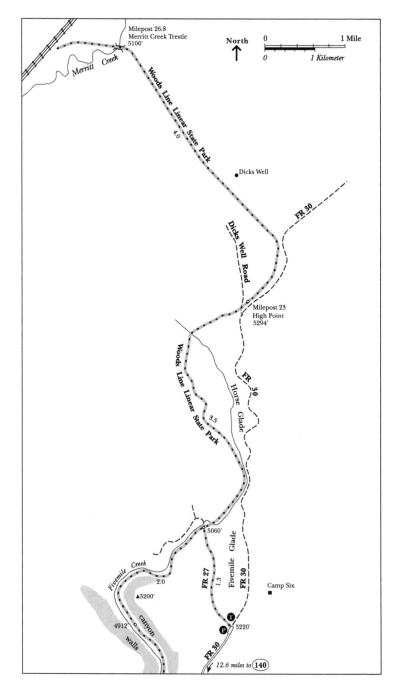

be possible to drive this stretch. Mileposts were marked along the rail-road line, starting at its intersection with the O.C. & E. line near Beatty. However, most markers are missing or damaged. Park plans call for new markers, but it may be years before they are put in. Forest Road 27 crosses the former rail line between miles 19 and 20. The milepost numbers increase when traveling north.

For a short tour on the Woods Line trail, ski south from Forest Road 27. The trail follows Fivemile Creek and passes under steep cliffs. It drops as it continues south and diminishing snow cover may limit trip distance. In 2 miles, the trail drops 150 feet. In late winter, elk may be seen in meadows along lower elevations of the creek.

Longer tours are possible skiing north from Forest Road 27, because the trail climbs gently and the snow cover is better. The first 2 miles north of Forest Road 27 are not particularly interesting, but the scenery improves farther out, passing through a mix of thin forest and clearings. The grade is easy. The trail peaks 3.5 miles from Forest Road 27 near milepost 23, though the grade is so gradual that "peak" is a bit misleading.

The trestle over Merritt Creek at milepost 26.8 is the best destination for a long ski tour. The trestle is 7.5 miles from Forest Road 27. After milepost 23, the trail drops gradually to the trestle. Climb the embankment just past the trestle for views of Winter Ridge and mountains to the north. The Woods Line leaves national forest and passes ranch houses shortly past the trestle.

The return trip can be shortened 1 mile by skiing the last few miles on Forest Road 30. The road passes just a short distance east of the Woods Line near milepost 23. This mile marker was still in good condition in 2002. Turn left onto Dicks Well Road, a short distance south of milepost 23, and ski 200 feet east to Forest Road 30. It is harder to use this shortcut on the way to the trestle, because Dicks Well Road may not be obvious from Forest Road 30. Snowmobilers use Forest Road 30, but few are encountered.

Reflection in pond near Woods Line

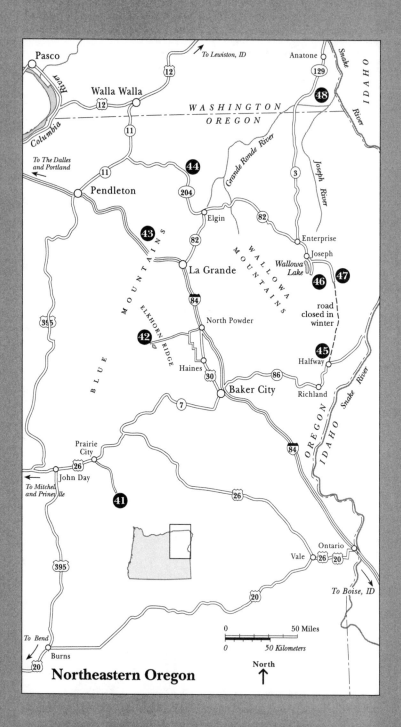

Northeastern Oregon

Northeastern Oregon

Northeastern Oregon is a vast region with few people, extending east and north from John Day and Pendleton to the borders of Idaho and Washington. The terrain includes high desert and sagebrush country, heavily forested ridges, and mountain peaks. Skiers will find colder air and drier snow here than in the Cascades. Sunshine is common over most of the region, though pockets of cloudy weather are found in the valleys.

Much of the region is dominated by the Blue Mountains, extending more than 150 miles from south of John Day to southeastern Washington. The Blues are characterized by high, rounded hills and forested ridges separated by deep canyons. Much more rugged peaks are found in the Elkhorns, which form a ridge on the east flank of the Blue Mountains near Baker City and in the Wallowa Mountains, spectacular peaks east of La Grande. The Wallowas have many peaks above 8000 feet and several above 9000 feet. The ski trails of northeastern Oregon are primarily in the Malheur, Umatilla, and Wallowa–Whitman National Forests. Trails at a state park in the Washington portion of the Blue Mountains are also included in this region in this guide.

41 SUMMIT PRAIRIE

Distance: 5.6 miles
Trails: Groomed snowmobile trails
Track Quality: Good classic skiing, good skating
Skill Level: Intermediate
Elevation: 5720 feet
Maximum Elevation Gain: 428 feet
Season: Mid-November to early April
Services and Facilities: Outhouse
Hours: NA
Fees: Sno-park permit
Information: Malheur National Forest, (541) 575-3000

Days are cold and clear and the snow is dry in the highlands near the Strawberry Mountains. Logan Valley and Summit Prairie are popular snowmobile destinations. The scenic, open terrain also attracts skiers, but budget cuts reduced snowplowing near both areas. Access to Logan Valley is now long and tedious. At Summit Prairie, however, the best views are still within easy reach and the road that was formerly plowed provides a new route to the prairie. Explore the huge open landscape and enjoy views of the steep ridges above. Snowmobilers use the area, but they are friendly. The groomed snowmobile trails here are well suited to skating.

From John Day follow Highway 26 east for 13 miles to Prairie City. Prairie City is 131 miles east of Prineville and 67 miles west of Baker City. At Prairie City, turn south onto Bridge Street, cross the John Day

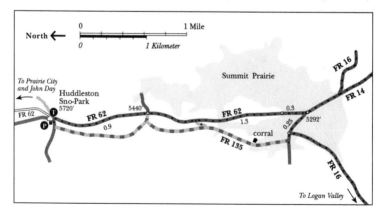

Snowmobile trail near Summit Prairie

River, and follow Bridge around a left curve. In two blocks, continue straight when Bridge makes a hard right. Follow Forest Road 62 south 20 miles to Huddleston Sno-Park. The road used to be plowed to Summit Prairie, but plowing now ends at Huddleston. While passing through Prairie City, check in front of the café for the local version of a celebrity sidewalk. Cattle brands, instead of footprints, are impressed in the concrete.

From the sno-park, groomed snowmobile trails head in several directions. When the road was plowed to Summit Prairie, the main snowmobile and ski route was a little west of Forest Road 62. That route is now Forest Road 135, an occasionally groomed alternate snowmobile trail that starts 100 yards west of the Huddleston Sno-Park, while unplowed Forest Road 62 is the main route. A good loop of less than 6 miles round trip descends Forest Road 62 to Summit Prairie and returns on the alternate trail.

From the end of the plowed road, ski south on Forest Road 62. The first mile is downhill and passes quickly. The track can be very fast on cold mornings. The road continues to descend, but only gradually, for another mile and then follows a level course to the wide-open expanse of Summit Prairie. Continue another 0.3 mile to a T intersection with Forest Road 16 at 2.5 miles from the sno-park. The open prairie is cradled between two steep north–south ridges. The ridge along the west side is heavily forested. To the east, the ridge has been opened by beetle infestation and forest fires and provides better views. Skiers with touring equipment can leave the packed trails and explore the flat, open terrain. Watch for fences. In deep snow, the barbed wire may not be obvious.

From the T, turn right and follow Forest Road 16 for a quarter mile. Continue straight when Forest Road 16 turns sharply left and heads into the woods. In a few yards, turn right onto Forest Road 135, the occasionally groomed return route. The road passes an old corral in 0.3 mile. The trail continues north to the sno-park, with two connections to Forest Road 62 along the way. It ends on a groomed snowmobile trail running east–west. Turn right and ski 100 yards east to the sno-park.

To add distance to this loop, ski out and back on Forest Road 16, heading west toward Logan Valley (5 miles) from Summit Prairie. For long loop tours from the sno-park, get a map of the snowmobile trails. Try these in late winter, when the days are longer. Some loop trails are hilly and not as well groomed as Roads 62 and 16.

42 ANTHONY LAKES

Distance: 2–11 kilometers (1.3–7 miles), 24 kilometers total
Trails: Groomed ski trails
Track Quality: Excellent classic skiing, excellent skating
Skill Level: Novice to advanced
Elevation: 7146 feet
Maximum Elevation Gain: 420 feet, main trails; 682 feet,
   Elkhorn Byway
Season: Mid-November to mid-April
Services and Facilities: Ski rentals, lessons, snacks, outhouse
Hours: 8:30 A.M.–4:00 P.M., Thursday–Sunday
Fees: $8, sno-park permit
Information: Anthony Lakes Mountain Resort, (541) 856-3277,
   www.anthonylakes.com

The groomed, high-elevation, cross-country trail system at Anthony Lakes Mountain Resort in northeast Oregon is a jewel unknown to most Oregon skiers. A mix of easy inner trails and roller-coaster outer trails creates as much opportunity for fun as can be found at larger ski areas. A new, 11-kilometer (7-mile) road loop, groomed on weekends and holidays, reaches open vistas and offers easy long-distance skiing. Reliable dry snow, stunning views of the rugged peaks of Elkhorn Ridge, and lots of sunshine are taken for granted here.

The Elkhorns extend southeast from the Blue Mountains. Their sharp features indicate that they are much younger mountains than the more rounded Blues. Situated at more than 7100 feet, Anthony Lakes is the highest, regularly groomed, cross-country ski area in Oregon.

Anthony Lakes is 315 miles from Portland and 285 miles from Bend. From Interstate 84, take exit 285 at North Powder, 24 miles south of La Grande and 19 miles north of Baker City. Drive west from the freeway on River Road, curving left onto Ellis Road in 4 miles. In another 0.7 mile, bear right at a poorly marked, three-way intersection where a sign points left to Haines. This road becomes Forest Road 73. The road is narrow and steep in places and reaches Anthony Lakes Mountain Resort 20.5 miles from the freeway. A left turn 100 feet before the alpine ski area leads into the Nordic lot. If this small lot is full, park in the alpine lot and follow a groomed connector trail to the Nordic system.

For a unique side trip on the way to Anthony Lakes, visit an Oregon

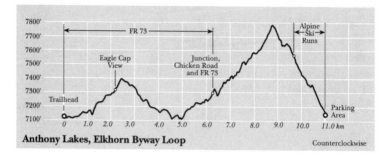

Anthony Lakes, Elkhorn Byway Loop Counterclockwise

Fish and Wildlife elk feeding station. Instead of turning onto Ellis Road, continue west on River Road 4.5 miles to the well-marked station. Ranching and farming have disrupted traditional winter elk feeding grounds, so Fish and Wildlife compensates with hay. On weekends, wagon rides bring visitors close to the elk. Other times, they can be viewed from a parking area above the feeding ground. An outdoor interpretive center depicts the life cycle of an elk and the human impact on its life.

Purchase a trail pass at the Nordic center next to the Nordic parking area. This small stone and log cabin built in 1939 is the most charming Nordic center in Oregon. The secluded, peaceful atmosphere is a contrast to the bustle of the alpine area just a short distance away. Seating is limited to a couple of small benches, but the atmosphere is friendly and the cabin is a good place to meet local skiers. The center rents good touring skis and a few high-performance skis. Coffee, juice, snacks, and a few ski supplies are available for purchase. Hot meals are served at the alpine lodge.

Trail grooming at Anthony Lakes is excellent, with double classic tracks and a wide skating platform. Trail junctions are well marked and the trails are easy to follow. Skiing at high altitude can be tiring, so ski slowly if you are not acclimated. Cold, dry snow is the rule here and selecting a kick wax is simple. Skiers accustomed to waxing for the wet snow of the Cascades will find their array of klisters and transition waxes unnecessary.

Anthony Lake Loop. The Nordic center is 60 feet off the north side of Anthony Lake Loop. Other trails are reached from this easy 1.9-kilometer loop. All trails can be skied in both directions, but ski counterclockwise on your first trip around Anthony Lake for an in-your-face view of Gunsight Mountain.

Coming out of the Nordic center, turn right and ski with the lake, visible through the trees, on your left. In 0.3 kilometer, the groomed connector trail from the alpine parking area is on the right. Turn left and ski south on the west side of the lake. The connector trail and the west leg of the Anthony Lake Loop are a common corridor for backcountry skiers heading to Angell Basin, a favorite destination for telemark skiing. Dogs and snowshoes are allowed on this short section as far as the backcountry trail.

Along the west side of Anthony Lake, the trees open up for views across the lake to Gunsight Mountain (8342 feet) and the Elkhorns. Novice skiers will appreciate that such dramatic views can be had from an easy trail. The loop continues around the lake with short gentle hills.

Lily Pad Loop and Gunsight. The Lily Pad Loop and the Gunsight Trail can be added to the Anthony Lake Loop for longer beginner tours. Ski counterclockwise on the Anthony Lake Loop from the Nordic center. Halfway around the lake, turn right onto Lily Pad Loop. In 0.1 kilometer, the Gunsight Trail splits right and Lily Pad continues left. Lily Pad heads east through marshes around tiny Lily Pad Lake for 0.4 kilometer of flat skiing to a four-way junction. Turn left and follow the winding east side of Lily Pad Loop through a series of short, sometimes steep, hills. Lily Pad rejoins the Anthony Lake Loop 0.4 kilometer from the Nordic center. Near this junction with the lake loop, the ski area often grooms a flat oval that is ideal for beginner ski lessons. The round trip from the Nordic center is 2.6 kilometers (1.6 miles).

Gunsight is a flat, 1-kilometer trail with views of Gunsight Mountain. It starts on Lily Pad Loop as described above. From there, it curves

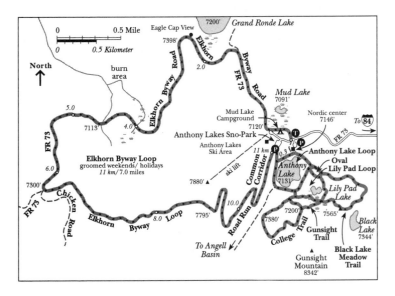

east, staying left at two junctions with the College Trail. It ends at a four-way junction with Lily Pad Loop and the Black Lake Meadow Trail. Continue on Lily Pad, going straight for some hills, or turning left for a flat return on Lily Pad to the lake loop.

College Trail. College Trail, which loops off the Gunsight Trail, is one of two hilly, advanced-level trails in the main trail system. The 1.7-kilometer trail was completed in 1994 with help from skiers from Eastern Oregon University. It has challenging downhill turns in either direction, but the downhill sections are steeper if skied clockwise. To go that way, ski clockwise on the Anthony Lake Loop 0.4 kilometer to Lily Pad and ski south on Lily Pad to Gunsight. Go 0.3 kilometer on Gunsight and turn left on College Trail. Ski clockwise on College, climbing and then descending through steep turns back to the Gunsight Trail. Continue straight to Anthony Lake Loop and return to the Nordic center for 4.2 kilometers (2.6 miles) round trip.

Black Lake Meadow Trail. The Black Lake Meadow Trail is the second advanced-level trail in the main trail system. From the Nordic center, ski clockwise on the Anthony Lake Loop 0.4 mile and bear left onto the Black Lake Meadow Trail. Ski east past the teaching oval on the right and start climbing. The trail loops back to the west and climbs steeply to its high point before descending a steep hill with tight turns. Good downhill skills are required here. The trail drops to the Lily Pad Loop. Turn right and ski north to the lake loop and return to the Nordic center for a 4.4-kilometer (2.8-mile) round trip.

Elkhorn Byway. In winter 2002, the ski area added an 11-kilometer (7-mile) road loop around the alpine ski hill that leads to expansive viewpoints. The Elkhorn Byway Loop, groomed only on weekends and holidays, should be skied counterclockwise because its final 2 kilometers descend an easy alpine ski run and skiing uphill here would risk collision with the alpine skiers. Beginners can ski to excellent views on the north side of the loop and return via the same route to avoid the alpine section. From the west side of the Nordic Center, ski north 100 yards on a narrow trail and walk across Forest Road 73 to the start of the Elkhorn Byway Loop. The groomed trail heads north and west through the Mud Lake Campground and connects to unplowed Forest Road 73, where it turns right and heads north. The trail runs adjacent to a snowmobile trail for several kilometers, but extra-wide grooming provides separation. In 2.5 kilometers, skiers reach views of Eagle Cap Peak and the Eagle Cap Wilderness, 50 miles to the northeast. From here, the Elkhorn Byway turns southwest and passes a 10-year-old burn area with views to the west. This is a good place for beginners to turn around. At 4.5 kilometers, it dips to the lowest point on the loop, 7113 feet, and then climbs to a junction with two other roads at 6.2 kilometers from the start. Forest Road 73 turns west. The road leading south is known as Chicken Road. The groomed ski loop turns and climbs toward the ski area on a narrow road. It passes quickly from Union County into Grant County. At 9 kilometers, it reaches yet a third, Baker County, at the loop's high point, 7795 feet. The road starts downhill and joins the Road Run alpine ski trail. This is a wide trail with plenty of room to maneuver, but advanced ski skills are required for the 650-foot drop on the 2-kilometer run back to the Nordic trails.

Skiing on Lily Pad Loop at Anthony Lakes

43 MEACHAM DIVIDE

Distance: 2.5–19 kilometers (1.6–12 miles)
Trails: Groomed ski trails
Track Quality: Good classic skiing, good skating
Skill Level: Novice to advanced
Elevation: 4131 feet
Maximum Elevation Gain: 350 feet
Season: Early December to late March
Services and Facilities: Outhouse
Hours: NA
Fees: $3 per person suggested donation, sno-park permit
Information: Blue Mountain Nordic Club, (541) 663-3239

Tucked in the Blue Mountains northwest of La Grande is a relatively new trail system developed and groomed by the Blue Mountain Nordic Club, a chapter of the Oregon Nordic Club. The trails mostly follow forest roads, but have a fine mix of challenging hills, rolling terrain, and flat stretches. On clear days there are excellent views of steep canyons and the northern Blues. Trails are groomed regularly with tracks for classic skiing and a wide skating platform. The trail system depends on volunteer support and donations from all users. The area does have a number of cloudy days, and its low elevation results in a shorter ski season than at nearby Anthony Lakes.

For La Grande skiers, the sno-park is only 19 miles west on Interstate 84. From Pendleton, it is 37 miles east along the interstate. Cabbage Hill, east of Pendleton, has severe driving conditions in winter storms. From Interstate 84 take exit 243 and drive east and north on Summit Road. Mount Emily Sno-Park is at the end of the plowed road 1.8 miles from the highway. Plowing is rough. Carry chains and a shovel. The Nordic parking lot is on the left and the snowmobile lot is on the right. The sno-park is on private timberland, but the ski trails are mostly in the Umatilla National Forest. A snowmobile route follows the ungroomed continuation of Summit Road and does not overlap the ski trails. A drive from Portland should take less than 5 hours.

Development of the ski area in the mid-1990s is a story of incredible cooperation. The ski club worked with a snowmobile club, local agencies, businesses, and rangers to develop the sno-park, set up the trails, and acquire and repair an old, 12-foot-wide grooming machine. Trail junctions are well marked, and distances are posted in kilometers. The club grooms on Wednesdays and weekends if donations and volunteer support are sufficient.

The backbone of the trail system is the 5-kilometer (3.2-mile) Loppet Trail, which follows Forest Road 3102 north and east from the sno-park. Seven side trails add a nice mix of trails for beginners to advanced skiers. A tour that includes the side trails on the way out and a direct return to the sno-park on Loppet is about 19 kilometers long. Three loops have short spurs to overlooks of Meacham Creek's steep canyon and the rounded summits of the Blue Mountains. Watch for wildlife. Elk and mule deer winter in the area and can outnumber skiers. Mountain lion tracks are occasionally seen along the trails.

Dogs are allowed on I Scream and Roller Coaster, two short ski trails near the sno-park, and on Loppet Trail as far as its junction with Roller Coaster. I Scream and Roller Coaster have steep hills, and dogs must be controlled to avoid hazards. Owners who take dogs on other trails risk a ban on dogs on all trails.

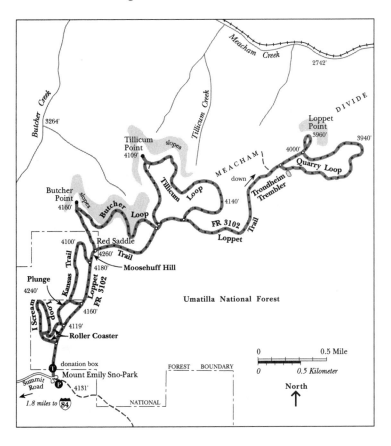

Loppet. The trailhead is in the northwest corner of the small parking lot. Loppet heads north from here on Forest Road 3102, connecting to all the side trails on the way. Look for the donation box on the right, 50 feet from the sno-park. Beginners can enjoy a 6-kilometer, out-and-back tour to Loppet's high point. A 10.4-kilometer round trip to Loppet Point is an intermediate tour. Loppet follows the wide road through small hills, climbing 150 feet from the sno-park. A steep uphill starting 1.5 kilometers from the sno-park is known locally as Moosehuff, an Americanization of a Norwegian term for interval training on hills. Beyond the top of Moosehuff, the road runs west on Red Saddle, a generally flat section.

Starting 3 kilometers from the sno-park, near a junction with Tillicum Loop, Loppet begins to descend and is mostly downhill for 2 kilometers. This section is difficult for beginners in icy conditions. A particularly steep, 0.2-kilometer downhill section is called the Trondheim Trembler (Trondheim, a Norwegian town, is the home of many fine skiers). A groomed cul-de-sac at the end of the road leads to Loppet Point, an overlook of Meacham Creek Canyon and Horseshoe Ridge to the north. Return along the same route, with plenty of uphill in the first 2 kilometers from Loppet Point. For a little more skiing before starting the return climb, ski around the Quarry Loop, which starts just south of Loppet Point. This 1.9-kilometer trail runs east and then loops back to Loppet, with some views of the Owsley Creek drainage and Spring Mountain to the east. It is mostly flat, but its north side has a steep downhill section when skied clockwise.

Roller Coaster and I Scream. The first side trail from Loppet is on the left 0.3 kilometer from the sno-park. This is Roller Coaster, which is a 1-kilometer, beginner trail with easy little hills. It heads west, passes two junctions with the I Scream Loop, and then leads northeast back to Loppet. I Scream is a 1-kilometer, intermediate loop around a small hill. Skiing clockwise on Roller Coaster, turn left at the first junction with I Scream and ski north along the west side of the hill to views from a clear-cut on its north slope. If there are no obvious ski tracks, this trail can be hard to follow. I Scream returns to Roller Coaster along a logging road on the east side of the hill.

Plunge and Kansas. Plunge, only 0.5 kilometer long, has short, steep hills with sharp turns. It starts on Loppet 0.6 kilometer from the sno-park, next to the end of Roller Coaster. It descends quickly on a narrow logging road. Before a gate in 0.2 kilometer, it makes a sharp right turn and climbs 0.3 kilometer through curves, ending on the Kansas Trail. (Skied in the opposite direction, these downhill curves

View from the Butcher Point overlook

are exciting.) Kansas is a 1-kilometer trail with one end on Loppet 1 kilometer from the sno-park and the other end emerging back onto Loppet 1.5 kilometers from the sno-park. It is a curving trail along clearings. Despite its name, Kansas ain't all flat. There are little hills, though beginners should enjoy them. It is more fun to ski counterclockwise, starting from Loppet 1.5 kilometers from the sno-park. This end is along Moosehuff Hill and is a difficult turn for skiers coming down the hill toward the sno-park.

Butcher. Butcher Loop is a generally easy trail that forms a 5.7-kilometer (3.6-mile) round trip with Loppet. A spur trail from its northwest corner leads to Butcher Point, one of the area's three major scenic overlooks. Ski 1.6 kilometers north from the sno-park on Loppet, passing junctions with Roller Coaster, Plunge, and Kansas. Turn left onto Butcher Loop and ski 0.6 kilometer, descending to the start of the spur to the overlook on Butcher Point. The spur continues straight here and the loop makes a hard right. Make the 0.1-mile detour to the Butcher Point overlook on a steep-sided ridge. Butcher Creek is 900 feet below to the west, flowing north through its steep canyon to Meacham Creek. Return 0.1 kilometer up the spur and continue clockwise around Butcher Loop, winding west 1.9 kilometers back to Loppet. Turn right and ski 2.6 kilometers to the sno-park.

Tillicum. Tillicum is the area's best-flowing trail, with rolling terrain and little hills. It is an excellent choice for beginners who have the stamina for a 9-kilometer (5.6-mile) round trip from the sno-park. The loop has several views of the surrounding Blue Mountains and a spur trail to Tillicum Point above the Meacham Creek Canyon. Ski 2.6 kilometers from the sno-park on Loppet. A few yards past Loppet's second junction with Butcher Loop, turn left onto Tillicum Loop for a clockwise loop. Ski north on easy terrain through forest and little clearings. In about 1 kilometer, the trail drops to a T. The loop continues to the right. The spur trail to the overlook at Tillicum Point is to the left. This spur drops quickly along a ridge and can be very difficult in icy conditions. It sits 1300 feet above Meacham Creek and a railroad line running through the canyon below. Ski back to the T and continue clockwise, climbing and rolling with views to the north and east over the Tillicum Creek canyon. In 2 kilometers from the overlook spur, it returns to Loppet. Turn right to return to the sno-park.

44 SPOUT SPRINGS

Distance: 2.8–4.5 miles
Trails: Groomed and ungroomed ski trails
Track Quality: Fair classic skating, fair skating
Skill Level: Novice to intermediate
Elevation: 5050 feet
Maximum Elevation Gain: 450 feet
Season: Early December to late March
Services and Facilities: Restaurant, lounge, ski rentals
Hours: 9:00 A.M.–4:00 P.M., Friday–Sunday
Fees: $5, sno-park permit
Information: Spout Springs Ski Area, (541) 566-0320,
www.skispoutsprings.com

The Spout Springs Ski Area in the Blue Mountains northeast of Pendleton has a rich history of cross-country skiing. Unfortunately, hard times hit this ski resort in the 1990s. Windstorm damage closed it for several years. New owners reopened the ski area in 1999, but the Nordic operation has been slow to reach its full potential. Currently, only short trails near the ski lodge are groomed.

The ski area has two cross-country trail systems. The lower system, which once had three groomed loops, is north of the ski lodge, in the woods below the alpine ski runs. The Stagecoach Loop is the only trail

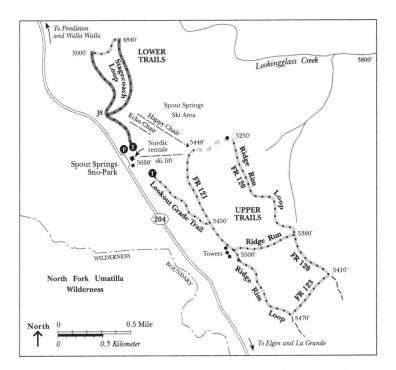

currently in use in the lower system. The upper trails are on a plateau 400 feet above the lodge. The U.S. Olympic cross-country ski team trained on this plateau in the 1950s. They could not have picked a more scenic training course. Skiers here are treated to views of the surrounding Blue Mountains, the distant Wallowa Mountains, and the Seven Devils in Idaho. There are 6 miles of trails on this plateau, but they have not been groomed since trees fell across some of the trails during a windstorm in November 2000. When these trails were groomed, a trail pass ($12 in 2000) included one chairlift ride to the plateau, eliminating a long uphill climb from the ski lodge. The upper trails are well worth a visit. Check with the ski area to find out if grooming has resumed.

Spout Springs Ski Area is on Highway 204, 14 miles southeast of Tollgate. From Interstate 84 at Pendleton, take exit 210, the Milton-Freewater exit. Follow signs through Pendleton toward Milton-Freewater and Highway 11. From Pendleton, drive north 22 miles on Highway 11 to Highway 204. Turn right onto Highway 204 and continue 24 miles to Spout Springs Ski Area on the left. From La Grande, follow Highway 82 18 miles to Elgin. Turn left onto Highway 204 and drive 18.8 miles to Spout Springs.

Ridge Rim overlook of the Blue Mountains

Stagecoach Loop. The Stagecoach Loop is a 2-mile beginner loop. From the Nordic rental shop, turn left and ski north toward the Echo chairlift. Before reaching the lift, turn left on an unmarked, but well-groomed trail through the trees. Continue to junction 8, the start of the Stagecoach Loop, 0.4 mile from the ski rental shop. The long east and west sides of the loop meet here. They are both groomed weekly and are easy to skate on. A short narrow section of the loop that climbs from the east side to the west side may not be groomed. In this case, skaters are limited to skiing out and back on the loop's two long legs. Classic skiers can make their own track on the ungroomed section to ski the whole loop. Turn right at junction 8 and ski north along the east side of Stagecoach Loop on gentle terrain for 0.8 mile. The loop turns left onto its connector section. This uphill stretch will challenge beginners; if skied in the opposite direction, it is an intermediate downhill. The connector climbs 0.4 mile to the groomed west side of the loop. Turn left and return, mostly downhill to junction 8. Round trip from the rental shop is about 2.8 miles.

Lookout Grade Trail. The Lookout Grade Trail angles steeply uphill to the west side of the upper trails. It starts 200 yards south of the ski lodge and follows a narrow but obvious road grade uphill, climbing 400 feet to the plateau in 0.5 mile. It ends on the plateau at Forest Road 121, which is the west side of the Ridge Rim Loop. The Lookout Grade was an advanced-level, groomed trail to the plateau. It is not groomed now, but skiers can still use it to reach the upper trails.

Ridge Rim Loop. The 3.5-mile Ridge Rim Loop, which circles the upper plateau, is part of the upper trail system. Do not expect to find tracks set by other skiers on this ungroomed loop. Most of the route is on forest roads, but a 0.3-mile section at the north end is on a narrow trail. Several feet of snow are required to easily get past trees that have fallen across this section.

For a 4.5-mile tour, ski 0.5 mile up the Lookout Grade Trail to Forest Road 121. Turn right to ski counterclockwise. There are plenty of westward views along this side. In 0.2 mile, the road passes communication towers on the right. Ridge Run, a shortcut trail to the east side of Ridge Rim Loop is on the left. It shortens the loop by 0.9 mile. Ridge Rim Loop continues on Forest Road 121 to Forest Road 123, turns left, and runs northeast to Forest Road 120, the east side of the loop. Turn left and ski about 1.4 miles to the end of the forest road. Near the north end of this section, there are clearings with views of the Seven Devils in Idaho. Turn left onto the loop's narrow section, following blue diamonds as you ski uphill. If it is difficult to get around fallen trees, return along Road 120 to the Ridge Run Trail and follow that shortcut to Road 121. In 0.4 mile, the trail reaches a clearing near the top of the Happy Chair ski lift and connects to Forest Road 121. From here, ski south on Forest Road 121 back to the Lookout Grade Trail. When the upper trails were groomed, most skiers reached the plateau via a 5-minute ride on the Happy Chair and started the Ridge Rim Loop at its north end.

45 CLEAR CREEK

Distance: 0.6–7.4 miles
Trails: Ungroomed ski trails
Track Quality: Good classic skiing, no skating
Skill Level: Novice to advanced
Elevation: 3740 feet
Maximum Elevation Gain: 655 feet
Season: Early December to early March
Services and Facilities: Outhouse
Hours: NA
Fees: Sno-park permit
Information: Pine Ranger District, Wallowa–Whitman National
    Forest, (541) 742-7511

The town of Halfway, 50 miles east of Baker City, sits in the Pine Valley on the southern edge of the Wallowa Mountains. Halfway serves as a gateway to the region's exciting backcountry. More moderate skiing can be enjoyed on the Clear Creek loops north of town. Ungroomed Forest Service trails offer something for all ability levels, as well as tours along a beautiful mountain stream. Visitors to Halfway may see signs referring to Half.com. This is the result of the town unofficially adopting that name for one year in a publicity deal with an Internet company in exchange for computer equipment.

From Baker City, drive 50 miles east on Highway 86 to Halfway. Turn left onto the Halfway–Cornucopia Highway, which is also Main Street. At the north end of town, across from the high school, turn right at a fork with Fish Lake Road. Drive 3.3 miles to Clear Creek Road on the left. Turn left onto the unpaved road, which becomes Forest Road 66 when it enters the Wallowa-Whitman National Forest. In 3.2 miles, Road 66 curves right into Clear Creek Sno-Park at the end of the plowing. Its unplowed continuation is a groomed snowmobile route.

Clear Creek has several ski loops marked with blue diamonds. Trails are not named. Loop names used here are invented to make description easier. Some junctions east of the creek are not obvious. Carry a map and compass.

North Easy and South Easy. Two short beginner loops start from the sno-park and stay between Forest Road 66 and Clear Creek. The more enjoyable of the two is North Easy Loop, which starts at the north end of the sno-park. This is a delightful, 1-mile loop with views of Clear Creek and just enough hills to be interesting. From the trailhead, bear left and ski north on the loop's west side for 0.5 mile to a three-way junction. A left leads to a bridge across Clear Creek. Turn right and ski south to the sno-park, with the creek close on the left.

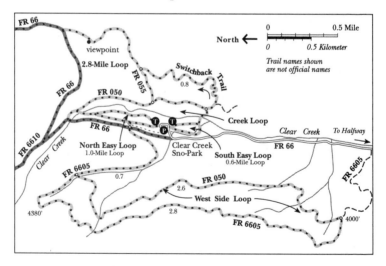

South Easy is a 0.6-mile loop that starts and finishes at the south end of the sno-park. If the snow depth is low, it is difficult to cross little streamlets along the marked route and it may be necessary to bushwhack to the west to get around these crossings.

Creek Loop. The 2.1-mile Creek Loop is an easy loop along both sides of Clear Creek. Ski south from the sno-park on the South Easy Trail. In 0.3 mile, turn east and follow blue diamond markers, crossing Clear Creek and smaller streams on three narrow footbridges. Make a hard left turn and follow blue diamonds north, climbing along Forest Road 050 for 1 mile. The north end of this section has good views of the creek to the left. At the north end, the route turns left and crosses Clear Creek on a footbridge. If this bridge crossing is intimidating, ski a short distance farther on Road 050 to Road 66. Cross the creek on Road 66 and follow the creek bank back to the Creek Loop. Ski south 0.1 mile to the North Easy Loop and return to the sno-park on the east leg of North Easy.

Switchback Trail. This 0.8-mile, advanced-level trail on the east side of Clear Creek starts at the south end of the Creek Loop. Switchback leads east from the Creek Loop where the Creek Loop turns north. It climbs a ridge on steep switchbacks through closely spaced trees. It turns north and follows a gentle grade to its end on Forest Road 055 and the 2.8-Mile Loop. The Switchback Trail should be considered a one-way trail; the switchback turns are too difficult to ski downhill safely.

2.8-Mile Loop. The 2.8-Mile Loop is plenty of fun but challenging. Short sections climb through the trees and the blue diamond markers may not be obvious. These sections are easier to follow if skied counterclockwise. Check for blue diamonds frequently to ensure you don't wander far from the trail. Reach the 2.8-Mile Loop via the North Easy Loop for a 4-mile round trip from the sno-park. Ski north from the sno-park on North Easy Loop and cross Deer Creek. Turn right onto Forest Road 050, the east leg of the Creek Loop. This is also the west side of the 2.8-Mile Loop. Ski south to Forest Road 055 and turn left. Ski east, climbing past the Switchback Trail on the right. The loop leaves the road in a short distance and leads through the trees for 0.7 mile before dropping to the end of a narrow logging road. Follow this road 50 feet to a sharp right turn and views to the northwest of the Wallowa Mountains. The road leads north 0.1 mile to an even better view and a junction with a wider logging road. Bear left here and left again at another intersection before dropping 0.2 mile to Forest Road 66, the groomed snowmobile route. Turn left and ski downhill to a junction with Forest Road 6610.

View of Wallowas from the 2.8-Mile Loop

Make a sharp left turn and continue on Forest Road 66 across Clear Creek. Connect to the North Easy Loop on the left and ski south to the sno-park.

West Side Loop. The West Side Loop west of Forest Road 66 is for advanced skiers. A round trip from the sno-park is 7.4 miles. Most of it follows forest roads, but the loop has long and steep hills. Ski north on the west leg of North Easy Loop 0.3 mile and turn left. Ski a few yards, climbing the bank to Forest Road 66, across from the start of Forest Road 6605. Follow Forest Road 6605 uphill, climbing steeply for 0.7 mile to a junction with Forest Road 050 on the left. This road is the return leg of a 5.4-mile loop. From here, continue on Forest Road 6605, which continues to climb and then loops to the south. It continues south 2 miles, dropping 400 feet, before turning east. Watch for blue diamonds on the left, where the West Side Loop breaks away from Forest Road 6605 and heads north. The West Side Loop continues north on trail and a narrow road for 2.6 miles to rejoin Forest Road 6605 and complete the loop. Turn right and return down Forest Road 6605 to Road 66 and the sno-park.

46 WALLOWA LAKE TRAMWAY

Distance: 2.5 miles
Trails: Groomed ski trails
Track Quality: Fair classic skiing, no skating
Skill Level: Novice to intermediate
Elevation: 8150 feet
Maximum Elevation Gain: 200 feet
Season: Thanksgiving weekend to late February
Services and Facilities: Cafe, ski rentals
Hours: 10:00 A.M.–3:00 P.M., weekends and Christmas week
Fees: $15.50
Information: Wallowa Lake Tramway, (541) 432-5331,
www.wallowalaketramway.com

Some of Oregon's most stunning mountain scenery awaits skiers at the top of Mount Howard on the edge of the rugged Wallowa Mountains. A 15-minute gondola ride on one of North America's steepest passenger tramways delivers visitors to the summit plateau at more than 8000 feet. Many visitors simply enjoy the extraordinary beauty from the top terminal, but skiers can circle the plateau for 360-degree views that extend to four states. More than 2 miles of groomed ski tracks enhance the experience but are secondary to the views.

From Interstate 84 at La Grande, take exit 261 and follow Highway 82 for 65 miles to Enterprise. The Forest Service Visitor Center on the north side of the highway just west of Enterprise is a good place for information on the tramway and nearby ski trails. Continue south on Highway 82, now called Wallowa Lake Highway. Reach Joseph 6 miles from Enterprise and the Wallowa Lake Lodge in another 6 miles from Joseph. Continue 0.2 mile to the tramway terminal on the left.

The gondola ride is the only practical way to the summit. The tramway opened in 1970. It lifts passengers 3700 feet over a 1.8-mile course. The four-passenger gondolas travel as high as 120 feet above the forest. For many years, winter operation was limited to a few weekends around the holidays. Recently, the schedule expanded to three months of weekend and holiday operation. Check ahead for current schedules.

The base terminal is in a glacial valley. Low clouds are not a good indication of conditions at the top. Tramway operators post weather conditions for the summit. The gondola may take only a few minutes to break through clouds to sunshine and panoramic views. Skis can

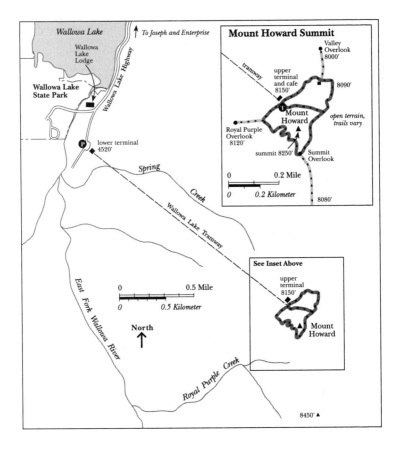

be rented at the base, but the selection is limited. It is better to bring your own or rent in Enterprise. The top terminal has restrooms and a café that serves cinnamon rolls, burgers, and soup. Beer and wine are also available. Remember that the effects of alcohol can be amplified at high altitude.

Most skiers experience some shortness of breath at this altitude. Minor headaches and dizziness are also common. Ski easily and enjoy the views. If serious problems occur, cut your visit short and return to the base.

Temperatures on the plateau generally stay below freezing and dry, powdery snow is the norm. Ski tracks are set with a snowmobile and a homemade track-setter. They are not for skating. Snowshoers and walkers also use the tracks. Their footprints make the tracks rough, but the trails are for their use, too. The views, not groomed tracks, are the reason for visiting the plateau. It is possible to telemark down to the base, but the slope is steep and the lower hill often has little snow. Most skiers return via the gondola.

The top terminal is on the west side of the plateau. The set tracks generally follow summer walking paths, but vary in the open terrain. There are three primary overlook points and more spots with views. Check the time of the last gondola to the base before exploring. Stay on the plateau and the gentle ridges at the three major lookouts. Carry a compass, as it is easy to get disoriented. The terrain off the plateau is steep and is only for those prepared for serious backcountry skiing.

Sparse stands of whitebark pine are scattered across the plateau. Though seldom much taller than 30 feet, some trees are estimated to be close to 1000 years old.

From the terminal, ski counterclockwise to a ridge that points to the peaks of the Wallowas and Eagle Cap Wilderness. An out-and-back trail descends the ridge to Royal Purple Lookout, named after a gold mine on Royal Purple Creek far below. Summit Overlook at the southeast corner of the plateau provides more views of the Wallowas. The ridge descending from this overlook can be followed to another overlook, but no track is set and the return climb is difficult. Skiing north on the east side of the plateau, skiers are treated to views of the Snake River territory and the Seven Devils Mountains in Idaho. On a clear day, peaks in Montana are visible. The Valley Overlook near the northwest corner of the plateau is above broad lowlands to the north and beautiful Wallowa Lake. Low clouds may obscure the lake. Outhouses near this overlook are open in winter.

Eagle Cap Wilderness from the Royal Purple Lookout

Once you return to the base, Wallowa Lake Lodge at the south end of the lake merits a visit. The lodge was built in the 1920s and was renovated twenty years ago. Rooms and cabins have no phones or televisions, a peaceful blessing. Wallowa Lake State Park, west of the lodge, is open in winter and rents cozy yurts for overnight stays. Non-guests may use hot showers for a fee. Gentle terrain in the park is good for an easy ski tour. Nights are long here, as steep valley walls delay the appearance of the sun and hasten its setting. Deer winter around the park and lodge. Many are too accustomed to people and are considered pests. Enjoy their beauty, but treat them as wild animals.

47 SALT CREEK SUMMIT

Distance: 1.3–5.6 miles
Trails: Ungroomed ski trails
Track Quality: Good classic skiing, no skating
Skill Level: Novice to advanced
Elevation: 6100 feet
Maximum Elevation Gain: 300 feet
Season: Mid-November to early April
Services and Facilities: Outhouse
Hours: NA
Fees: Sno-park permit
Information: Wallowa Mountains Visitor Center, (541) 426-5546

The Salt Creek Summit ski loops are in the Wallowa–Whitman National Forest, 50 miles east of La Grande. The Wallowa Mountains are just to the west and Hells Canyon and the Idaho border are 12 miles east. A sign in the parking lot claims three groomed ski loops, but trail grooming stopped in the early 1990s. The volunteers got tired. A snowmobile club packs wide trails that skiers can use, but the best skiing is on the formerly groomed loops and a fourth challenging trail across the road. Even without grooming, trails in this mixed terrain—with views of the Wallowa Mountains and Idaho's Seven Devils—are fun for skiers from beginner to advanced level.

The town of Joseph, on the edge of the Wallowas, is 71 miles from La Grande on Highway 82. In Joseph, turn east onto the Imnaha Road (County Road 350). Drive 8.4 miles and turn sharply right on Wallowa Mountain Road, which becomes Forest Road 39. Continue 10 miles, climbing to the end of the plowing. The sno-park is on the left. Forest Road 39 continues along the east side of the Wallowas to the town of Halfway, but is unplowed and normally not clear until late April.

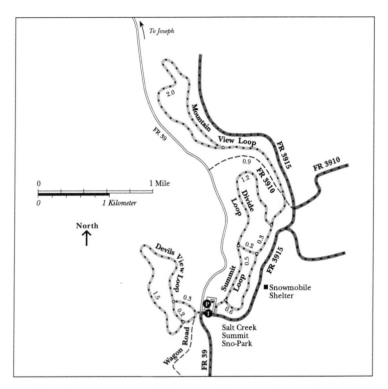

Three loops start east of the sno-park. Long sections of these loops pass through open landscape created by the 1989 Canal Burn. A fourth loop starts across Forest Road 39 from the sno-park.

Summit Loop. The Summit Loop is a 1.3-mile novice loop that travels over flat meadows and gentle hills. It passes numerous dead trees, casualties of the Canal Burn. The burn areas yield beautiful views of the Seven Devils Mountains in Idaho. Start at the southeast corner of the sno-park next to Forest Road 3915, which is a groomed snowmobile trail. The Summit Loop heads north along the east side of the sno-park before turning east and up a small hill to a split in the trail. Turn right for a counterclockwise loop that returns to this junction. The trail runs east 0.1 mile and then north another 0.5 mile to a junction with the Divide Loop. To continue on Summit Loop, turn left and ski 0.2 mile to another junction with the Divide Loop. Turn left and ski south back to the sno-park.

Divide Loop. The 1.5-mile Divide Loop starts on the north end of the Summit Loop, for a 2.6-mile round-trip tour from the sno-park. The loop has some steep hills on its west side that will challenge intermediate skiers. Ski clockwise on Summit Loop 0.5 mile to a junction with Divide Loop. Continue straight on Divide and descend a steep hill. Divide continues north and then curves south, passing a junction with Mountain View Loop and reconnecting to Summit Loop in 1.5 miles. Continue clockwise on Summit Loop 0.6 mile to the sno-park.

Mountain View Loop. Mountain View is an intermediate-level trail that starts on the east side of Divide Loop. Ski counterclockwise on Summit and Divide 0.9 mile from the sno-park. Turn right onto Mountain View and cross unplowed Forest Road 3910. Mountain View continues northwest between Forest Roads 3910 and 3915, a groomed snowmobile route. This is an out-and-back section of Mountain View. In 0.9 mile, it reaches a fork in an open burned area. The two sides of the fork are the start and return sides of a 2-mile loop with steep ups and downs. The east side of the loop is mostly through the burn area. Much of the west side is along a logging road. The Forest Service may stop maintaining trail markers on this loop, so

be prepared to look for blue diamonds. After completing the 2-mile loop, return on the out-and-back trail to Divide Loop and continue to the sno-park for a 5.6-mile round trip.

Devils View Loop. Devils View Loop starts across Forest Road 39 from the sno-park entrance. It is a hilly, 1.8-mile loop for intermediate skiers. Most of the trail is gentle, but beginners will have problems with several steep uphill and downhill sections. Much of the loop is in the woods, but it crosses clearings on a steep hillside with excellent views of the Seven Devils. From Forest Road 39, follow the Wagon Road Trail south for 0.1 mile and turn right onto Devils View. The loop heads north to the best views, and then turns south and returns to the Wagon Road.

Vestiges of the 1989 Canal Burn

48 FIELDS SPRING STATE PARK

Distance: 1–4 miles
Trails: Groomed ski trails
Track Quality: Excellent classic skiing, no skating
Skill Level: Novice to intermediate
Elevation: 3990 feet
Maximum Elevation Gain: 590 feet
Season: Mid-December to mid-March
Services and Facilities: Group lodges, heated bathrooms, showers
Hours: 8:00 A.M.–dusk
Fees: Sno-park permit
Information: Fields Spring State Park, (509) 256-3332

Nine miles north of the border, Washington's Fields Spring State Park supplements northeast Oregon skiing with a fine groomed ski trail system. Fields Spring is also popular with skiers and sledders from Lewiston, Idaho. The park has great views of the rounded hills at the north end of the Blue Mountains and opportunities for wildlife viewing. The park rangers who set ski tracks are also skiers who are enthusiastic about the trails. Groups can rent one of two lodges for an overnight stay in the park.

The park is on Washington State Route 129, 30 miles south of Clarkston, Washington. From La Grande, drive 65 miles east on Highway 82 to Enterprise, and then drive north on Highway 3, which becomes Washington Route 129. The road drops steeply into the Grande Ronde Canyon, crossing the river 48 miles from Highway 82 and then climbing steeply from the river to the park in 9.5 miles. Turn sharply right on the park access road. Continue to the park entrance and turn right and then left in a few yards. Drive 0.1 mile south to the park campground and a sno-park. There is also a small county sno-park 0.5 mile south of the park entrance at the end of the access road. There is no trail fee. The Washington sno-park program pays grooming expenses. The park ranger sells sno-park permits, which are required at both sno-parks. Oregon permits are honored.

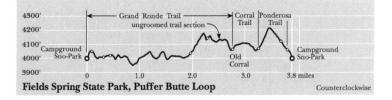

Fields Spring State Park, Puffer Butte Loop   Counterclockwise

Get gas or groceries before leaving Enterprise. Boggan's Oasis at the highway crossing of the Grande Ronde River serves great milkshakes. There are no other restaurants, groceries, or motels near the park. Groups can rent two lodges with rustic sleeping accommodations and kitchen facilities. Reserve them through the State Parks Environmental Learning Centers program at (360) 902-8600. Winter camping is possible, if arranged with the ranger. The heated bathrooms at the campground sno-park have coin-operated showers.

The park rangers groom mostly for weekends and holidays with a snowmobile pulling a track-setter. Most trails are groomed with two passes, making an 8-foot-wide trail with two sets of ski tracks. Dogs are not allowed on the groomed trails. Snowshoes are not allowed on groomed trails but are allowed on other trails.

Be alert for signs of wildlife throughout the park. Wild turkeys are common near the ranger station and on the access road. Deer, hare, woodpeckers, and other wildlife are also found.

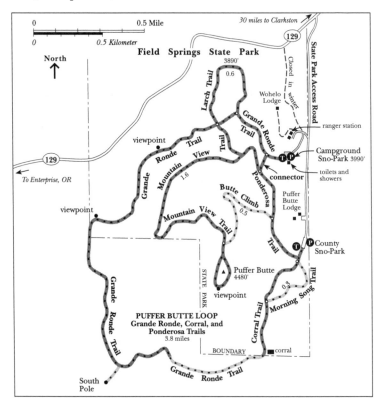

Puffer Butte Loop. Puffer Butte (4480 feet) stands at the center of the trails. The Puffer Butte Loop, which follows the Grande Ronde, Corral, and Ponderosa Trails, is a generally easy, 3.8-mile loop around the base of the butte. A 0.5-mile section of this loop is not groomed due to snowdrift conditions. From the west side of the campground sno-park, ski west on the Grande Ronde Trail past a short trail on the left and junctions with Larch and Mountain View Trails. At 1 mile from the sno-park, an opening in the trees yields a fine view of the Blue Mountains to the north. Grande Ronde curves south through rolling terrain to an open ridge above the Grande Ronde Valley 2 miles from the sno-park. Enjoy views in three directions of deep canyons and the rounded hills of the Blue Mountains. Descend the ridge for a glimpse of the Grand Ronde River far below. This lower viewpoint, called the South Pole, is a good turnaround point for those not wishing to complete the loop. Grooming ends a short distance beyond the South Pole. The 0.5-mile, ungroomed section traverses an open hillside with steep drifts but is not difficult to ski. The ungroomed trail ends at an old stock corral. From here, the Corral Trail, which is groomed, leads north to the county sno-park described earlier. In 0.4 mile from the corral, turn left onto Ponderosa, which climbs from Corral. In 0.5 mile, turn right onto a short, unnamed connector trail to Grand Ronde and back to the campground sno-park.

Mountain View. An intermediate-level tour to the top of the butte ends at an excellent overlook of the Grande Ronde Valley. From the campground sno-park, ski west on Grande Ronde 0.4 mile to Mountain View on the left. Mountain View climbs 1.6 miles to the top of Puffer Butte. The downhill return is along the same route. A challenging return option, Butte Climb, starts to the right just below the summit and drops to the Ponderosa Trail. Butte Climb trail is packed periodically.

Larch. Larch is a short beginner trail off the north end of Grande Ronde that is groomed only 4 feet wide. Starting 0.3 mile from the campground sno-park, the east leg of Larch descends gently to the north. It continues along a flat stretch, then turns south and climbs a steep hill back to Grande Ronde for a 0.6-mile, counterclockwise loop. For a little more challenge on the downhill, ski the loop clockwise.

Corral and Morning Song. The Corral and Morning Song Trails are nice beginner tours with easy-to-reach views. Start at the county sno-park. Skiers staying at Puffer Butte Lodge can walk or ski 0.1 mile

Puffer Butte overlook of the Blue Mountains

south to this sno-park. From the sno-park, ski south on Corral 0.1 mile and turn left onto Morning Song, a 0.3-mile, ungroomed ski trail. Morning Song drops to a picnic bench at a viewpoint to the south and east and then climbs back to Corral. Turn left and ski south to the old corral and the end of the groomed trail for more views. Return to the county sno-park on Corral for an easy 1-mile round trip.

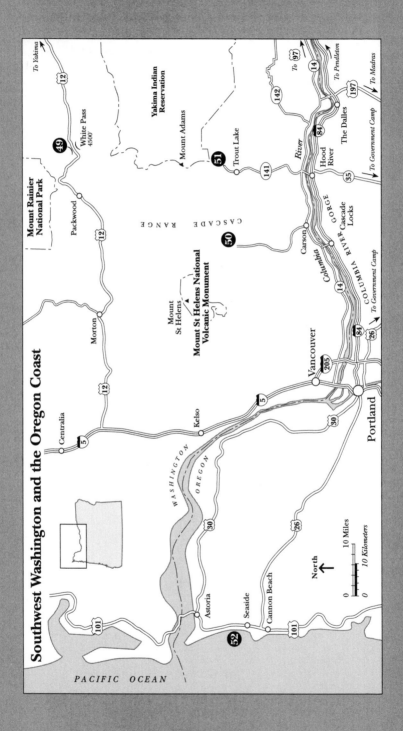

Southwest Washington and the Oregon Coast

Southwest Washington and the Oregon Coast

Portland skiers tend to overlook the Cascade Mountains of southwest Washington. Trails in the hills north of the Columbia River are a little farther from Portland than Mount Hood is, but the drive seldom has traffic problems. Mount St. Helens and Mount Adams dominate the scenery. Views of Mount Rainier and Mount Hood are also possible. As in Oregon, the chance of sunshine noticeably improves east of the Cascade crest.

An Oregon sno-park permit is valid at Washington sno-parks, but vehicles with Washington license plates must display a Washington permit. Washington State Park funds help pay for trail grooming throughout the state, including Wind River and Pineside. Farther north, the commercial ski area at White Pass provides more groomed trail opportunities.

While these accessible wintertime ski areas are often overlooked, the beaches of western Oregon are virtually ignored. They see little snow, but the beaches do offer a unique opportunity for skiers with a sense of adventure looking for an off-season outing. Route 52 digresses from typical ski trail descriptions to describe unusual beach "trails."

49 WHITE PASS

Distance: 3–10 kilometers (2–10 miles); 16 kilometers total
Trails: Groomed ski trails
Track Quality: Excellent classic skiing, excellent skating
Skill Level: Novice to advanced
Elevation: 4500 feet
Maximum Elevation Gain: 290 feet
Season: Late November to early April
Services and Facilities: Ski rentals, lessons, food
Hours: 9:00 A.M.–4:00 P.M., Thursday–Sunday
Fees: $8 per day
Information: White Pass Ski Area, (509) 672-3100,
www.skiwhitepass.com

The White Pass Ski Area offers some of the most enjoyable rolling and winding groomed trails in the Northwest. Sixteen kilometers of excellently groomed trails cross varied terrain. Sitting on the crest of the Cascades, the area gets plenty of cloudy days, but the fine trails and relaxed atmosphere more than compensate. Condominiums next to the trailhead are available to rent, making it possible to step out the door and ski. Portland skiers used to weekend trips to Mount Bachelor should visit White Pass for an enjoyable alternative with about the same travel time.

The ski area is at the summit of the pass on Highway 12 between the small westside town of Packwood and the eastside city of Yakima. From Portland, drive north 70 miles on Interstate 5 to exit 68, Highway 12. Drive east 87 miles to the pass. The final 22 miles from Packwood to the pass climb 3000 feet. The cross-country trails are across the highway from the alpine ski area. Turn left into the parking area and park near the condominiums. If approaching from Yakima, drive 50 miles west on Highway 12.

The main trailhead is at the west end of the condominiums, close to the parking lot. It overlooks Leech Lake, 90 feet below. A spacious new yurt serves as a ticket booth, a rental shop, and a gathering place for cross-country skiers. Ski lessons from a very competent staff are available. A store/delicatessen east of the condominiums is a quiet place for a break or for lunch. A short, unnamed, groomed trail starting behind the store leads to the trailhead by the yurt.

Lake Loop. The Lake Loop Trail is the start of all tours. It is good for novice skiers and has fine views of the lake. Signs show distances in kilometers. From the yurt, a trail bears left and drops on a short, steep

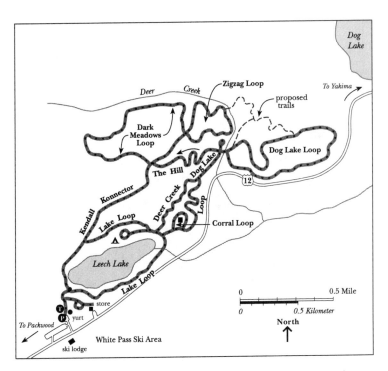

pitch to a junction at the start of the Lake Loop. A left turn leads to a relentless, 1.7-kilometer climb to the upper trails. If there is no hurry to reach the upper trails, turn right and descend another short hill to ski the 3.2-kilometer (2-mile) Lake Loop counterclockwise. The 1.5-kilometer south shore leg is easy enough for novice skiers, but gentle bumps and turns will entertain more experienced skiers. The trail crosses a creek and curves around the lake's east end to a junction with the Corral Loop, a short and very flat loop on the right. Turn left to continue to the Lake Loop. In 0.2 kilometer, there is a fork with a short, unnamed cul-de-sac through a campground on the lake. Bear right and climb two short, steep pitches before merging with the Kendall Konnector. A right here leads up to the upper trails, while a left begins a fast 0.7-kilometer downhill above the lake back to the start of the Lake Loop.

Deer Creek and Dog Lake Loops. Deer Creek and Dog Lake Loops are two of the most interesting trails at White Pass. Dick Kendall, a popular White Pass ski instructor since the early 1980s, designed these trails to roll and twist, and added some exciting downhill curves. Kendall, now a retired Forest Service engineer, helped design other Forest Service ski trails throughout the Northwest.

Leech Lake below the White Pass Trailhead

Deer Creek Loop, skied counterclockwise, starts from the south side of the Corral Loop. It heads north, making several sharp turns and rolling up and down for 1.5 kilometers before reaching a junction with the Dog Lake Trail. Here, Deer Creek Loop drops to the left for a quick, 0.7-kilometer return to the Lake Loop near the Corral Loop junction.

From its start at the middle of the Deer Creek Loop, the Dog Lake Trail climbs 0.4 kilometer and passes a left turn for The Hill, a steep route to the upper trails. It crosses Deer Creek and splits into the north and south legs of Dog Lake Loop. Bear right to ski the loop counterclockwise. The south leg descends and climbs short hills, dropping to its lowest elevation before turning back to the west. The north leg will be rerouted when a connector trail between Dog Lake Loop and the Zigzag Trail is completed.

Dark Meadows and Zigzag Loops. The upper trails, the Dark Meadows and Zigzag Loops, are 300 feet higher than the lake. They normally have snow well before the lower trails do. Neither has impressive viewpoints, but the terrain is ample attraction. Dark Meadows is an easy, rolling, 3.5-kilometer (2.2-mile) loop with gentle turns but continuous ups and downs. Zigzag, added in 1996, is a challenging, 2-kilometer (1.3-mile) loop that leads off of Dark Meadows Loop. It can be skied in either direction, but the downhills are easier going counterclockwise. From its start, it zigzags down 1 kilometer and then climbs back to its start.

Connector trails. The drawback to the upper trails is that they are hard to reach. There are two routes up and one down. The 0.7-kilometer (0.4-mile) trail known simply as The Hill is brutal. It begins from Dog Lake Trail with a steep uphill grade and then gets steeper. Hairpin turns uphill make it impossible to maintain momentum. An opening near the top provides a view of rugged mountains to the south. The view is nice but poor compensation for the effort. The Hill is the area's only one-way trail and must not be skied downhill. It ends at a junction with the Dark Meadows Loop and the Kendall Konnector.

The other route to the upper trails is a continuous 1.7-kilometer (1.1-mile) uphill from the start of the Lake Loop. It climbs the west leg of the Lake Loop and the Kendall Konnector to join the Dark Meadows Loop. Though boring as an uphill route, it is a quick and stimulating downhill return to the trailhead. Watch for two-way traffic on the wide and generally straight trail.

A third route to the upper trails has been flagged and hopefully will be completed soon. It will connect Dog Lake Loop to the low end of Zigzag, meandering near a beaver marsh and small waterfall. The new route will break the elevation gain into stages and will be more interesting than the two existing routes.

50 WIND RIVER

Distance: 1.2–11 miles
Trails: Groomed ski trails
Track Quality: Very good classic skiing, no skating
Skill Level: Novice to intermediate
Elevation: 3000 feet
Maximum Elevation Gain: 500 feet
Season: Mid-December to early March
Facilities and Services: Outhouses at sno-parks
Hours: NA
Fees: Sno-park permit
Information: Wind River Ranger District, Gifford Pinchot National
   Forest, (509) 427-5171

Portland skiers tend to overlook the upper Wind River winter recreation area, though the Forest Service has a fine system of groomed trails here through varied terrain. Wind River lies northeast of Portland in the Gifford Pinchot National Forest. Several loops are groomed weekly with two sets of ski tracks. Logging clear-cuts provide excellent views of the region's volcanic peaks. The area is mostly below 3000 feet, but it has unusually good snow for such low elevation. The drive from Portland to these ski trails is slightly longer than the drive to Mount Hood, but traffic is lighter.

From Portland, drive Interstate 84 to Cascade Locks. Cross the Bridge of the Gods, a toll bridge across the Columbia River, to Washington and turn east (right) onto Highway 14. Drive 2.5 miles past Stevenson, and turn north onto unmarked Wind River Road toward Carson. Continue north through Carson. At 14.5 miles from Highway 14, the road forks right just after a fish hatchery. The road becomes Forest Road 30. It is 11 miles farther to Old Man Pass Sno-Park on the left. The last 5 miles are steep. In heavy snow years, the county may limit plowing to conserve funds. Check in advance with the Wind River Ranger Station. Carry a shovel and tire chains.

Trail information is available at the ranger station, 7.5 miles north of Carson on Wind River Road and then 1.5 miles west on Hemlock Road. It is closed on weekends, but trail and road conditions are posted

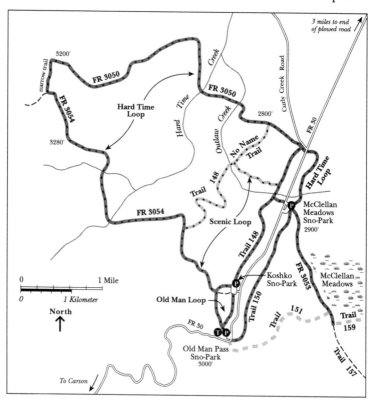

outside. Trails are groomed on Friday or Saturday. Grooming is managed by the Forest Service but funded through Washington State Parks.

The sno-park at Old Man Pass (3000 feet) is one of three near the groomed trails along Forest Road 30. Koshko Sno-Park is named after a ranger who helped develop the trail system. It is on the left, 0.5 mile beyond Old Man Pass and 0.2 mile west on an access road. McClellan Meadows Sno-Park (2900 feet) is on the right 1.5 miles beyond Old Man Pass. All three sno-parks have toilets. Old trail signs may mention Hard Time Sno-Park, which was eliminated when Curly Creek Road was rerouted in 2000. More sno-parks farther north provide access to snowmobile trails. Dogs are not allowed on the groomed trails. Unfortunately, some dog owners take advantage of weak enforcement.

Old Man Loop. Old Man Loop is a short novice trail starting from either Old Man Pass or Koshko Sno-Park. Ski counterclockwise for easier downhill sections. The 1.2-mile triangle is suitable for young children. From the information board at Old Man Pass Sno-Park, ski 20 yards to the start of the loop. Bear right and ski north on an old skid road that parallels Forest Road 30 to Koshko Sno-Park. Old Man Loop continues west, climbing from Koshko Sno-Park, to a junction with Forest Road 3054. The road to the right is the Hard Time Loop. Taking a left on this road, which is not an official ski trail, leads you gently back to Koshko Sno-Park. Ski across Forest Road 3054 on Old Man Loop and climb a little more before descending to the start of the loop at Old Man Pass Sno-Park.

Hard Time Loop. The 11-mile Hard Time Loop, suitable for strong intermediate skiers, is mostly on forest roads and offers views of Mount St. Helens, Mount Adams, and Mount Rainier. The distance requires stamina. A less ambitious option is to ski out and back on the loop's north leg starting from McClellan Meadows Sno-Park. This option is 7 miles round trip to the best views.

For the loop, from the north end of McClellan Meadows Sno-Park, ski north on the groomed trail to a junction with Curly Creek Road and Forest Road 30. Walk across Forest Road 30. The trail briefly follows the shoulder of Curly Creek Road, with an inspiring view of Mount St. Helens straight ahead. In 200 yards, it connects to Forest Road 3050, the north leg of the loop. This leg climbs gently as it leads west. Along the way, enjoy more views of St. Helens's tattered peak. The best vista point is a small clear-cut 3 miles from Forest Road 30. Continue 200 yards on the road around a sharp curve for equally fine views of Mount Adams and Mount Rainier. Forest Road 3050 ends at 5 miles. Turn left onto a narrow but well-marked trail and climb

Old Map Loop, a good trail for children

0.4 mile to Forest Road 3054. Turn left. Road 3054 climbs to its high point in 0.6 mile. It then descends 3.5 miles to the Old Man Loop and Old Man Pass Sno-Park, losing 280 feet and passing more volcano viewpoints. From the Sno-Park, cross the road and ski north on Trail 150 to complete the loop at McClellan Meadows Sno-Park.

Scenic Loop. The Scenic Loop is an intermediate-level route that combines groomed and ungroomed trails. It is 5.3 miles round trip from Old Man Pass Sno-Park. It also can be skied from McClellan Meadows Sno-Park via a short connector trail that starts across Forest Road 30 from the sno-park. From Old Man Pass Sno-Park, ski north to Koshko Sno-Park and continue north on groomed Trail 148. After passing the connector trail from McClellan Meadows Sno-Park on the right, Trail 148 crosses Outlaw Creek and soon reaches a junction with its first ungroomed leg. (Groomed Trail 148 continues north from here to Forest Road 3050.) Turn left and ski west on the ungroomed trail. Shortly after passing a junction with No Name Trail in 0.5 mile, the Scenic Loop trail again crosses Outlaw Creek. This crossing offers a good view of the creek. The loop turns south and its ungroomed west leg passes through heavy woods and some clear-cuts. In 1.5 miles past the stream, it reaches Road 3054, where the loop returns to groomed trail. Turn left and return to the sno-park to complete the loop.

The Scenic Loop tour can be extended 0.8 mile at its north end by skiing north on Trail 148, west on Forest Road 3050, and south on the No Name Trail back to the Scenic Loop.

51 PINESIDE

Distance: 1.5–7 miles
Trails: Groomed ski trails
Track Quality: Good classic skiing, no skating
Skill Level: Novice to intermediate
Elevation: 2760 feet
Maximum Elevation Gain: 952 feet
Facilities and Services: Outhouse at sno-park
Season: Late December to mid-March
Hours: NA
Fees: Sno-park permit
Information: Mount Adams Ranger District, Gifford Pinchot
  National Forest, (509) 395-3400

A little-known system of groomed ski loops starts from Pineside Sno-Park on the south flank of Mount Adams, north of Trout Lake. The loops pass through heavy timber on generally easy forest roads but have long uphill sections. There are few views, but the ease of skiing on groomed trails and the area's relative solitude are sufficient attractions. The trails have unusually good snow for their low elevation. They are groomed on Fridays and set with double tracks but are too narrow for skating. Unmarked and ungroomed logging roads connecting to the groomed loops create more possibilities for those who like to explore.

From Portland, drive east on Interstate 84 to Hood River and cross the toll bridge to Highway 14 in Washington. Turn west (left) and drive 1.5 miles. Turn right onto Alternate Route 141 and drive 2 miles north to Route 141. Follow Route 141 north 19.2 miles to a fork with Mount Adams Recreation Road. The diner behind the gas station here is a good place to stop after skiing. The left fork leads to the Mount Adams Ranger Station in 0.8 mile. To reach Pineside, bear right and stay right in another 1.5 miles. The road becomes Forest Road 82. At 4.8 miles from the gas station, Pineside Sno-Park (2760 feet) is on the right immediately after a sharp right turn. There is also space for a few cars on the left side of the road. In 1.7 miles farther, Pipeline Sno-Park is on the left. The Forest Service expects to rename this lot Snowking Sno-Park in winter 2002–3. Forest Road 82 is usually plowed an additional 2 miles beyond this to Smith Butte Sno-Park. Smith Butte is used by snowmobilers and does not access the groomed ski trails. When plowing funds are low, the road is only plowed to Pipeline (Snowking) Sno-Park.

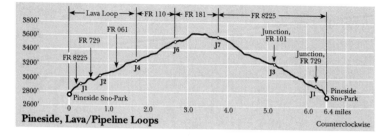

Pineside, Lava/Pipeline Loops

Counterclockwise

Trails generally run uphill when heading north toward Mount Adams. East–west sections are flat or rolling. Some trail junctions are posted with junction numbers 1–7.

Eagle Loop. With one exception, the ski loops at Pineside are north of Forest Road 82. The exception is Eagle Loop, a short trail leading south from the Pineside Sno-Park. It descends quickly through sharp turns, levels off along a logging road, and climbs back to Forest Road 82 in 0.8 mile. Ski 0.4 mile along Forest Road 82 for a quick return to the sno-park. A longer and more enjoyable return option is to cross Forest Road 82 and ski a 1.1-mile loop back to the sno-park. This loop climbs 0.4 mile on Forest Road 061 and turns left onto Lava Loop (Forest Road 729). It leads west 0.4 mile and then returns downhill on Forest Road 8225 to the sno-park.

Big Tree Loop. The main trailhead is across Forest Road 82 from Pineside Sno-Park. Two trails start here. A groomed trail on the left leads west along narrow Forest Road 041. In 0.7 mile, it reaches a fork for the Big Tree Loop. This is a good, albeit long, beginner trail. It is 4.6 miles round trip from the sno-park. Ski in either direction. The north leg has brief views of Mount Adams. Several unmarked roads connect to the loop and provide easy opportunities for exploring. Along the northwest leg, look for a "must do" side trip to the trail's namesake, Washington's largest ponderosa pine standing 7 feet wide and more than 200 feet tall.

Forest Road 8225. The second trail from the main trailhead follows Forest Road 8225, which climbs steadily as it heads north. This road is groomed wide but may not have classic ski tracks. It is shared with snowmobiles and dogsled teams, but such traffic is minimal. Forest Road 8225 forms the west leg of both Lava Loop, a beginner trail, and Pipeline, an intermediate loop. Both loops are well marked and are best skied counterclockwise, with a downhill return on Forest Road 8225. Road 8225 continues beyond these loops and connects to many miles of groomed snowmobile trails.

Lava Loop. Ski north from the main trailhead on Forest Road 8225 0.3 mile to Forest Road 729 on the right. This is junction 1, the start of Lava Loop, a 2.7-mile beginner trail. Turn right and ski less than 0.5 mile to junction 2 at Forest Road 061. Go left and in another 0.9 mile of climbing, reach junction 4 at Forest Road 101. Lava Loop continues to the left to Forest Road 8225 and the downhill to the sno-park to complete the loop.

Pipeline Loop. The intermediate-level Pipeline Loop starts at the north end of Lava Loop. Its name is derived from a nearby livestock water supply pipe. From junction 4 on Lava Loop, ski northeast a few yards to junction 5. Turn left on Forest Road 110 and climb, steeply at times, to junction 6 at Road 181. An ungroomed trail a few yards east of the junction is a nice side trip, leading north to clear-cuts with views of Mount Adams. To continue the loop, turn left on Forest Road 181 and ski through alternating uphill and level sections, cresting 900 feet above Pineside Sno-Park before dropping gently to Forest Road 8225 and a long downhill return to the sno-park. Pipeline Loop is 6.4 miles round-trip from the sno-park.

Spruce budworms are responsible for a large number of dead pine trees along the northeast side of Pipeline Loop. The dead trees create severe fire danger. This part of the forest will eventually be cleared, either by cutting or by fire.

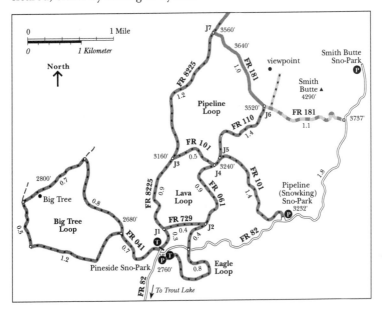

Groomed tracks on the Pipeline Loop

Pipeline (Snowking) Sno-Park is 500 feet higher than Pineside. It provides the easiest route to Pipeline Loop and is a good starting point when snow is marginal at Pineside. From the Pipeline (Snowking) Sno-Park, a 1.4-mile trail follows Forest Road 101 to junction 5 and the Pipeline and Lava Loops. Forest Road 101 has gentle ups and downs with little net climb to junction 5. For tours with net elevation loss, use a car shuttle to start at Pipeline (Snowking) Sno-Park and ski Forest Roads 101 and 8225 to Pineside.

Forest Road 181. Another option is to drive on Forest Road 82 nearly 2 miles beyond Pipeline (Snowking) Sno-Park to where space for three cars is plowed at the end of Forest Road 181. This snow-covered road is not a marked ski trail, but it is often groomed with the other trails. It is a rolling trail along the south flank of Smith Butte that leads 1.1 miles to the Pipeline Loop Trail. It usually has better snow than the lower trails.

52 OREGON BEACHES

Distance: As far as you want to go
Trails: NA
Track Quality: Good classic skiing, poor skating
Skill Level: Intermediate
Elevation: Sea level
Max Climb: 10 feet
Season: Early June to late October
Services and Facilities: Sand castles
Hours: Early ebb to late high tide
Fees: None
Information: NA

Cross-country skiing in Oregon does not have to end with the change to spring or even to summer. Without much effort, skiers can find snow-covered trails from early November to June. With some effort, they can reach high-elevation snow the rest of the year. Some skiers eschew the high elevation effort, however, and enjoy a little summer skiing at sea level. Beach skiing is an occasional diversion for racers and others who cannot wait until November. All the sandy stretches of the Oregon coastline are potential ski trails. Honeyman State Park at the north end of the Oregon Dunes, Gleneden Beach south of Lincoln City, and the Seaside beaches have all been tested and approved by summer skiers.

Summer skiing along the Pacific Ocean

Gliding is a part of skiing, even on sand. There is a zone of firm wet sand above the tide line where the skis glide best. Experiment to find the best "ski trail." Some skiers put hard glide wax on the skis. Others think bare polyethylene bases are best. No-wax skis are okay, but the grip pattern is not needed. The sand provides plenty of grip. Grip wax is an obvious no-no, unless you want a gooey mess underfoot. The only special equipment recommendation is that the skis should be old. Standard recommendations about dressing in layers for skiing do not apply for beach skiing. Likewise, you can ignore the caution to always carry a trail map. Just keep the ocean on one side.

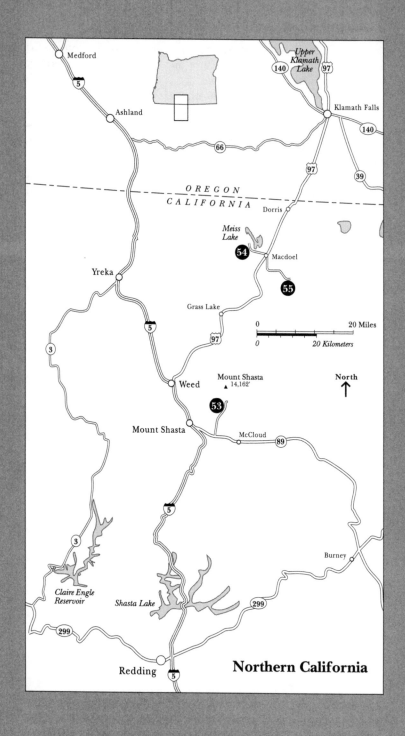

Northern California

The Mount Shasta area in northern California is an accessible playground for Oregon residents of Ashland and Klamath Falls. Skiers heading to Sacramento or the Bay Area can enjoy a day of skiing to break up the long drive. For those planning to spend several days, added attractions around Mount Shasta include monuments to a rich gold mining history and winter feeding grounds for thousands of eagles and waterfowl.

Mount Shasta, 14,162 feet, dominates the scenery. The origin of its name is uncertain. Early Russian explorers along the coast spotted the snow-covered peak. The name may be from a Russian word for pure or white. A commercial ski area on the south flank of the mountain has excellent groomed trails. Ungroomed trails in the Bunny Flats area on the mountain's north side are popular with many skiers. Snowmobile parks along Highway 97 are little known to skiers but offer miles of easy skiing.

The town of Mount Shasta is a good choice for an overnight stay. It has a mix of accommodations and dining and enough shops to be interesting without being offensive. The original name of the town was Strawberry Valley for the nearby abundant fields of wild strawberries. Fifth Season Sports rents cross-country skis and can provide trail information.

The California Department of Parks and Recreation has two winter parking and recreation programs. The sno-park program is similar to Oregon's. California recognizes Oregon Sno-Park permits, but the northernmost sno-parks are near Lake Tahoe, far from the Oregon border. The second winter program is the Green Sticker program, which uses snowmobile fees to plow access roads and snowmobile parks and to groom snowmobile trails. Some snowmobile parks along Highway 97 are close enough for day trips from Klamath Falls or Ashland. Snowmobiles must display Green Stickers, but skiers can use the snowmobile parks for no fee.

53 MOUNT SHASTA SKI PARK

Distance: 1–6 kilometers (0.6–3.8 miles); 30 kilometers total
Trails: Groomed ski trails
Track Quality: Excellent classic skiing, excellent skating
Skill Level: Novice to advanced
Elevation: 5254 feet
Maximum Elevation Gain: 455 feet
Season: Late November to early May
Services and Facilities: Nordic center, ski rentals, lessons, snacks
Hours: 9:00 A.M.–4:00 P.M. daily
Fees: $14
Information: Mount Shasta Board & Ski Park, (800) ski-shasta,
www.skipark.com

The Nordic Lodge at Mount Shasta Board & Ski Park is Ashland's closest full-service Nordic ski area. Though part of a large resort, the cross-country trails are far from the alpine activity and offer a tranquil atmosphere. The mix of easy, intermediate, and challenging trails provides some of the best variety in the region. Trails are wide and grooming is excellent for skating and classic skiing. Trail fees are higher than at Oregon ski areas, but the extra dollars will be a small part of total expenses for most ski trips. Annual snowfall is more than 10 feet and the Nordic Lodge takes advantage of it, staying open until early May.

Mount Shasta, a dormant volcano, erupted only 200 years ago. Native Americans called the mountain Ieka. European visitors dubbed it Shasta. Mount Shasta legends abound. Stories of the mystical race of Lemurians living within the mountain have persisted since the 1880s. More "conventional" stories about Bigfoot, leprechauns, and other beings are common. The only mysterious creatures skiers will encounter are snow snakes, which are to blame for most embarrassing and otherwise unexplainable tumbles into the snow.

The drive south from Ashland, mostly on Interstate 5, takes 1.5 hours in good weather. Siskiyou Pass at the state border can be treacherous in a storm. From Ashland, drive 64 miles south on Interstate 5 to the south end of the town of Mount Shasta and the Highway 89–McCloud exit. Turn left off the exit and drive east on Highway 89, which climbs steadily into the snow zone. In 5.3 miles, turn left onto Forest Road 88 (Ski Park Highway) and continue 3.4 miles to the Nordic Lodge parking lot on the left, 1 mile before the downhill ski area. Free shuttle buses run between the two lots.

The Nordic Lodge sells snacks, coffee, and limited ski accessories. It has benches for a few skiers taking a break. The Temple Hut, a roomy shelter along the ski trails, is a comfortable place for a lunch stop. A third of the ski trails are one-way. For the safety of all, do not ski in the wrong direction. Mount Shasta accommodates snowshoers and dog owners while avoiding conflict with skiers. The ski area designates separate trails for snowshoes and skiers with dogs. Snowshoe-clad staff pack those trails daily.

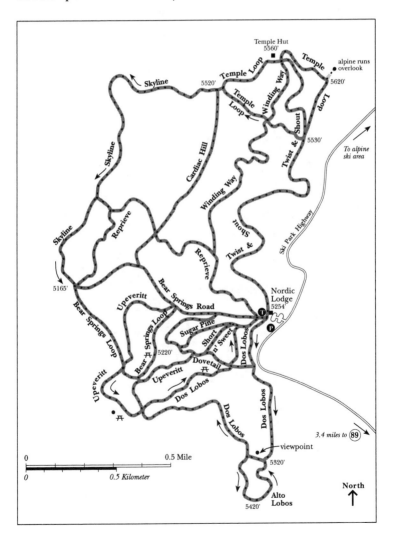

The many interconnecting trails can be divided into three areas. The central trails are west of the Nordic Lodge. They have a mix of flat terrain and easy hills and are excellent for beginner tours and easy training. These trails are reached from Bear Springs Road, the main trail leaving the Nordic Lodge. The north-end trails head up

Temple Hut trailside shelter at Mount Shasta Board & Ski Park

the flank of Mount Shasta. They have long uphill stretches going away from the Nordic Lodge and equally long, but considerably more fun, downhill returns. Hardcore racers use these trails for uphill interval training. The Lobos trails south of the Nordic Lodge are on steep terrain, with challenging ups and downs. There are many route options. The ones described here are just a sample.

Sugar Pine. Sugar Pine is an easy 1.2-kilometer loop that is a fine choice for children. Turn left off Bear Springs Road just a short distance from the Nordic Lodge to follow the loop back to Bear Springs Road. Turn right and follow Bear Springs Road back to the lodge.

Reprieve–Bear Springs Loop. A particularly fun route combines three trails with moderate ups and downs that will extend the abilities of strong beginners and entertain experienced skiers. From the Nordic Lodge, ski 0.1 kilometer on Bear Springs Road to Reprieve. Turn right onto Reprieve, a 2-kilometer trail that climbs, descends a short hill, and crosses the Cardiac Hill trail. It climbs again before descending a long gradual hill to the Bear Springs Road. Cross the road to Bear Springs Loop and ski 0.5 kilometer on gentle terrain to Upeveritt. Bear Springs Loop continues straight, but a short loop on Upeveritt is rewarding. Turn right onto Upeveritt and enjoy a climb to a bench with a stellar view of Mount Shasta. After sufficient oohing and aahing, continue on Upeveritt. After a short steep downhill, the trail flattens. In 0.5 kilometer from the bench, use a short connector on the left and ski a few feet to rejoin the Bear Springs Loop. Turn right and ski 0.5 kilometer north to Bear Springs Road. Turn right and return to the Nordic Lodge for a 4-kilometer (2.5-mile) round-trip tour.

Twist & Shout–Skyline. The spacious Temple Hut on the Temple Loop is a good destination for a break. Many skiers need a break after the 300-foot climb from the Nordic Lodge. There are three trails to choose from for the long climb. Pick Twist & Shout for a tough but reasonable 2-kilometer climb with some views along the way. For a scenic detour near the top, turn right 1.5 kilometers from the Nordic Lodge onto Temple Loop, which climbs steeply to an overlook of the alpine ski area and then continues downhill to the Temple Hut. This detour adds 0.2 kilometer and some extra climbing.

After visiting Temple Hut, ski down Temple Loop and turn right onto Skyline, which is a challenging 1.7-kilometer downhill run to Bear Springs Road. Skyline is a one-way trail in the downhill direction. Return to the Nordic Lodge on Bear Springs Road for about 5.5 kilometers round trip.

Dos Lobos. This route is for advanced skiers. Heed the one-way signs. Dos Lobos heads south from the Nordic Lodge and does some serious climbing for 1 kilometer to a large open area with views of Mount Shasta. A side loop, Alto Lobos, leaves from here and loops along the southern edge of the open area. This 0.6-mile side loop runs through steep ups and downs for 0.6 kilometer and returns to its starting point on Dos Lobos. Dos Lobos continues another 1.3 kilometer with a long, exciting downhill run to Sugar Pine. Turn right and return to the Nordic Lodge. The round trip including Alto Lobos is 3 kilometers (1.9 miles).

54 JUANITA LAKE

Distance: 6–10 miles
Trails: Occasionally groomed ski trails
Track Quality: Fair classic skiing, no skating
Skill Level: Intermediate
Elevation: 4268 feet
Maximum Elevation Gain: 850 feet
Season: Early January to late February
Services and Facilities: None
Hours: NA
Fees: None
Information: Goosenest Ranger District, Klamath National Forest, (530) 398-4391

Juanita Lake is a lovely mountain lake in the Klamath National Forest 15 miles south of the California border. It is an easy drive from Klamath Falls. The area does not get a lot of snow, and the tour includes a long uphill climb. Still, the lake is exceptionally stunning in winter and there are views of Mount Shasta and Mount McLoughlin along the trails. Klamath National Forest winter recreation brochures describe groomed ski trails here. Forest Service personnel occasionally use a snowmobile and grooming sled to set ski tracks for classic skiing, but it does not happen often. When there is adequate snow, Forest Service personnel may be committed to other duties. Check with the Goosenest Ranger District for current grooming information.

From Klamath Falls, drive 27 miles south on Highway 97 to the south end of the town of Macdoel and turn right onto Meiss Lake Road. Drive 4.2 miles to the first of two trailheads. Park on the right in a Butte Valley Wildlife Area lot. Walk across Meiss Lake Road to the trailhead at a gate on Mistletoe Road. A second sno-park and the other trailhead are 2.5 miles farther up Meiss Lake Road on the left, at a junction with North Juanita Lake Road.

From the Mistletoe Road trailhead, ski uphill on Mistletoe Road. This narrow forest road climbs gradually, heading southwest and passing through forest and small clearings with views to the north of the Butte Valley. Mistletoe Road passes an unnamed ski trail on the right in about 2.5 miles. This side trail is a difficult route to the east side of Juanita Lake. Stick with Mistletoe, continuing to Forest Road 46N04. Cross that road and follow blue diamonds, curving north to the south end of Juanita Lake, 4 miles from the trailhead. The 55-acre lake is known for trout fishing. You may find people ice fishing on the lake during winter. In late winter, eagles or osprey may be seen if the lake is not frozen.

There is an easy, 1.7-mile loop around the lake, mostly along a paved summer trail. A short out-and-back side trail leads from the northwest corner of Juanita Lake to Musgrave Creek. The lake loop crosses a dam at the north end of the lake. A round trip from the Mistletoe Road trailhead, including a loop around the lake, is 9.9 miles.

The route from the North Juanita Lake Road trailhead on Meiss Lake Road follows North Juanita Lake Road to a picnic area at the northeast corner of Juanita Lake, close to the dam. This road, 2.9 miles, is a shorter but steeper route to the lake. When there is no snow at the trailhead, drive up North Juanita Lake Road to the snow line to start the tour to Juanita Lake.

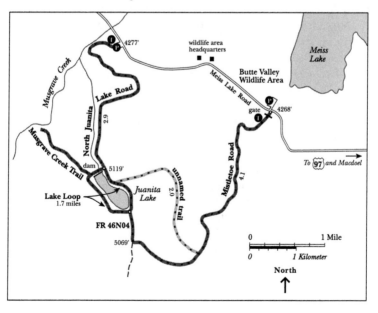

55 FOUR CORNERS

Distance: 10.8 miles
Trails: Groomed snowmobile trails
Track Quality: Fair classic skiing, good skating
Skill Level: Intermediate
Elevation: 5314 feet
Maximum Elevation Gain: 1070 feet
Season: Mid-December to late March
Services and Facilities: Outhouse, rustic warming hut
Hours: NA
Fees: None
Information: Goosenest Ranger District, Klamath National Forest, (530) 398-4391

The Four Corners Snowmobile Park in the Goosenest Ranger District of the Klamath National Forest provides access to 50 miles of groomed snowmobile trails. Green Sticker snowmobile fees pay for plowing and trail grooming. Skiers can use the trails but must be courteous to motorized users. The wide trails are groomed once or twice each week and are normally fine for skating.

From Klamath Falls, drive south 27 miles on Highway 97 and turn left onto Meiss Lake Road at the south end of Macdoel. Turn right in 0.2 mile and drive 0.5 mile on Old State Highway to a left onto Red Rock Road. This paved road becomes Forest Road 15 and climbs 1000 feet in 28 miles to Four Corners Snowmobile Park. Look for trail maps near the bulletin board.

Three groomed trails leave the park, heading east, west, and south. The loops they form are scaled for snowmobile travel and are much too long for a ski tour. The trail leading west has the least snowmobile traffic, but the most interesting tour is south for an out-and-back trip on Forest Road 15. A 10.8-mile round trip leads to views of Pumice Stone and Little Glass Mountains. The terrain is not challenging, but the distance merits an intermediate rating.

Ski south on Forest Road 15, which climbs steadily but not steeply. It is easy to cover the miles quickly. Ungroomed side roads along the way provide tour opportunities for those who don't want to ski all the way to Pumice Stone. In 3 miles, groomed Forest Road 77 curves left at junction 20. Continue straight, climbing to junction 19. Forest Road 15 climbs for a short distance past junction 19 to the divide between

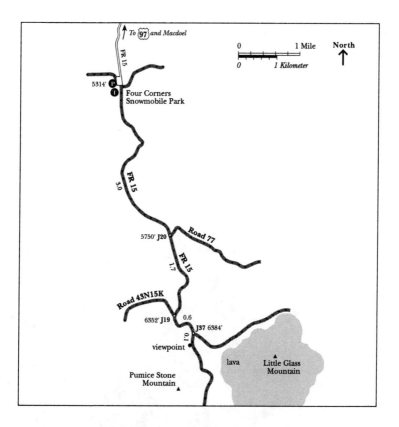

the Klamath and Trinity National Forests. From there, it makes a quick descent to junction 37 and southeast views of the craggy ridge of Little Glass Mountain. Continue a couple hundred yards for views of Pumice Stone Mountain on the right (west). The top of the mountain is usually heavily corniced. Seeing such obvious cornices from below is a good reminder of the risk of skiing near the edge when on top of any steep hill. This point, 5.4 miles from the sno-park, is a good place to turn around and return along the same route.

Little Glass Mountain

APPENDIX A: ANNUAL EVENTS

Oregon ski clubs and ski areas sponsor numerous on-snow events. A few have become traditions and attract skiers from throughout the Northwest. Most include a race but also appeal to skiers who seldom race. These events, which include activities for kids, illustrate that racing and touring are not separate and exclusive pursuits. This is a great way to participate in the Nordic community.

TEACUP CLASSIC, MOUNT HOOD

The trails at Teacup Lake are ideal for classic skiing, and the races on the last Sunday in January are strictly classic. Skating is not allowed. Volunteers have organized this race annually for more than twenty years. Race entrants range from first-time racers to former and prospective Olympic team members. The course is challenging with tough hills. Contact the Teacup Lake chapter of the Oregon Nordic Club (ONC).

SENIOR WEEK, DIAMOND LAKE RESORT

Senior skiers, loosely defined as those 50 and older, get together in January for 4 days of lessons, touring, good food, wine, and fun at a comfortable resort with incredible views. The event is so popular that a second Senior Week in February was added.

CRATER LAKE WILDERNESS RACE

Traditionally held the first Saturday of February, this race attracts many skiers who seldom race, as well as a few hot shots. It is a "wilderness race" because the course is set by skiers rather than by machine. There are several course lengths. The race follows East Rim Road, starting at 6480 feet and climbing. Crater Lake is not visible from the course, but after-race festivities are held at Rim Village. The event is organized by Alla Mage, which is the Klamath Falls chapter of the ONC.

LADD CANYON LOPPET, LA GRANDE

For years the Blue Mountain Nordic Club has hosted this informal long race and tour. This event, held in early February, is now open to nonmembers and attracts skiers from the Willamette Valley, Washington, and Idaho. It is a 50-kilometer point-to-point tour from Anthony Lakes to the mouth of Ladd Canyon. The catch is the amazing elevation loss—nearly 3700 feet from start to finish. Sections are steep and skiers must be confident skiing downhill on rough tracks.

JOHN DAY MEMORIAL, DIAMOND LAKE

This popular day of races honors one of Oregon's cross-country pioneers. It is held on the third Sunday of February along a generally easy course. A 20-kilometer event allows skating; the 10-kilometer event is strictly classic technique. The day's events include Special Olympics Nordic races for disabled skiers. A fine dinner and ceremonies follow the race. Contact the Southern Oregon chapter of the ONC.

JOHN CRAIG MEMORIAL, SISTERS

The John Craig Memorial is the granddaddy Nordic event in the Northwest. John Templeton Craig perished trying to cross McKenzie Pass to deliver mail in 1877. The earliest commemorative race was in the 1930s. Since 1970, the statewide Oregon Nordic Club has made this an annual early spring event. Activities include a Mail Carry to Craig's gravesite, a casual tour, and races. The course length varies, depending on the snow line. Contact any Oregon Nordic Club chapter for information.

CASCADE CREST, MOUNT BACHELOR

Mount Bachelor is the venue for several races every year. The most famous, attracting skiers from throughout North America, is the late-season Cascade Crest. This is a freestyle race on a challenging course along Bachelor's Nordic trails and extending north to Dutchman Flat. Spring sunshine is almost guaranteed, and views of surrounding volcanoes make for one of the prettiest racecourses anywhere. The Crest is a fundraiser for young Nordic racers. It is usually held in early April.

POLE PEDAL PADDLE, BEND

The Pole Pedal Paddle (PPP) is Bend's famous multisport relay race, attracting athletes from around the world. Thousands of runners, bikers, boaters, and skiers participate. The mid-May event starts at Mount Bachelor with a downhill ski leg and an 8-kilometer Nordic leg. Nordic skiers are in high demand. Teams compete, but the emphasis is fun and after-race festivities are part of the PPP. For information, contact the Mount Bachelor Ski Education Foundation.

Racer at Diamond Lake

APPENDIX B: SKI AREAS AND RESORTS

MOUNT HOOD AND SOUTHWEST WASHINGTON
Inn at Cooper Spur
(541) 352-6692
www.innatcooperspur.com

Cooper Spur Ski Area
(541) 352-7803
www.cooperspur.com

Mount Hood Meadows Ski Resort
(503) 337-2222, ext. 262
Snow phone: (503) 227-7669
www.skihood.com

Summit Meadows Cabins
Trillium Lake
(503) 272-3494
www.summitmeadow.com

Timberline Lodge
(503) 272-3311
Snow phone: (503) 222-2211
www.timberlinelodge.com

White Pass Ski Area
(509) 672-3100
www.skiwhitepass.com

SANTIAM PASS
Hoodoo Ski Area
(541) 822-3337
www.hoodoo.com

CENTRAL OREGON

Mount Bachelor Ski Area
(541) 382-2442
Snow phone: (541) 382-7888
www.mtbachelor.com

Elk Lake Resort
(541) 480-7228
www.elklakeresort.com

Paulina Lake Resort
(541) 536-2240

WILLAMETTE PASS

Odell Lake Lodge
(541) 433-2540
www.odelllakeresort.com

Shelter Cove Resort
(541) 433-2548/(800) 647-2729
www.sheltercoveresort.com

Willamette Pass Ski Area
(541) 345-7669
www.willamettepass.com

SOUTHERN OREGON AND NORTHERN CALIFORNIA

Diamond Lake Resort
(800) 733-7593
www.diamondlake.net

Mount Shasta Board & Ski Park
(800) ski-shasta
Snow phone: (530) 926-8686
www.skipark.com

NORTHEASTERN OREGON

Anthony Lakes Mountain Resort
(541) 856-3277
www.anthonylakes.com

Fields Spring State Park
(509) 256-3332
Lodge reservations: Call the State Parks Environmental Learning
Centers program at (360) 902-8600

Spout Springs Ski Area
(877) 577-8445
(541) 566-0320

Wallowa Lake Tramway
(541) 432-5331
www.wallowalaketramway.com

Wallowa Lake Lodge
(541) 432-9821
www.wallowalake.com

APPENDIX C: LAND AGENCIES

Bureau of Land Management
Hyatt Lake Recreation Complex
(541) 482-2031
www.or.blm.gov/Medford/recreationsites/Medbuckprairierecsite.html

Crater Lake National Park
(541) 594-3000
www.nps.gov/crla

Deschutes National Forest
1645 Highway 20 East
Bend, OR 97701
(541) 383-5300
www.fs.fed.us/r6/centraloregon

> Bend–Fort Rock Ranger District
> Bend, Oregon
> (541) 383-4000
>
> Crescent Ranger District
> Crescent, Oregon
> (541) 433-3200
>
> Sisters Ranger District
> Sisters, Oregon
> (541) 549-7700

Fremont National Forest
1301 South G Street
Lakeview, OR 97630
(541) 947-2151
www.fs.fed.us/r6/fremont/trails

Gifford Pinchot National Forest
500 W 12th Street
Vancouver, WA 98660
(360) 696-7500

Mount Adams Ranger District
Trout Lake, Washington
(509) 395-3400

Wind River Ranger District
Carson, Washington
(509) 427-5171

Klamath National Forest
1312 Fairlane Road
Yreka, CA 96097-9549
(530) 842-6131
www.r5.fs.fed.us/klamath

Goosenest Ranger District
37805 Hwy 97
Macdoel, CA 96058
(530) 398-4391

Malheur National Forest
P.O. Box 909
431 Patterson Bridge Road
John Day, OR 97845
(541) 575-3000
www.fs.fed.us/r6/malheur

Mount Hood National Forest
16400 Champion Way
Sandy, OR 97055
(503) 668-1700
www.fs.fed.us/r6/mthood

Mount Hood Information Center
Welches, Oregon
(503) 622-7674
(888) 622-4822
www.mthood.org

High school racer

Barlow Ranger District
Dufur, Oregon
(541) 467-2291

Hood River Ranger District
Parkdale, Oregon
(541) 352-6002

Zigzag Ranger District
Zigzag, Oregon
(503) 622-3191

Ochoco National Forest
3160 NE 3rd Street
Prineville, OR 97754
(541) 416-6500
www.fs.fed.us/r6/centraloregon

Rogue River National Forest
Ashland Ranger District
645 Washington Street
Ashland, OR 97520-1402
(541) 482-3333
www.fs.fed.us/r6/rogue/about02.html

Umpqua National Forest
Diamond Lake Ranger District
2020 Toketee Ranger Station Road
Ideyld Park, OR 97447
(541) 498-2531
Online snow report: *www.fs.fed.us/r6/umpqua/rec/dlsnow.html*

Wallowa–Whitman National Forest
P.O. Box 907
Baker City, OR 97814
(541) 523-1405
www.fs.fed.us/r6/w-w

La Grande Ranger District
La Grande, Oregon
(541) 963-7186

Pine Ranger District
Halfway, Oregon
(541) 742-7511

Wallowa Mountains Visitor Center
88401 Highway 82
Enterprise, OR 97828
(541) 426-5546

Willamette National Forest
P.O. Box 10607
Eugene, OR 97440
(541) 225-6300

McKenzie Ranger District
McKenzie Bridge, Oregon
(541) 822-3381

Oakridge Ranger District
Westfir, Oregon
(541) 782-2291

Winema National Forest
2819 Dahlia Street
Klamath Falls, OR 97601
(541) 883-6714
www.fs.fed.us/r6/winema

Chemult Ranger District
Chemult, Oregon
(541) 365-7001

Klamath Ranger District
Klamath Falls, Oregon
(541) 885-3400

APPENDIX D: SKI CLUBS AND ORGANIZATIONS

OREGON NORDIC CLUB (ONC)
www.onc.org

Alla Mage ONC
932 Hanks Street
Klamath Falls, OR 97601

Blue Mountain ONC
P.O. Box 2764
La Grande, OR 97850
(541) 663-3239

Central Oregon ONC
P.O. Box 744
Bend, OR 97709-0744
www.conc.freehosting.net

Columbia Gorge ONC
420 W 10th Street
The Dalles, OR 97053

Grants Pass ONC
P.O. Box 742
Grants Pass, OR 97526

Ochocos ONC
2644 SE Mill Street
Prineville, OR 97754

Portland ONC
P.O. Box 3906
Portland, OR 97208-3906
(503) 222-9757
www.onc.org/pdx.html

Southern Oregon ONC
P.O. Box 1209
Phoenix, OR 97535

Teacup Lake ONC
5317 SE Center Street
Portland, OR 97206
www.teacupnordic.org

Tumalo Langlauf ONC
1293 NW Wall Street, #1454
Bend, OR 97701
www.tumalolanglauf.com

Willamette ONC
P.O. Box 181
Salem, OR 97308

OTHER CROSS-COUNTRY SKI GROUPS
Eagle Cap Nordic
107 Barton Heights
Joseph, OR 97846

Edelweiss Ski Club
P.O. Box 755
Roseburg, OR 97470

Mount Hood Nordic Patrol
www.skipatrol.mount-hood.or.us

Willamette Pass Backcountry Nordic Patrol
www.wbsp.org

CROSS-COUNTRY SKI RACING
Mount Bachelor Ski Education Foundation
www.mbsef.org/xc.htm

Oregon Interscholastic Ski Racing Association
www.oisra.org/xcountry/index.html

Pacific Northwest Ski Association
www.pnsa.org/nordic/general.htm

XC Oregon
www.xcskiworld.com/xcoregon

OUTDOOR CLUBS WITH CROSS-COUNTRY ACTIVITIES

Bergfreunde
Portland, Oregon
(503) 245-8543
www.bergfreunde.org

Chemeketans
Salem, Oregon
www.chemeketans.org

Mazamas
Portland, Oregon
(503) 227-2345
www.mazamas.org

Ptarmigans
Vancouver, Washington
www.ptarmigans.org

WEATHER AND SNO-PARK INFORMATION

National Weather Service
www.wrh.noaa.gov

Oregon Department of Transportation
(800) 977-6368
Outside Oregon: (503) 588-2941
www.tripcheck.com/RoadCams/roadcams.htm
Sno-park Information: *www.tripcheck.com/winter/snoparks.htm*

Washington Department of Transportation
www.traffic.wsdot.wa.gov/cameras.htm

INDEX

ABOUT THE AUTHOR

Mike Bogar started skiing in Michigan in 1975. He holds a bachelor's degree in mechanical engineering from Michigan State University. He moved to Oregon in 1981 and has spent twenty years exploring ski trails in the Northwest. Bogar is an active citizen ski racer and has raced in ski marathons throughout North America and Europe. Bogar gives back to the sport through volunteer service organizing races and clinics, instructing, and working on trail development and grooming. He has served as a race director, Oregon Nordic Club (ONC) state board member, Winter Recreation Advisory Committee member for the Oregon Department of Transportation, and president of the Teacup Lake chapter of the ONC. He lives near Portland. When he is not skiing, he spends his free time birdwatching, sea kayaking, hiking, and solving crossword puzzles.

THE MOUNTAINEERS, founded in 1906, is a nonprofit outdoor activity and conservation club, whose mission is "to explore, study, preserve, and enjoy the natural beauty of the outdoors.... " Based in Seattle, Washington, the club is now the third-largest such organization in the United States, with 15,000 members and five branches throughout Washington State.

The Mountaineers sponsors both classes and year-round outdoor activities in the Pacific Northwest, which include hiking, mountain climbing, ski-touring, snowshoeing, bicycling, camping, kayaking and canoeing, nature study, sailing, and adventure travel. The club's conservation division supports environmental causes through educational activities, sponsoring legislation, and presenting informational programs. All club activities are led by skilled, experienced volunteers, who are dedicated to promoting safe and responsible enjoyment and preservation of the outdoors.

If you would like to participate in these organized outdoor activities or the club's programs, consider a membership in The Mountaineers. For information and an application, write or call The Mountaineers, Club Headquarters, 300 Third Avenue West, Seattle, WA 98119; (206) 284-6310.

The Mountaineers Books, an active, nonprofit publishing program of the club, produces guidebooks, instructional texts, historical works, natural history guides, and works on environmental conservation. All books produced by The Mountaineers Books fulfill the club's mission.

Send or call for our catalog of more than 500 outdoor titles:

The Mountaineers Books
1001 SW Klickitat Way, Suite 201
Seattle, WA 98134
(800) 553-4453

mbooks@mountaineersbooks.org
www.mountaineersbooks.org

The Mountaineers Books is proud to be a corporate sponsor of Leave No Trace, whose mission is to promote and inspire responsible outdoor recreation through education, research, and partnerships. The Leave No Trace program is focused specifically on human-powered (nonmotorized) recreation.

Leave No Trace strives to educate visitors about the nature of their recreational impacts, as well as offer techniques to prevent and minimize such impacts. Leave No Trace is best understood as an educational and ethical program, not as a set of rules and regulations.

For more information, visit *www.LNT.org*, or call (800) 332-4100.

Other titles you might enjoy from The Mountaineers Books

Available at fine bookstores and outdoor stores, by phone at (800) 553-4453, or on the World Wide Web at www.mountaineersbooks.org

The Complete Guide to Cross-Country Ski Preparation by Nat Brown. $18.95 paperbound. 0-89886-600-6.

Staying Alive in Avalanche Terrain by Bruce Tremper. $17.95 paperbound. 0-89886-834-3.

Wilderness Navigation: Finding Your Way Using Map, Compass, Altimeter, & GPS by Bob Burns and Mike Burns. $9.95 paperbound. 0-89886-629-4.

Free-Heel Skiing: Telemark and Parallel Techniques for All Conditions, 3rd Edition by Paul Parker. $19.95 paperbound. 0-89886-775-4.

Snowshoe Routes: Oregon by Shea Andersen. $16.95 paperbound. 0-89886-833-5.

Snowshoeing: From Novice to Master, 5th Edition by Gene Prater, edited by Dave Felkley. $16.95 paperbound. 0-89886-891-2.

Backcountry Snowboarding by Christopher Van Tilburg. $18.95 paperbound. 0-89886-578-6.

100 Hikes in™ Oregon, 2nd Edition by Rhonda and George Ostertag. $14.95 paperbound. 0-89886-619-7.

75 Hikes in™ Oregon's Coast Range & Siskiyous, 2nd Edition by Rhonda and George Ostertag. $14.95 paperbound. 0-89886-620-0.

50 Hikes in™ Hell's Canyon and Oregon's Wallowas by Rhonda and George Ostertag. $14.95 paperbound. 0-89886-521-2.

Best Hikes with Children® in Western & Central Oregon, 2nd Edition by Bonnie Henderson. $14.95 paperbound. 0-89886-575-1.

Hiking Oregon's Geology by Ellen Morris Bishop and John Eliot Allen. $16.95 paperbound. 0-89886-485-2.

Exploring Oregon's Wild Areas: A Guide for Hikers, Backpackers, Climbers, Cross-Country Skiers, and Paddlers, 4th Edition by William L. Sullivan. $18.95 paperbound. 0-89886-793-2.

Oregon Campgrounds Hiking Guide by Rhonda and George Ostertag. $14.95 paperbound. 0-89886-547-6.

Oregon Desert Guide: 70 Hikes by Andy Kerr. $15.95 paperbound. 0-89886-602-2.

Oregon State Parks: A Recreation Guide, 2nd Edition by Jan Bannan. $16.95 paperbound. 0-89886-794-0.